Hart-Davis, Guy.
iPad geekery : 50
insanely cool hacks and
2013.
33305226270431
ha            02/26/13

P9-AFT-178

# iPad® Geekery

## 50 Insanely Cool Hacks and Mods for Your Apple Tablet

Guy Hart-Davis

New York  Chicago  San Francisco
Lisbon  London  Madrid  Mexico City
Milan  New Delhi  San Juan
Seoul  Singapore  Sydney  Toronto

*The McGraw-Hill Companies*

Cataloging-in-Publication Data is on file with the Library of Congress

McGraw-Hill books are available at special quantity discounts to use as premiums and sales promotions, or for use in corporate training programs. To contact a representative, please e-mail us at bulksales@mcgraw-hill.com.

iPad® Geekery: 50 Insanely Cool Hacks and Mods for Your Apple Tablet

Copyright © 2013 by The McGraw-Hill Companies. All rights reserved. Printed in the United States of America. Except as permitted under the Copyright Act of 1976, no part of this publication may be reproduced or distributed in any form or by any means, or stored in a database or retrieval system, without the prior written permission of publisher, with the exception that the program listings may be entered, stored, and executed in a computer system, but they may not be reproduced for publication.

All trademarks or copyrights mentioned herein are the possession of their respective owners and McGraw-Hill makes no claim of ownership by the mention of products that contain these marks.

1234567890   DOC DOC   1098765432

ISBN       978-0-07-180755-5
MHID       0-07-180755-1

**Sponsoring Editor**
Roger Stewart

**Editorial Supervisor**
Janet Walden

**Project Manager**
Anupriya Tyagi, Cenveo
Publisher Services

**Acquisitions Coordinator**
Ryan Willard

**Copy Editor**
Bill McManus

**Proofreader**
Claire Splan

**Indexer**
Claire Splan

**Production Supervisor**
Jean Bodeaux

**Composition**
Cenveo Publisher Services

**Illustration**
Cenveo Publisher Services
and Lyssa Wald

**Art Director, Cover**
Jeff Weeks

**Cover Designer**
Ty Nowicki

Information has been obtained by McGraw-Hill from sources believed to be reliable. However, because of the possibility of human or mechanical error by our sources, McGraw-Hill, or others, McGraw-Hill does not guarantee the accuracy, adequacy, or completeness of any information and is not responsible for any errors or omissions or the results obtained from the use of such information.

*This book is dedicated to Teddy.*

*No iPads were harmed during the writing of this book.*

## About the Author

**Guy Hart-Davis** is the author of more than 80 computer books, including *iPhone Geekery; Kindle Fire Geekery; How to Do Everything: iPhone 4S; How to Do Everything: iPod touch; How to Do Everything: iPod & iTunes, Sixth Edition; The Healthy PC, Second Edition; PC QuickSteps, Second Edition; How to Do Everything with Microsoft Office Word 2007;* and *How to Do Everything with Microsoft Office Excel 2007.*

# Contents

# Acknowledgments

I'd like to thank the following people for their help with this book:

- Roger Stewart for proposing and developing the book
- Ryan Willard for handling the acquisitions end
- Bill McManus for editing the manuscript with a light touch
- Janet Walden for assisting with the production of the book
- Anupriya Tyagi for coordinating the production of the book
- Cenveo Publisher Services for laying out the pages
- Claire Splan for creating the index

# Introduction

Do you want to take your iPad to its limits—and then beyond them?

If so, this is the book for you.

This book shows you how to get the very most out of your iPad by using to the max all the features Apple intends you to use—and then extend your iPad with capabilities Apple *doesn't* intend it to have.

## What Does This Book Cover?

Here's what this book covers:

- Chapter 1, "Music and Audio Geekery," kicks off by showing you how to sync music and other content onto your iPad from multiple computers rather than a single computer. You then learn how to use your iPad as your home stereo and car stereo, how to create custom ringtones for free from your songs, and how to share your music smoothly among all your devices. I show you how to record high-quality audio on your iPad, play your guitar through your iPad, and record your live band on your iPad. I even show you how to fix your off-key singing—if it's not as bad as mine—and use your iPad to replace your live band.

- Chapter 2, "Photo and Video Geekery," tells you how to put your videos and DVDs on your iPad for viewing anywhere, either on the iPad's screen or on a TV you connect it to. We then dig into photography, sharing your photos easily using Photo Stream and capturing time-lapse movies. After that, we mount your iPad on a tripod for rock-steady, pro-grade filming, and then build a Steadicam rig to stabilize your iPad when shooting on the move. Finally, we look at how to view your computer's webcam on your iPad from anywhere—and how to turn your iPad into a chunky webcam.

Note paragraphs with this icon provide extra information. For example, Chapter 2 also shows you how to turn your iPad into an extra display for your computer and into an in-car entertainment system.

- Chapter 3, "iPad as Your Main Computer Geekery," shows you how to tap into the iPad's powerful computing capabilities and actually use your iPad as your main computer. First, you connect a Bluetooth keyboard or other hardware keyboard so that you can hammer in text at full speed. Then you learn expert tricks for entering text quickly and accurately with the onscreen keyboard. We then go through creating full-fat business documents—Word, Excel, PowerPoint, and PDFs—on your iPad and using your iPad as not only a portable drive but also as a file server for your home network or workgroup. We finish the chapter by turning you into a power user of the Mail app and setting you up to give presentations directly from your iPad.
- Chapter 4, "Security and Troubleshooting Geekery," teaches you how to secure your iPad against theft or intrusion, how to track it down if you lose it, and how to wipe the data from your iPad if you can't recover it. You also learn how to use

**DOUBLE GEEKERY**

## Why Is This Book Better Than Other iPad Books?

Unlike other iPad books, this book assumes that you already know how to use your iPad—how to navigate the user interface, browse the Web, install apps, and so on. This is the kind of stuff you learn in regular books about the iPad.

*iPad Geekery* assumes you're already an intermediate or advanced iPad user—and that you want to become even more advanced. So it starts from that point, giving you a full book's worth of the good stuff you actually want, instead of grinding through all the basics you already know and then ending with a few pages of advanced material.

your iPad safely in wet or dirty conditions, troubleshoot software and hardware problems, and restore your iPad to factory settings if it has software problems or if you're ready to sell it.

 Tip paragraphs with this icon provide tips, tricks, hints, and workarounds. For example, if you need to make your iPad safe for your kids to use, don't miss Chapter 4.

- Chapter 5, "Cellular, Wi-Fi, and Remote Geekery," starts by showing you how to unlock your cellular iPad from its carrier so that you can connect it to a different carrier's network. You then learn how to share your iPad's Internet connection with your computers or devices, how to take control of your PC or Mac from your iPad, and how to connect your iPad to your company network across the Internet using a virtual private network.

 Caution paragraphs with this icon warn you of pitfalls and tell you how to avoid them.

- Chapter 6, "Jailbreaking and Advanced Geekery," starts by showing you how to back up your iPad for safety, and then shows you how to "jailbreak" your iPad, freeing it from the restraints that Apple has placed upon it. You then discover how to find and install third-party apps that Apple hasn't approved, how to connect to your iPad via SSH and transfer files to its file system, and how to manage the file system using an app on the iPad. You also find out how to connect to your iPad from your computer using VNC, which can be fun, useful, or both. You then learn how to apply themes to change your iPad's user interface, make Wi-Fi–only apps run over 3G connections, and play console and arcade games under emulation. Finally—and only if you want to—we put your iPad back in its Apple jail.

# Conventions Used in This Book

To make its meaning clear without using far more words than necessary, this book uses a number of conventions, several of which are worth mentioning here:

- Note, Tip, and Caution paragraphs highlight information to draw it to your notice.
- Double Geekery sidebars provide in-depth focus on important topics.
- The pipe character or vertical bar denotes choosing an item from a menu on the PC or Mac. For example, "choose File | Open" means that you should click the File menu and select the Open item on it. Use the keyboard, mouse, or a combination of the two as you wish.
- The ⌘ symbol represents the COMMAND key on the Mac—the key that bears the Apple symbol and the quad-infinity mark on most Mac keyboards.

- Most check boxes have two states: *selected* (with a check mark in them) and *cleared* (without a check mark in them). This book tells you to *select* a check box or *clear* a check box rather than "click to place a check mark in the box" or "click to remove the check mark from the box." Often, you'll be verifying the state of the check box, so it may already have the required setting—in which case, you don't need to click at all.

# 1 Music and Audio Geekery

Your iPad is a great device for playing music wherever you take it, whether you use its built-in speaker, the headset or another pair of headphones, or a speaker system. I'm sure you know how to play music on your iPad, so we won't cover it in this book. But to put exactly the music you want on your iPad, you will quite likely need to connect your iPad to not just your main computer but also other computers. So we'll start the chapter by looking at how to sync music and other content from multiple computers.

Next, we'll look at how you can use your iPad as your home stereo and as your car stereo. We'll then explore how to create your own custom ringtones for free from your music and how to share your music among your iPad, your computers, and your other iOS devices by using Apple's Home Sharing feature and the iCloud service.

Toward the end of the chapter, we'll examine how you can turn your iPad into a recording studio for capturing high-quality audio. We'll look at how you can play your guitar through your iPad, how you can use your iPad to record your live band, and how you can fix your off-key singing. Finally, you'll learn how to use your iPad as your backing track for when your band is absent.

## Project 1: Load Your iPad with Content from Multiple Computers

As you know, you can sync your iPad in either of two ways: by using Apple's iCloud online service, or by using your computer.

Cloud computing is the wave of the future, and iCloud can be a great way to keep your music and other content synced among your iPad, your computer, and other iOS devices you have (for example, an iPhone or an iPod touch). In fact, you don't even need a computer—you can do all your computing with your iPad or other iOS devices.

But if you have a large collection of music and videos, or if you have a poky or unreliable Internet connection, you're probably better off syncing with your computer. Apple has got you covered here—you can download the latest version of iTunes, install it on your PC or Mac, and get your iPad syncing underway inside a few minutes.

But what if you want to load content onto your iPad from multiple computers rather than a single one?

Apple has designed your iPad and iTunes to assume you'll be syncing all your information from a single computer. This is what many people—perhaps most—will do. But given that you're reading this book, you're most likely among those special ones who wants to load your iPad from multiple computers.

This section shows you how to do that. We'll start with the limitations.

## Understand What You Can and Can't Sync

Here's what you need to know about syncing your iPad with multiple computers:

- Your iPad can sync only with a single iTunes library at a time. So if you sync your desktop's iTunes library with your iPad, you can't then sync your laptop's iTunes library without wiping the desktop library from your iPad. You can *load* music and other items from more than one library, but you can *sync* only a single library.
- The iTunes library includes music, movies, TV shows, ringtones, podcasts, and books. To sync any of these items with the iTunes library of a computer other than your iPad's home computer's iTunes library, you must wipe out your iPad's existing library.
- Apps are separate from the iTunes library, but you can sync only one computer's set of apps to an iPad. This can be a different computer than the computer whose iTunes library you're syncing for music, movies, and so on. Syncing apps with another computer removes all the existing apps from your iPad. (Not the built-in apps—you'd need a virtual bulldozer to shift those.)
- Photos are also separate from the iTunes library you're using for syncing music, but you can sync photos from only one computer with your iPad. Syncing photos with another computer removes your iPad's existing photos (but not any photos or videos in your iPad's Camera Roll).

 The Camera Roll contains the photos you've taken on your iPad's cameras plus any photos you've saved from web pages or e-mail messages.

- The items that appear on the Info tab of your iPad's control screens—contact information, calendar information, mail accounts, bookmarks, and notes—are also handled separately from music. When you start to sync your iPad's information items with another library, you can choose between merging the new information with the existing information and simply replacing the existing information.
- You can tell iTunes that you want to manage your iPad's music and videos manually. After you tell iTunes this, you can connect your iPad to a computer other than its home computer and add music and videos to it from that computer. But if you switch your home computer's library back to automatic syncing, you'll lose any music and videos you've added from other computers.

- For copyright reasons, iTunes puts limitations on which music and video files you can copy from your iPad to a computer. For example, you can't connect your iPad to your friend's computer and copy all the songs from your iPad to the computer using iTunes. See the sidebar at the end of this section for instructions on working around this limitation—for example, to recover your iTunes library after your computer crashes.

# Set Your iPad to Sync Data from Multiple Computers

Now that you understand the restrictions on syncing, let's look at how to set your iPad to sync data from multiple computers rather than a single computer.

 When you set your iPad to sync music or photos with another computer, the initial sync may take hours, because of the amount of data involved. By contrast, syncing information (contacts, calendars, and so on) usually takes only seconds, and syncing apps takes a few minutes, depending on how many apps there are and how chunky their developers have made them. So don't start syncing music or photos a few minutes before you need to rush off somewhere with your iPad.

## Sync All Your iPad's Data with Its Current Computer

Before you start making changes, connect your iPad to its current home computer and run a sync. This makes sure that you have a copy of the latest information from your iPad on your computer in case you need it later.

## Change the iTunes Library Your iPad Is Syncing Music With

To change the iTunes library your iPad is syncing music with, follow these steps:

1. Connect your iPad to the computer that contains the music you want to sync.
2. Click your iPad's entry in the Devices category of the Source list in the iTunes window to display its control screens.
3. Click the Music tab to display the Music screen.
4. Select the Sync Music check box.
5. Use the controls to specify which music you want to sync (see Figure 1-1). For example, either select the Entire Music Library option button to sync the whole library (assuming your iPad has enough room for it), or select the Selected Playlists, Artists, Albums, And Genres option button, and then select the check box for each item you want to include.

 At this point, you can also choose sync settings for the other items that changing the music library will affect: ringtones, movies, TV shows, podcasts, and books.

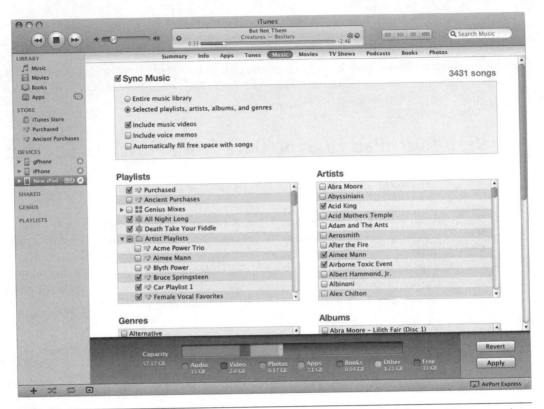

**FIGURE 1-1** On the Music screen, choose whether to sync all the music in your library or only the playlists, artists, albums, and genres whose check boxes you select.

6. Click the Apply button, which replaces the Sync button when you make changes. iTunes displays a dialog box asking if you want to erase and sync the library, as shown here.

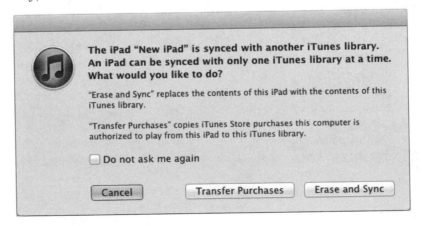

If the dialog box contains the Transfer Purchases button, you'll normally want to click it to transfer to iTunes all your purchased items from your iPad that this computer is authorized to play.

7. Click the Erase And Sync button. iTunes replaces the existing library items on your iPad with the items you chose from the new library.

## Change the Computer Your iPad Is Syncing Information With

To change the computer your iPad is syncing contacts, calendars, mail accounts, and other information with, follow these steps:

1. Connect your iPad to the computer that contains the information you want to sync.
2. Click your iPad's entry in the Devices category in the Source list in the iTunes window to display its control screens.
3. Click the Info tab to display the Info screen (see Figure 1-2).
4. Select the appropriate check boxes. For example, on a Mac, select the Sync Contacts check box, the Sync Calendars check box, and the Sync Mail Accounts check box; and select the Sync Safari Bookmarks check box and the Sync Notes check box in the Other box as needed.
5. Use the controls in each box to specify which items you want to sync. For example, select the check box for each mail account to sync in the Selected Mail Accounts list box.
6. Click the Apply button, which replaces the Sync button when you make changes. iTunes displays a dialog box (shown here) that offers you the choice between replacing the information on your iPad and canceling.

The information on the iPad "iPad3" is synced with another user account. Do you want to sync this iPad with the information from this user account instead?

"Replace Info" replaces the information on this iPad with the information from this user account.

Cancel    Replace Info

 Depending on which information you're syncing, iTunes may offer you the choice of merging the new information with the existing information. If so, click the Merge Info button in the dialog box instead of the Replace Info button.

7. Click the Replace Info button if you want to replace the information.

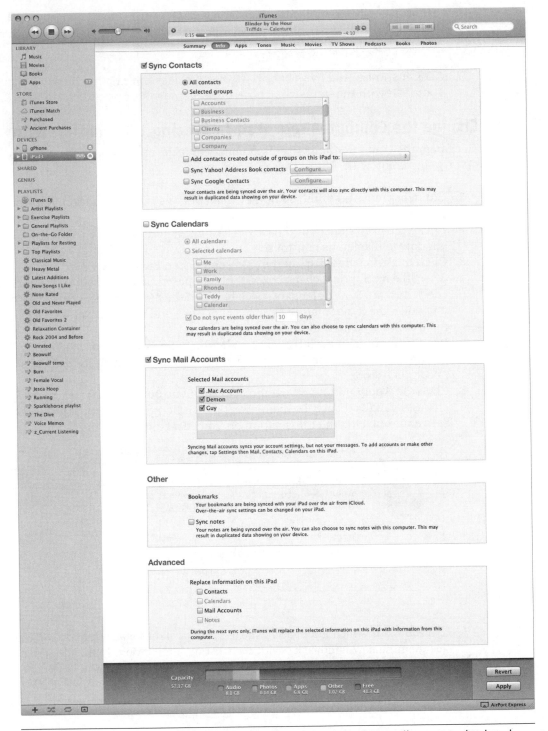

**FIGURE 1-2**    On the Info screen, choose which contacts, calendars, mail accounts, bookmarks, and notes to sync from your computer to your iPad.

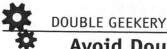

DOUBLE GEEKERY

## Avoid Double-Syncing
## Your Contacts and Calendars

If you're syncing your contacts and calendars using iCloud, make sure you don't sync them using iTunes as well. Syncing twice like this is likely to create duplicated contacts and appointments, which are a real headache to remove.

If you've set iCloud to sync your contacts and calendars, iTunes displays the warning dialog box shown here if you select the Sync Contacts check box or the Sync Calendars check box on the Info screen in iTunes. Click the OK button to dismiss the dialog box, and then clear the Sync Contacts check box or the Sync Calendars check box, as needed.

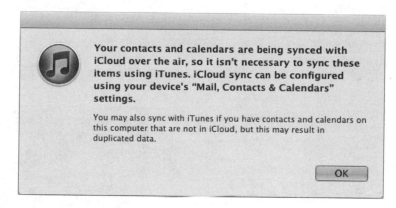

## Change the Computer Your iPad Is Syncing Apps With

To change the computer your iPad is syncing apps with, follow these steps:

1. Connect your iPad to the computer that contains the apps you want to sync.
2. Click your iPad's entry in the Devices category of the Source list in the iTunes window to display its control screens.
3. Click the Apps tab to display the Apps screen (see Figure 1-3).
4. Select the Sync Apps check box.
5. In the list box, clear the check box for each app you don't want to sync. These check boxes are all selected by default.
6. Select the Automatically Sync New Apps check box if you want iTunes to automatically sync new apps with your iPad. (This is usually helpful.)

7. Click the Apply button. iTunes displays a dialog box (shown here) to confirm that you want to replace all your iPad's apps with the apps in this computer's iTunes library.

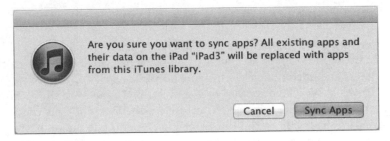

Are you sure you want to sync apps? All existing apps and their data on the iPad "iPad3" will be replaced with apps from this iTunes library.

Cancel    Sync Apps

8. Click the Sync Apps button. iTunes syncs the apps.

**FIGURE 1-3**   On the Apps screen, choose which apps to sync with your iPad.

## Change the Computer Your iPad Is Syncing Photos With

To change the computer your iPad is syncing photos with, follow these steps:

1. Connect your iPad to the computer that contains the photos you want to sync.
2. Click your iPad's entry in the Devices category of the Source list in the iTunes window to display its control screens.
3. Click the Photos tab to display the Photos screen (see Figure 1-4).
4. Select the Sync Photos From check box.
5. In the Sync Photos From drop-down list, choose the source of the photos. For example, choose the Pictures folder on Windows or choose iPhoto on Mac OS X.
6. Use the controls to specify which photos to sync. For example, select the All Photos, Albums, Events, And Faces option button if you want to sync all the photos (assuming they'll fit on your iPad). Or select the Selected Albums, Events, And Faces, And Automatically Include option button, choose a suitable item in the drop-down list, and then select the check box for each album, event, and face you want to sync.

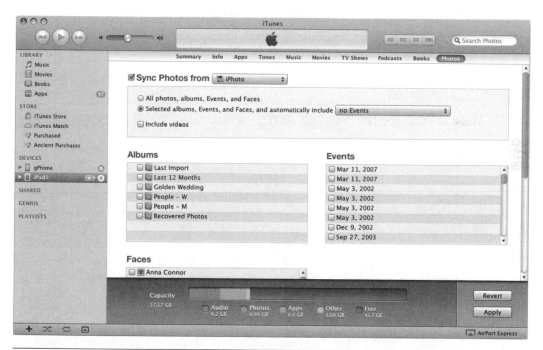

**FIGURE 1-4**   On the Photos screen, choose which photos to sync with your iPad.

7. Click the Apply button. iTunes displays a dialog box (shown here) to confirm that you want to replace the synced photos on your iPad.

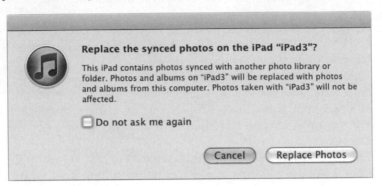

**Replace the synced photos on the iPad "iPad3"?**

This iPad contains photos synced with another photo library or folder. Photos and albums on "iPad3" will be replaced with photos and albums from this computer. Photos taken with "iPad3" will not be affected.

☐ Do not ask me again

[ Cancel ]    [ Replace Photos ]

8. Click the Replace Photos button. iTunes replaces the photos.

 If you're using a Mac, you can use iPhoto or Image Capture to copy photos from your iPad to your Mac. Use iPhoto when you want to gather your photos into Events, edit them, and manage them in iPhoto. Use Image Capture when you just want to get the photos (or screen captures, or saved images) from your iPad into your Mac's file system.

 DOUBLE GEEKERY

# Recover Your Songs and Videos from Your iPad

When you sync your iPad with your computer, any songs and videos on your iPad are also in your library on your computer, so you don't need to transfer the songs and videos from your iPad to your computer. This includes the songs and videos you purchase on your iPad from the iTunes Store. But if you have a computer disaster, or if your computer is stolen, you may need to recover the songs and videos from your iPad to your new or repaired computer.

To recover songs and videos from your iPad, you need a utility that can read your iPad's file system. To help you avoid losing your music and videos, iPad enthusiasts have developed some great utilities for transferring files from your iPad's hidden music and video storage to a computer.

At this writing, several utilities are available for copying your music and videos from your iPad to your computer. The best utility for both Windows and the Mac is DiskAid from DigiDNA ($24.90; www.digidna.net; trial version available). DiskAid (shown next) reads your iPad's library database and displays its contents so that you can easily copy them back to a computer.

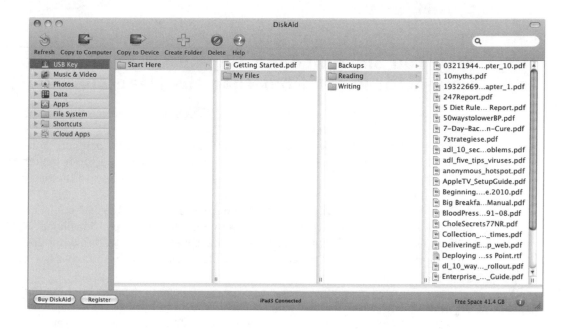

# Project 2: Use Your iPad as Your Home Stereo

Your iPad is great for music on the go, but you can use it as your home stereo as well. In this project, we'll look at the four best ways of doing so:

- Using an iPad speaker dock
- Connecting your iPad directly to your stereo with a cable
- Connecting your iPad to your stereo or speakers via Bluetooth or a radio transmitter
- Using the AirPlay feature to play music to an AirPort Express or Apple TV

## Use an iPad Speaker Dock

The simplest way to get a decent volume of sound from your iPad is to connect it to a pair of powered speakers (speakers that include their own amplifier). You can buy speakers designed especially for the iPad, which use the Dock Connector port for high-quality output. But you can also get good sound using your iPad with any powered speakers that accept input via a miniplug connector (the size of connector used for the iPad's headset).

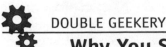

## Why You Should Connect Speakers to the Dock Connector Port Rather Than the Headphone Port

When you connect external speakers to your iPad, you have a choice of ports: the headphone port or the Dock Connector port.

If possible, use the Dock Connector port rather than the headphone port. You can use it either directly with a speaker or cable that has a Dock Connector or indirectly, by connecting your iPad to a dock and then connecting the speakers to the line-out port on the dock.

The Dock Connector port delivers a fixed output level and better audio quality than the headphone port (whose output level varies depending on the volume setting), so it's a much better choice. Most speakers designed specifically for use with the iPad have a Dock Connector that enables them to receive audio at line-out quality and a constant volume.

When you need to connect speakers to the headphone port rather than the Dock Connector port, turn your iPad's volume all the way down at first. The headphone port puts out up to 60 milliwatts (mW) altogether—30 mW per channel—and can deliver a high enough signal to cause distortion or damage to an input that's expecting a standard line-out volume. After you make the connection, start playing audio and turn your iPad's volume up gradually until you get a suitable level on the input.

# Connect Your iPad to Your Existing Stereo

If you have a good stereo, you can play music from your iPad through it. In this section, we'll look at how to connect your iPad to your stereo using a cable, using Bluetooth, and using a radio transmitter.

## Connect Your iPad to a Stereo with a Cable

The most direct way to connect your iPad to a stereo system is with a cable. For a typical receiver, you'll need a cable that has a miniplug at one end and two RCA plugs at the other end. Figure 1-5 shows an example of an iPad connected to a stereo via the amplifier.

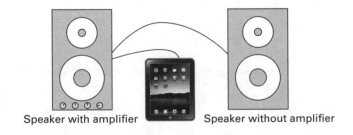

Speaker with amplifier        Speaker without amplifier

**FIGURE 1-5**   A miniplug-to-RCA-plugs cable is the most direct way of connecting an iPad to your stereo system.

Some receivers and boom boxes use a single stereo miniplug input rather than two RCA ports. To connect your iPad to such devices, you'll need a stereo miniplug-to-miniplug cable. Make sure the cable is stereo, because mono miniplug-to-miniplug cables are common. A stereo cable has two bands around the miniplug (as on most headphones), whereas a mono cable has only one band.

If you have a high-quality receiver and speakers, get a high-quality cable to connect your iPad to them. After the amount you've presumably spent on your iPad and stereo, it'd be a mistake to degrade the signal between them by sparing a few bucks on the cable.

 You can find various home-audio connection kits that contain a variety of cables likely to cover your needs. These kits are usually a safe buy, but unless your needs are peculiar, you'll end up with one or more cables you don't need. So if you do know which cables you need, make sure a kit offers a cost savings before buying it instead of the individual cables.

Connect your iPad to your receiver as follows:

1. Connect the miniplug to your iPad's headphone port. If you have a dock, connect the miniplug to the dock's line-out port instead, because this gives a more consistent volume and better sound quality than the headphone port.
2. If you're using the headphone port, turn down the volume on your iPad all the way.
3. Whichever port you're using, turn down the volume on the amplifier as well.
4. Connect the RCA plugs to the left and right ports of one of the inputs on your amplifier or boom box—for example, the AUX input or the Cassette input (if you're not using a cassette deck).

 Don't connect your iPad to the Phono input on your amplifier. The Phono input is built with a higher sensitivity to make up for the weak output of a record player. Putting a full-strength signal into the Phono input will probably blow it.

5. Start the music playing. If you're using the headphone port, turn up the volume a little.
6. Turn up the volume on the receiver so that you can hear the music.
7. Increase the volume on the two controls in tandem until you reach a satisfactory sound level.

 Too low a level of output from your iPad may produce noise as your amplifier boosts the signal. Too high a level of output from your iPad may cause distortion.

## Use a Bluetooth Connection Between Your iPad and Your Stereo

Connecting your iPad to your stereo with a cable gives you great quality, but it means your iPad is anchored in place (unless you get a cable long enough for you to roam the room like a 1970s guitarist). If you want to keep your iPad at hand while you play music through your stereo, try Bluetooth instead.

To connect your iPad to your stereo via Bluetooth, get a device such as the Belkin Bluetooth Music Receiver ($49.95; http://store.apple.com and other retailers). This is a Bluetooth device that connects via a cable to your stereo. You then connect your iPad to the receiver via Bluetooth and play music across the airwaves. Quality is lower than with a cable, but you'll be able to use your iPad without it being tethered.

## Use a Radio Transmitter Between Your iPad and a Stereo

If you don't want to connect your iPad directly to your stereo system or pay for a Bluetooth receiver, you can use a radio transmitter to send the audio from your iPad to the radio on your stereo.

The sound you get from this arrangement typically will be lower in quality than the sound from a wired connection, but it should be at least as good as listening to a conventional radio station in stereo. If that's good enough for you, a radio transmitter can be a neat solution to playing music from your iPad throughout your house.

 Using a radio transmitter has another advantage: You can play the music on several radios at the same time, giving yourself music throughout your dwelling without complex and expensive rewiring.

To use the radio transmitter, you connect it to your iPad's headphone socket or Dock Connector port, set the frequency to transmit, and then set the music playing. When you tune your radio in to that frequency, it receives the broadcast just like a regular radio station.

 For more detail on using a radio transmitter, see the section "Use a Radio Transmitter with Your iPad" in the next project.

# Use Your iPad's AirPlay Feature

Your iPad includes a feature called AirPlay that enables it to play music on remote speakers connected to an AirPort Express wireless access point or Apple TV, or to speakers that implement Apple's AirPlay standard.

If you have an AirPort Express (a wireless access point that Apple makes), you can use it not only to network your home but also to play music from your iPad or your computer through your stereo system. Similarly, if you have an Apple TV, you can use AirPlay to play music from your iPad through the speakers connected to the Apple TV.

To play music through an AirPort Express, first set it up like this:

1. Connect the AirPort Express to the receiver via a cable. The line-out port on the AirPort Express combines an analog port and an optical output, so you can connect the AirPort Express to the receiver in either of two ways:
   - Connect an optical cable to the AirPort Express's line-out socket and to an optical digital-audio input port on the receiver. If the receiver has an optical input, use this arrangement to get the best sound quality possible.

- Connect an analog audio cable to the AirPort Express's line-out socket and to the RCA ports on your receiver.

2. If your network has a wired portion, connect an Ethernet port on the AirPort Express to the switch or hub using an Ethernet cable. If you have a DSL that you will share through the AirPort Express, connect the DSL via the Ethernet cable.

3. Plug the AirPort Express into an electric socket.

To play music through an Apple TV, set it up like this:

1. Connect the Apple TV to the receiver, speakers, or TV. For a receiver or speakers, use an optical audio cable. For a TV, use an HDMI cable or an optical audio cable.

2. If your network has a wired portion, connect the Ethernet port on the Apple TV to the switch or hub using an Ethernet cable.

3. Connect the Apple TV's power supply and turn on the Apple TV.

You can now play music from your iPad by tapping the AirPlay icon, the icon showing a solid triangle superimposed on a hollow rectangle, as shown in the upper-right corner of the screen in Figure 1-6. In the AirPlay dialog box that opens, tap the AirPort Express button.

When you need to switch back to your iPad's speakers, tap the AirPlay icon again, and this time tap the iPad button.

 You can also play music from iTunes through your AirPort Express or Apple TV. Click the AirPlay icon near the lower-right corner of the iTunes window to display the pop-up menu with the speakers you can use. Then click the AirPort Express item or the Apple TV on the menu to direct iTunes' output to the appropriate device. You can also click the Multiple Speakers item on the pop-up menu and use the Multiple Speakers dialog box to direct the output to multiple output devices simultaneously and adjust the relative volume for each.

**FIGURE 1-6**   Tap the AirPlay icon (the triangle and rectangle in the upper-right corner of the screen) to display the AirPlay dialog box, and then tap the AirPort Express button.

# Project 3: Use Your iPad as Your Car Stereo

If you take your iPad everywhere you go, you'll probably want to use it to play music in the car. Most new and recent cars nowadays have some form of built-in connection for connecting an iPod or iPhone, but many of these are not designed to hold an iPad—so you may need to use a different means of connection.

Apart from using a built-in connection, you have three main possibilities:

- Use a cassette adapter to connect your iPad to the car's cassette player.
- Use a radio transmitter to play your iPad's output through the car's radio.
- Wire your iPad directly to the car stereo and use it as an auxiliary input device.

Each of these methods has its pros and cons. The following sections tell you what you need to know to choose the best option for your car stereo.

## Use a Cassette Adapter with Your iPad

If the car stereo has a cassette player, your easiest option is to use a cassette adapter to play audio from your iPad through the cassette deck. You can buy such adapters for between $10 and $20 from most electronics stores or from an iPad specialist.

The adapter is shaped like a cassette and uses a playback head to input analog audio via the head that normally reads the tape as it passes. A wire runs from the adapter to your iPad.

A cassette adapter can be an easy and inexpensive solution, but it's far from perfect. The main problem is that the audio quality tends to be poor, because the means of transferring the audio to the cassette player's mechanism is less than optimal. But if your car is noisy, you may find that road noise obscures most of the defects in audio quality.

If the cassette player's playback head is dirty from playing cassettes, audio quality will be that much worse. To keep the audio quality as high as possible, clean the cassette player regularly using a cleaning cassette.

 If you use a cassette adapter in an extreme climate, try to make sure you don't bake it or freeze it by leaving it in the car.

## Use a Radio Transmitter with Your iPad

If the car stereo doesn't have a cassette deck, your easiest option for playing music from your iPad may be to get a radio transmitter. This device plugs into your iPad and broadcasts a signal on an FM frequency to which you then tune your radio to play the music. Better radio transmitters offer a choice of frequencies to allow you easy access to both your iPad and your favorite radio stations.

Radio transmitters can deliver reasonable audio quality. If possible, try before you buy by asking for a demonstration in the store (take a portable radio with you, if necessary). If you're buying online, read the user reviews closely.

The main advantages of these devices are that they're relatively inexpensive (usually between $15 and $50) and they're easy to use. They also have the advantage that you can put your iPad out of sight without any telltale wires to help the light-fingered locate it.

On the downside, most of these devices need batteries (others can run off the 12-volt accessory outlet or cigarette-lighter socket), and less expensive units tend not to deliver the highest sound quality. The range of these devices is minimal, but at close quarters, other radios nearby may be able to pick up the signal. If you use the radio transmitter in an area where the airwaves are busy, or you drive through areas that use different frequencies, you may need to keep switching the frequency to avoid having the transmitter swamped by the full-strength radio stations.

If you decide to get a radio transmitter, you'll need to choose between getting a model designed specifically for iOS devices with Dock Connector ports and getting one that works with any audio source. Radio transmitters designed for iOS devices typically mount on the device, making them a neater solution than general-purpose ones that dangle from the headphone socket. Radio transmitters designed for use with iOS devices in cars often mount on the accessory outlet or dash and secure the device as well as transmitting its sound. Most of these devices are designed for iPhones and iPods rather than iPads, so you'll probably need a different form of mount—for example, a dashboard mount.

A radio transmitter works with radios other than car radios, so you can use one to play music through your stereo system (or someone else's). You may also want to connect a radio transmitter to a PC or Mac and use it to broadcast audio to a portable radio. This is a great way of getting streaming radio from the Internet to play on a conventional radio.

DOUBLE GEEKERY

## Find a Suitable Frequency for a Radio Transmitter

In most areas, the airwaves are busy these days—so to get good reception on your car's radio from your iPad's radio transmitter, you need to pick a suitable frequency. To do so, follow these steps:

1. With your iPad's radio transmitter turned off, turn on your car radio.
2. Tune the car radio to a frequency on which you get only static, and for which the frequencies one step up and one step down give only static as well. For example, if you're thinking of using the 91.3 frequency, make sure that 91.1 and 91.5 give only static as well.
3. Tune the radio transmitter to the frequency you've chosen, and see if it works. If not, identify and test another frequency.

This method may sound obvious, but what many people do is pick a frequency on the radio transmitter, tune the radio to it—and then feel disappointed by the results.

## Wire Your iPad Directly to a Car Stereo

If neither the cassette adapter nor the radio transmitter provides a suitable solution, or if you simply want the best audio quality you can get, connect your iPad directly to your car stereo. How easily you can do this depends on how the stereo is designed:

- If your car stereo has a miniplug input built in, get a Dock Connector–to-miniplug cable to connect your iPad's Dock Connector port to the miniplug input. You can also use a miniplug-to-miniplug cable from your iPad's headphone port to the miniplug input, but the Dock Connector gives you better quality and a fixed volume.
- If your stereo is built to take multiple inputs—for example, a CD player (or changer) and an auxiliary input—you may be able to simply run a wire from unused existing connectors. Then all you need to do is plug your iPad into the other end and press the correct buttons to get the music going.
- If no unused connectors are available, you or your local friendly electronics technician may need to get busy with a soldering iron.

# Project 4: Use Home Sharing and Library Sharing to the Max

Both iTunes and your iPad are designed to share your music with other computers and devices. You can share music either among computers and devices linked to the same iTunes account or with any compatible computer or device on the same network.

## Understand the Difference Between Home Sharing and Library Sharing

iTunes gives you two different types of sharing:

- **Home Sharing**   Home Sharing lets you share your entire library with up to five computers and with your iPad, iPod touch, or iPhone. You can copy media files from one computer to another, so you can make sure each of your computers contains the same library. You can also set Home Sharing to automatically copy any new media files or apps you buy.
- **Library sharing**   Library sharing lets you share either your entire library or selected playlists with other computers on your network. The other computers can only play the songs or other media files; they cannot copy the files.

 The big difference between Home Sharing and iTunes' library sharing is that Home Sharing enables you to copy files, whereas library sharing doesn't. Home Sharing is for sharing media files among your computers; library sharing is for sharing your media files with other people.

To use Home Sharing, you set up each of the computers to use the same Apple ID. Using the same Apple ID is the mechanism for making sure that you're not violating copyright by giving copyrighted content to other people. If you don't have an Apple ID yet, you can create one from the Home Sharing screen.

 Your iPad can access both the libraries you share via Home Sharing and libraries or playlists you share via library sharing. Your iPad can also access libraries or playlists other people share via library sharing.

## Set Up Home Sharing on Each Computer

To set up Home Sharing, follow these steps:

1. Open iTunes.
2. In the Source list on the left, see if the Shared category is expanded, showing its contents. If not, expand it by holding the mouse pointer over the Shared heading and then clicking the word "Show" when it appears.
3. Click the Home Sharing item to display its contents.
4. Type your Apple ID in the Apple ID box.

 If you don't yet have an Apple ID, click the Need An Apple ID? link, and then follow through the process of signing up for one. Once you're armed with your Apple ID, go back to the Home Sharing screen.

5. Type your password in the Password box.
6. Click the Create Home Share button. iTunes checks in with the iTunes servers and sets up the account.

 If iTunes displays a dialog box saying that Home Sharing could not be activated because this computer is not authorized for the iTunes account associated with the Apple ID you provided, click the Authorize button.

7. When the Home Sharing screen displays the message that Home Sharing is now on, click the Done button. iTunes then removes the Home Sharing item from the Shared category in the Source list, and you have access to the libraries of the other computers on which you've set up Home Sharing.

## Copy Files Using Home Sharing

After setting up Home Sharing, you can quickly copy files from one installation of iTunes to another. To do so, follow these steps:

1. In the Source list in iTunes, make sure the Shared category is expanded, showing its contents. If the Shared category is collapsed, expand it by holding the mouse pointer over the Shared heading and then clicking the word "Show" when it appears.

2. Click the Home Sharing library whose contents you want to see. The library's contents appear in the main part of the iTunes window, and you can browse them as usual (see Figure 1-7). For example, choose View | Column Browser | Show Column Browser to display the column browser so that you can browse by genres, artists, albums, or whichever other items you prefer.

The Home Sharing libraries appear in the Shared category with a Home Sharing icon next to them. The Home Sharing icon shows a house containing a musical note.

3. In the Show drop-down list at the bottom of the iTunes window, choose which items to display:
   - **All Items** This is the default setting. Use it when you want to get an overview of what the library contains.
   - **Items Not In My Library** Use this setting to display only the items you may want to copy to your library.
4. Select the items you want to import to your library. If you've switched to the Items Not In My Library view, you may want to choose Edit | Select All (or press CTRL-A on Windows or ⌘-A on the Mac) to select everything.
5. Click the Import button. iTunes imports the files.

**FIGURE 1-7**   You can browse a Home Sharing library using the same techniques as for browsing your own library.

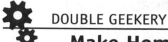

## Make Home Sharing Automatically Import New Purchases from Your Other Computers

You can set Home Sharing to automatically import your new purchases from the iTunes Store to your computer. So if you buy a song on your laptop computer, you can have iTunes automatically import it to your desktop computer as well. If you buy a song on your iPad from the iTunes Store, iTunes syncs the song first to whichever computer you use for syncing, and then imports it to the other computers you've set up for Home Sharing.

To set Home Sharing to automatically import new purchases, follow these steps:

1. In the Source list in iTunes, click a Home Sharing library to display its contents and the Home Sharing control bar.
2. Click the Settings button to display the Home Sharing Settings dialog box (shown here).
3. Select the Music check box, the Movies check box, the TV Shows check box, the Books check box, and the Apps check box, as needed.
4. Click the OK button to close the Home Sharing Settings dialog box.

# Set Up Home Sharing on Your iPad

Next, you need to set up Home Sharing on your iPad to enable it to access the libraries you've shared using Home Sharing in iTunes.

To set up Home Sharing on your iPad, follow these steps:

1. Press the Home button to display the Home screen.
2. Tap the Settings icon to display the Settings screen.
3. Tap the Music button to display the Music screen (shown in Figure 1-8).
4. In the Home Sharing box at the bottom, tap the Apple ID box, and then type your Apple ID and password.

You can now access your shared libraries from the Music app. See the section "Play Shared Music from Your iPad," later in this chapter, for details.

# Set Up Library Sharing in iTunes on Your Computer

You can share either your entire library or selected playlists with other users on your network. You can share most items, including MP3 files, AAC files, Apple Lossless

**FIGURE 1-8** In the Settings app, tap the Music button to display the Music screen, and then enter your Apple ID and password in the Home Sharing box.

Encoding files, AIFF files, WAV files, and links to radio stations. You can't share Audible files or QuickTime sound files.

At this writing, you can share your library with up to five other computers per day, and your computer can be one of up to five computers accessing the shared library on another computer on any given day.

The shared library remains on the computer that's sharing it, and when a participating computer goes to play a song or other item, that item is streamed across the network. This means that the item isn't copied from the computer that's sharing it to the computer that's playing it in a way that leaves a usable file on the playing computer.

When a computer goes offline or is shut down, library items it has been sharing stop being available to other users. While the computer is online, participating

DOUBLE GEEKERY

# Understand Why iTunes May Not Be Able to Access Other Computers on the Same Network

Technically, iTunes' sharing is limited to computers on the same TCP/IP subnet as your computer is on. (A *subnet* is a logical division of a network.) A home network typically uses a single subnet, so your computer can "see" all the other computers on the network. But if your computer connects to a medium-sized network, and you're unable to find a computer that you know is connected to the same network somewhere, it may be on a different subnet.

computers can play the shared items but can't do anything else with them; for example, they can't burn shared songs to CD or DVD, download them to an iPod or iPad, or copy them to their own libraries.

To share either your entire library or selected playlists with other users of iTunes or iPads (or iPod touches, or iPhones) on your network, follow these steps:

1. Display the iTunes dialog box or the Preferences dialog box:
   - In Windows, choose Edit | Preferences or press CTRL-COMMA or CTRL-Y to display the iTunes dialog box.
   - On the Mac, choose iTunes | Preferences or press ⌘-COMMA or ⌘-Y to display the Preferences dialog box.
2. Click the Sharing tab to display it. Figure 1-9 shows the Sharing tab of the iTunes dialog box with settings chosen.
3. Select the Share My Library On My Local Network check box. (This check box is cleared by default.) By default, iTunes then selects the Share Entire Library option button. If you want to share only some playlists, select the Share Selected Playlists option button. Then, in the list box, select the check box for each playlist you want to share.
4. By default, your shared library items are available to any other user on the network. To restrict access to people with whom you share a password, select the Require Password check box, and then enter a strong (unguessable) password in the text box.

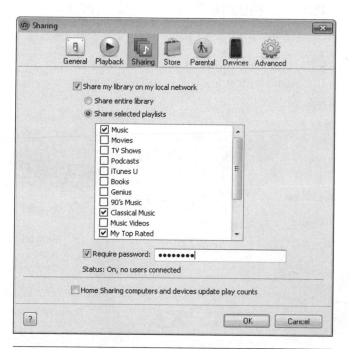

**FIGURE 1-9** On the Sharing tab of the iTunes dialog box or the Preferences dialog box, choose whether to share part or all of your library.

If there are many computers on your network, use a password on your shared music to help avoid running up against the five-users-per-day limit. If your network has only a few computers, you may not need a password to avoid reaching this limit.

5. Select the Home Sharing Computers And Devices Update Play Counts check box if you want iTunes to update the play count for a song whenever any computer plays it, not just this computer.

6. Click the General tab to display its contents. In the Library Name text box near the top of the dialog box, set the name that other users trying to access your library will see. The default name is *username's* Library, where *username* is your username—for example, Anna Connor's Library. You might choose to enter a more descriptive name, especially if your computer is part of a well-populated network (for example, in a dorm).

7. Click the OK button to apply your choices and close the dialog box.

 When you set iTunes to share your library, iTunes displays a message reminding you that "Sharing music is for personal use only"—in other words, remember not to violate copyright law. Select the Do Not Show This Message Again check box if you want to prevent this message from appearing again.

## Play Shared Music from Your iPad

To play shared music from your iPad, follow these steps:

1. Press the Home button to display the Home screen.
2. Tap the Music button to display the Music app.
3. Tap the More button to display the More panel (shown here).

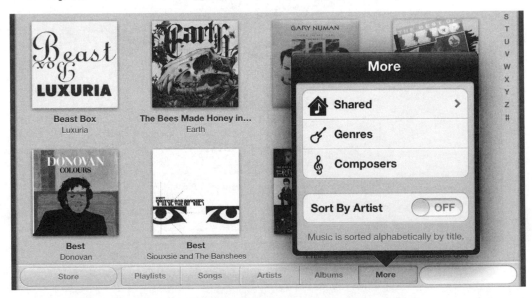

4. Tap the Shared button to display the Shared panel (shown here).

5. Tap the shared music library you want to access.

   If the Shared button doesn't appear on the More panel, Home Sharing is turned off on your iPad. Turn it on as described in the section "Set Up Home Sharing on Your iPad," earlier in this chapter.

# Project 5: Create Your Own Custom Ringtones for Free

To make your iPad sound unique and to give yourself a clear indication of when you receive FaceTime calls, texts, voicemail, tweets, and so on, you can create custom ringtones and sync them to your iPad. This is a great way to get ringtones that you not only like but that enable you to distinguish crucial notifications from ignorable ones by ear.

   Earlier versions of iTunes included a feature for making ringtones from songs bought from the iTunes Store. But Apple has removed this feature from iTunes 10, so you need to create your ringtones manually as described here.

To create a ringtone from a song, follow these steps:

1. Play the song and identify the part you want to use. This can be up to 30 seconds long. Note down the start time and end time.

2. Right-click (or CTRL-click on the Mac) the song, and then click Get Info on the context menu to display the Item Information dialog box for the song.

The Item Information dialog box doesn't actually show the words "Item Information" in its title bar. On Windows, the title bar shows the word "iTunes"; on the Mac, the title bar shows the song's title rather than the words "Item Information."

3. Click the Options tab to bring it to the front of the Item Information dialog box (see Figure 1-10).

4. Click in the Start Time box and enter the start time for the ringtone section—for example, 1:23.200. iTunes automatically selects the Start Time check box for you, so you don't need to select it manually.

When setting the Start Time value and Stop Time value, use a colon to separate the minutes and seconds but a period to separate the seconds and thousandths of seconds.

5. Click in the Stop Time box and enter the end time for the ringtone section. Again, iTunes automatically selects the Stop Time check box for you.

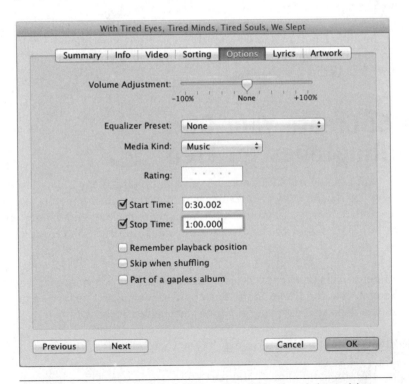

**FIGURE 1-10**   Use the Item Information dialog box (whose title bar shows "iTunes" on Windows and the song's name on the Mac) to cut a ringtone out of a song.

6. Click the OK button to close the Item Information dialog box.

7. Right-click or CTRL-click the song, and then click Create AAC Version on the context menu. iTunes creates a new song file containing just the section of the song you specified by using the Start Time value and Stop Time value.

If the command on the context menu is not Create AAC Version, you need to change the current encoder. Choose Edit | Preferences on Windows or iTunes | Preferences on the Mac to display the iTunes dialog box or the Preferences dialog box. On the General tab, click the Import Settings button. In the Import Settings dialog box, choose AAC Encoder in the Import Using drop-down list and iTunes Plus in the Setting drop-down list. Then click the OK button to close each dialog box in turn.

8. Right-click (or CTRL-click on the Mac) the new, shorter song file, and then click Show In Explorer (on Windows) or Show In Finder (on the Mac) on the context menu. iTunes opens a Windows Explorer window or Finder window showing the song file.

9. Press ENTER or RETURN to display an edit box around the song name.

10. Change the file extension from m4a to m4r, and then press ENTER or RETURN to apply the change. The m4r extension indicates the file type for a ringtone.

11. Leave the Windows Explorer window or Finder window open for the moment and go back to iTunes.

12. With the new song file still selected, choose Edit | Delete. iTunes displays a dialog box confirming you want to remove the file, as shown here.

13. Click the Remove button. iTunes displays a second dialog box asking if you want to move the file to the Recycle Bin (on Windows) or the Trash (on the Mac), as shown here.

14. Click the Keep File button.
15. In the Windows Explorer window or Finder window, click the ringtone file and drag it to the Library category of the Source list in the iTunes window.
16. You're almost done, but you've set the original song file to play only your ringtone section. Restore it to normality by following these substeps:
    a. Right-click or CTRL-click the original file in the iTunes window, and then choose Get Info to display the Item Information dialog box.
    b. If the Summary tab doesn't appear at the front, click it to bring it there.
    c. Clear the Start Time check box and the Stop Time check box.
    d. Click the OK button to close the Item Information dialog box.
17. Now click the Tones item in the Library category of the Source list to display your ringtones. The file you created appears there, and you can start using it.

# Project 6: Spread Your Music Across Your Computers and Devices with iCloud and iTunes Match

Apple's iTunes Match service is a great way of spreading your music automatically among the computers and devices you use. iTunes Match gives you access to online versions of all the songs in your iTunes library. These online versions are stored in iCloud, Apple's new online service.

 In order to use iCloud and iTunes Match, your iPad must be running iOS 5 or later, and preferably the latest version available. This isn't usually a problem, because Apple has made updating your iPad easy whether you use iTunes to perform the upgrade or simply upgrade on your iPad itself.

## Understand How iTunes Match Works

To get your music to spread through iCloud, you need to buy an iTunes Match subscription. iTunes Match is Apple's service for giving you access to music online. Here's how iTunes Match works:

- You buy an iTunes Match subscription, which costs $24.99 per year at this writing.
- iTunes then scans all the songs in your music library to see which of them are available in the iTunes Store. The iTunes Store has more than 20 million songs, so chances are that a good proportion of your songs are in it.
- iTunes gives you access to the matching songs in iCloud. These songs are encoded using Advanced Audio Coding (AAC) at the 256 Kbps bitrate, which means they sound good but are compressed small enough for easy streaming.
- iTunes uploads to iCloud all the songs that are in your library but not in iCloud. This takes a while, depending on how many songs are involved and how fast your Internet connection can shift them, but you need to do it only once for each song.

# Set Up iTunes Match in iTunes on Your PC or Mac

To set up iTunes Match on your PC or Mac, you use iTunes. Follow these steps:

1. Open iTunes if it's not running, or activate it if it is running.
2. In the Store category in the Source list, click the iTunes Match item to display the iTunes Match screen (see Figure 1-11).
3. Click the Subscribe button. iTunes displays the Sign In To Subscribe To iTunes Match dialog box.
4. Type your password, and then click the Subscribe button. The iTunes Match screen then displays a progress readout (see Figure 1-12) as it goes through the steps of gathering information about your iTunes library, matching your music with songs available in the iTunes Store, and uploading your artwork and unmatched songs.

 The iTunes Match process may take several hours—or several days if your library has many songs that need uploading. You can stop it if necessary by clicking the Stop button in the lower-right corner of the iTunes Match screen.

5. Use your computer normally while iTunes Match runs.

**FIGURE 1-11**   To start setting up iTunes Match, click the iTunes Match item in the Source list, and then click the Subscribe button on the iTunes Match screen.

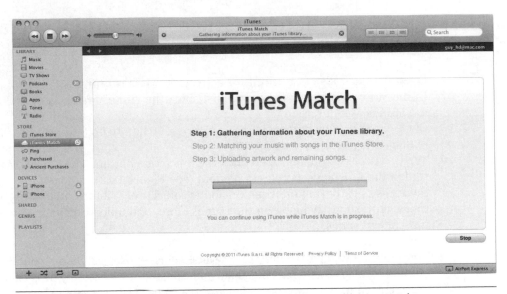

**FIGURE 1-12** iTunes Match goes through the songs in your library, matches as many as possible with songs in the iTunes Store, and uploads your artwork and unmatched songs.

When iTunes Match finishes running, all the songs in your music library are available to your iPad, your other iOS devices, and your other computers through iCloud.

 If you stop iTunes Match before it finishes uploading your songs that aren't available in the iTunes Store, iTunes Match restarts automatically each time you launch iTunes. This can come as a surprise, especially as you may find iTunes Match hogging your Internet connection. To turn iTunes Match off until you want to run it again, choose Store | Turn Off iTunes Match.

## Turn On iTunes Match on Your iPad

Now that you've set up your iTunes Match subscription and identified your songs, you can turn on iTunes Match on your iPad and any other iOS devices.

 Turning on iTunes Match on your iPad (or other iOS device) replaces the music library on your iPad. If you prefer to load your iPad manually with just some of the songs you have in iTunes, don't turn on iTunes Match.

To set up iTunes Match on your iPad, follow these steps:

1. Press the Home button to display the Home screen.
2. Tap the Settings icon to display the Settings screen.
3. Tap the Music button to display the Music screen.
4. Tap the iTunes Match switch and move it to the On position. Your iPad displays the Apple ID Password dialog box.

5. Type your password, and then tap the OK button. Your iPad displays the dialog box shown here, telling you that iTunes Match will replace the music library on your iPad.
6. Tap the Enable button to turn on iTunes Match.
7. At the top of the Music screen, choose settings for the two extra switches that appear (see the illustration at right).
   - **Use Cellular Data**   Move this switch to the On position if you want to play music from iCloud even when your iPad is using the cellular network rather than Wi-Fi. This switch appears only if your iPad has cellular connectivity.

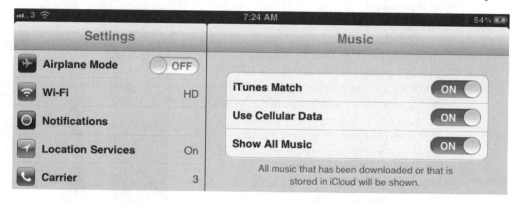

   - **Show All Music**   Move this switch to the On position if you want to see all the songs you have available in iCloud. Move this switch to the Off position if you want to see only the songs that are available on your iPad. For example, when you have no Internet connection, it's helpful to view only the available songs so you don't try to play songs that aren't available.

# Project 7: Record High-Quality Audio Using an External Microphone

Your iPad's built-in microphone is fine for chatting on video calls via FaceTime, and for recording voice notes into apps that support them. So is the microphone built into your iPad's headset controls. But if you need to record high-quality audio, you'll normally want to use an external microphone.

If you plan to use an external microphone, you'll normally need to use a third-party app to record audio from it. This section first explains your options for connecting an external microphone and then introduces you to four third-party apps for recording audio.

## Choose an External Microphone

You can get miniature external microphones that plug into your iPad's headphone port and capture audio better than the built-in microphone, but these are mostly suitable for capturing spoken audio such as lecture notes. If you're planning to record music at a quality you'll be able to enjoy afterward, you'll normally want to get a handheld condenser microphone.

You have two basic options here:

- **Get a microphone specifically designed for iOS devices**   At this writing, the main contender in this category is the iRig Mic from IK Multimedia ($59.99; www .ikmultimedia.com and various online stores). The iRig Mic (see Figure 1-13) is a full-size unidirectional condenser microphone with a cable leading to a 3.5-mm jack that connects to your iPad's headphone socket. The connector also has a headphone socket so that you can listen to the audio.

- **Get a microphone adapter and connect your own microphone**   If you want to be able to connect any regular microphone (for example, a high-quality microphone you have already), get a microphone adapter that converts from a 1/4-inch microphone jack or a 1/8-inch microphone jack to your iPad's 3.5-mm microphone input jack. You can find many such adapters on sites such as Amazon.com and eBay, for prices starting at a handful of dollars. Usually, you'll want to pay enough to get an adapter of a quality at least as high as your microphone so that you don't degrade the signal.

## Choose an App for Recording Audio from Your External Microphone

**FIGURE 1-13**   The iRig Mic connects to your iPad's headphone socket and provides its own headphone socket for monitoring the input. (Photo courtesy of IK Multimedia Production srl.)

Now that you've chosen your external microphone, you need to get a third-party app that can record audio via that microphone. Here are four of the leading contenders, all of which you can get from the App Store:

- **FiRe (Field Recorder)**   If you need to capture live audio, FiRe ($5.99) is a good choice. FiRe can record in either mono or stereo using either your iPad's built-in microphone or an external microphone that you connect. As you record, FiRe displays a waveform in real time, so you can see what you're getting. The left screen in Figure 1-14 shows FiRe's input screen, on which you can control the gain, choose the quality, decide whether to play audio through, turn audio processing on or off, and choose which preset to use. You can choose among different presets, such as Male Voice Enhancer, Female Voice Enhancer, Live Concert Outdoors, and Noise Gate. The right screen in Figure 1-14 shows FiRe in action recording audio.

At this writing, most recording apps are designed for the iPhone and iPod touch. But they run on the iPad as well, even though they don't make the most of its screen space.

- **iRig Recorder**   If you went with the iRig Mic as your microphone, iRig Recorder may seem the obvious choice as your recording app. Your best approach is to start with the free version, iRig Recorder FREE, and then either buy the full version of iRig Recorder for $4.99 or buy only the add-ons you want. For example, you may want to buy the editing add-on but not the processing add-on.
- **ISW Recorder and Editor**   ISW Recorder and Editor is free, so it's well worth trying to see if it meets your needs. You can cut recordings down to only the parts you

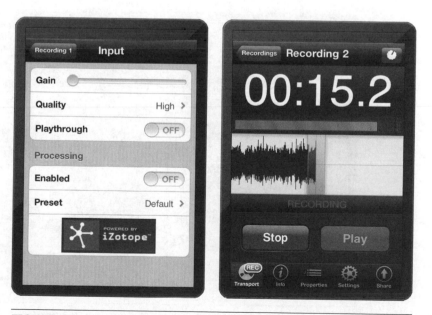

**FIGURE 1-14**   After choosing options such as Gain, Quality, and Playthrough on the Input screen (left), you can set FiRe recording (right) and see the waveform of the audio you're capturing.

need, rearrange audio snippets into your preferred order, and share them via e-mail, Twitter, or Facebook. The left screen in Figure 1-15 shows ISW Recorder and Editor.

- **iProRecorder** iProRecorder ($4.99) is a business-oriented recorder intended mainly for dictation and transcription, although you can of course use it to record any other audio as well. iProRecorder (shown on the right in Figure 1-15) features adjustable playback speed and a jog/shuttle wheel, both of which are helpful when you're transcribing a recording.

# Project 8: Play Your Guitar Through Your iPad

If you play electric guitar, you can connect it to your iPad and play it through your iPad. This is great because you can not only play your guitar through headphones so that you blast your own ears rather than the neighbors, but also use your iPad as a bunch of effects pedals to get the sound you want. Your iPad is easier to carry than a bagful of effects pedals, and the apps for producing the effects cost much less than the physical pedals.

You can use this technique for any instrument that has a pickup—electric bass, electric violin, or whatever.

In this section, we'll first get your guitar connected to your iPad with a cable. We'll then look at special-effects apps you can use to enhance the sound.

**FIGURE 1-15** ISW Recorder and Editor (left) is a free recorder that includes basic editing capabilities. iProRecorder (right) is a business-oriented recorder that features adjustable playback speed and a jog/shuttle wheel for making transcription easier.

# Connect Your Guitar to Your iPad

To connect your guitar to your iPad, you'll need either a cable that goes from your guitar's 1/4-inch output to your iPad's headphone port or an adapter that lets you make this connection. Here are two of the leading possibilities:

- **GuitarConnect Cable**  The GuitarConnect Cable from Griffin Technology ($29.99; www.griffintechnology.com) is a guitar cable with a built-in splitter. You plug the GuitarConnect's 1/4-inch jack into your guitar, plug the 1/8-inch jack on the other end into your iPad's headphone socket, and optionally plug your headphones into the headphone port on the GuitarConnect.
- **AmpliTube iRig**  The AmpliTube iRig from IK Multimedia ($39.99; www .ikmultimedia.com or sites such as Amazon.com) is a guitar connector and splitter. You plug your regular guitar lead into one end of the iRig (see Figure 1-16), plug the cable at the other end into your iPad's headphone socket, and optionally plug your headphones into the other port on the iRig.

 You can also connect the headphone port on the GuitarConnect Cable or the AmpliTube iRig to an amplifier or stereo.

Now that you've connected your guitar, what you play goes into your iPad, where you can record it or run it through an effects app, as discussed next.

**FIGURE 1-16**   The AmpliTube iRig gives you an easy way to connect your guitar to your iPad's headphone socket. You can also plug your headphones into the iRig to listen to what you're playing.

# Apply Special Effects to Your Guitar

Now that your guitar input is going into your iPad, you can apply effects to it by using an app such as one of these:

- **AmpliTube**    AmpliTube is a family of effects apps from IK Multimedia designed to work with the iRig. There are enough versions to be confusing. You'll probably want to start with AmpliTube FREE for iPad or AmpliTube Fender FREE for iPad before moving on to AmpliTube for iPad ($19.99), AmpliTube Fender ($14.99), or AmpliTube LE ($2.99). At this writing, AmpliTube Fender and AmpliTube LE don't have iPad-specific versions. Figure 1-17 shows AmpliTube.
- **iShred LIVE**    iShred LIVE is a stompbox effects app. iShred LIVE is free, but you have to pay for effects—Adrenaline, Kömpressör, Trembler, Screamer, Octavinator, and so on. Most effects cost $0.99 each, but some cost $1.99 or more. You can also buy a Power Pack that contains all the effects. Figure 1-18 shows iShred LIVE.

Having your iPad do the work of effects pedals is great, but it means that you need to tap your iPad's screen to change effects. If you want to be able to change effects without interrupting your playing, consider getting the StompBox controller from Griffin Technology ($59.99; www.griffintechnology.com or various online retailers). The StompBox (shown in Figure 1-19 connected to an iPad) is a physical pedal that you can connect to your iPad and use to control the effects in iShred LIVE.

**FIGURE 1-17**    AmpliTube is a family of effects apps that works with the iRig guitar connector.

**FIGURE 1-18**    iShred LIVE is an effects app that works with the GuitarConnect Cable.

FIGURE 1-19 Add the Griffin StompBox to your iPad guitar setup if you want to control your effects with your feet as you play. (Photo courtesy of Griffin Technology, Inc.)

 To keep your effects at your fingertips, get a case or holster that lets you sling your iPad across your body. Alternatively, get an iPad holder such as the iKlip (around $40; www.ikmultimedia.com) that lets you mount your iPad on a mike stand, where you can use it both for effects and for your set list.

# Project 9: Record Your Band on Your iPad

If you play live in a band, you'll probably want to record it. Your iPad is a great tool for the task once you equip it with suitable hardware and software.

 You can record audio using your iPad's built-in microphone and a third-party recording app such as those discussed in Project 7, but you will normally get better results by using an external microphone. See Project 7, "Record High-Quality Audio Using an External Microphone," for suggestions on which microphone to choose.

In this section, you'll first choose how to input your audio into your iPad. You'll then choose a recording app that can capture the audio.

## Choose Your Input

If you want to record a live performance, you can simply use a microphone as discussed in Project 7, "Record High-Quality Audio Using an External Microphone," and an app such as iRig Recorder or FiRe. But you can also use your iPad as a multi-track recorder by installing the right app. You can then lay down a single track at a time, just as you would with a physical multi-track recorder, and mix the tracks together to produce the result you want.

To capture input from a voice or from an acoustic instrument without a pickup, use a microphone as mentioned above, but record it as a track on a multi-track recorder.

To capture input directly from a "real" instrument such as a guitar or bass, connect it using a cable such as the Griffin GuitarConnect Cable or the AmpliTube iRig. See the previous project for details on these connectors.

To capture MIDI input from a keyboard, drum machine, or other device that has a MIDI output, get a MIDI interface such as the iRig MIDI ($69.99; www.ikmultimedia .com) or the MIDI Mobilizer II ($99.99 list but widely available for much less; http:// line6.com/midimobilizer/).

## Choose a Recording App

What you need next is a suitable app for recording the audio that the microphone or input picks up. Here are three apps to consider:

- **Multi Track DAW**   Multi Track DAW (shown in Figure 1-20; $9.99) is a digital audio workstation (DAW) that can record up to eight tracks. You can view the tracks as either waveforms or as volume meters, and you can set the volume of each track to a suitable level to create the overall mix. You can import songs from your iPad's music library into tracks, which can be a great way of getting a song started quickly. Multi Track DAW is an iPad app, so it makes the most of the iPad's screen.
- **FiRe Studio**   FiRe Studio ($4.99) can record and mix up to eight tracks, giving you plenty of flexibility. You can scroll quickly through the waveforms, place the playback head where you want to start playback, and lock finished tracks to prevent changes. At this writing, FiRe Studio is designed for the iPhone and iPod touch but also works on the iPad.

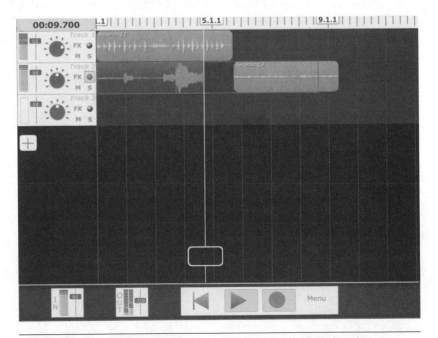

**FIGURE 1-20**   Multi Track DAW is a digital audio workstation that can record up to eight tracks.

- **StudioApp**    StudioApp ($4.99) is a recorder that enables you to add up to four tracks to instrumental tracks. StudioApp targets hip-hop artists, rappers, and singers, but it works for any audio you input. Like FiRe Studio, StudioApp is designed for the iPhone and iPod touch.

# Project 10: Fix Your Off-Key Singing with Your iPad

If you record your singing, or if you sing live, you'll likely want it to sound as good as possible. To help, you can get various iPad apps that can improve the sound of your vocals and even fix off-key singing. Here are two apps to start with:

- **improVox**    improVox ($3.99) is a vocals app that provides real-time pitch adjustment and can also apply harmonies to your vocals. To use improVox (see Figure 1-21), you drag the dot on the left side to adjust the harmony and the dot on the right side to adjust the effects (Stutter, Reverb, Echo, and Cavern). At the bottom of the screen, you can set the key, choose the style, and pick a mood.
- **VocaLive**    If you want to record and process vocals, try VocaLive for iPad (see Figure 1-22). Start with the free version, VocaLive Free for iPad, and graduate to the paid version (called VocaLive for iPad and costing $19.99) if it suits you. The full version includes a real-time vocal processor and a dozen vocal effects— including Pitch Fix, Choir, De-Esser, and Chorus—that enable you to make your vocals sound substantially different (better, unless you prefer it otherwise).

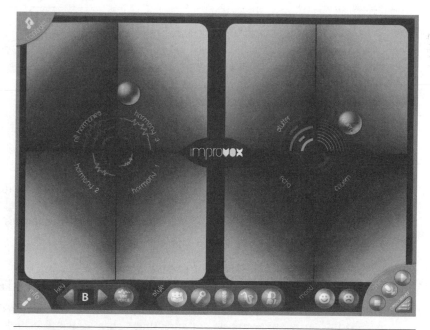

**FIGURE 1-21**    improVox lets you correct your pitch in real time and apply harmonies to what you sing.

**FIGURE 1-22** VocaLive is an app for recording and processing vocals.

# Project 11: Use Your iPad as Your Backing Track

Playing music along with your band is great, but chances are you'll sometimes need to play on your own. When this happens, you don't need to play alone, because you can use your iPad as your backing track.

 In this section, I'm assuming you want to play music you've created as your backing track. If you want to play along to someone else's music, you can pick up karaoke mixes or guitar-free mixes of many songs from various sites on the Internet.

## Choose a Suitable App as Your Backing Track

Which app will suit you best to provide your backing track depends on what you need to do—but here are four examples of apps that you may want to look at:

- **GarageBand**   GarageBand ($4.99) is Apple's app for composing and recording music on both the Mac and the iPad. In GarageBand, you can quickly assemble backing tracks by using either the audio loops provided with the app or loops you purchase elsewhere, record audio from live instruments (such as guitars or drums), and mix the tracks together. Figure 1-23 shows GarageBand on the iPad.
- **BeatMaker**   BeatMaker ($9.99) and BeatMaker 2 ($19.99) are high-powered sequencing apps. You can load an existing kit or develop a custom kit, play it live or record it, and arrange patterns into tracks that sound the way you want them to. Figure 1-24 shows the pads in a BeatMaker kit loaded and ready to play or record.
- **GigBaby**   GigBaby ($0.99) is a four-track recorder with a built-in rhythm section. You can set the rhythm you want, record other backing tracks to play along with it, and then use GigBaby either as your accompaniment or to record your lead performance. Figure 1-25 shows GigBaby at work. At this writing, GigBaby is designed for the iPhone and iPod touch but also works on the iPad.
- **Band**   Band ($3.99) is an app for playing virtual instruments onscreen—bass, grand piano, and two drum kits (see Figure 1-26). You can play the instruments in real time at a pinch, but what you'll normally want to do is record your instrumental parts so that Band can play them back while you play along on a real

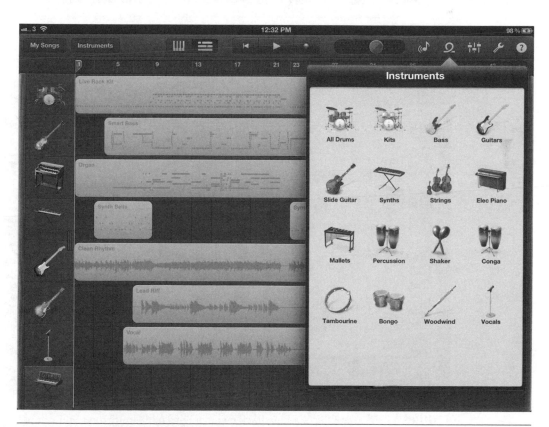

**FIGURE 1-23**   GarageBand is a powerful app for composing and recording music on your iPad.

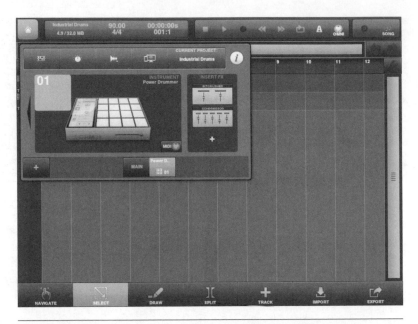

**FIGURE 1-24** BeatMaker is a sequencing app that lets you play existing kits or develop custom kits containing the sounds you want.

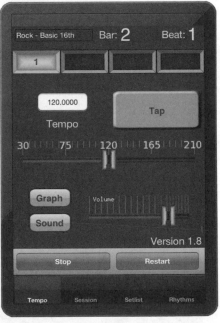

**FIGURE 1-25** GigBaby is a four-track recorder with built-in rhythms you can use as a base for your songs.

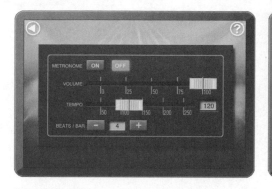

**FIGURE 1-26**    Band provides a set of virtual instruments that you can either play live or record as your accompaniment.

instrument. At this writing, Band is designed for the iPhone and iPod touch but also works on the iPad.

## Connect Your iPad to Your Amp or Sound Board

To get your backing track to play along with you, you'll need to connect your iPad to your amp or to your sound board.

You can connect your iPad via its headphone socket using a cable with a 3.5-mm plug at the iPad's end and whatever is needed at the amplifier's end—for example, a 1/4-inch plug or two RCA plugs. But if you have the choice, use a cable that has a Dock Connector at the iPad's end. Using the iPad's Dock Connector port gives you a line-level output, which has a constant volume and is much easier to work with than the output of the headphone port, whose volume depends on the volume setting.

 If you have an iPad dock that has a line-out port, you can use that instead of getting a cable with a Dock Connector.

# 2

# Photo and Video Geekery

Equipped with its high-resolution camera at the back and the user-facing camera at the front, your iPad is ready to capture photos and video either fore or aft. It's also pretty good at playing back video, either on its screen for your enjoyment or on an external monitor or a TV so that you can share it with others without necessarily getting intimate.

We'll start this chapter by looking at how you can turn your iPad into an extra display for your computer. I'll then show you how to put your videos and DVDs on your iPad so you can watch them wherever you want. We'll then move on to the procedure for watching video from your iPad on your TV. We'll then look at how to share your photos among your iPad and your other devices by using Apple's Photo Stream feature.

After that, I'll show you how to use your iPad as an in-car entertainment system, and how to take time-lapse movies and shoot video at different frame rates.

Toward the end of the chapter, I'll show you how to build your own Steadicam rig to hold and stabilize your iPad so that you can shoot good-quality video while you're moving. And last, we'll go through how to view your webcam on your iPad, either as a party trick (if you have that kind of party) or to keep tabs on home when you're away.

## Project 12: Use Your iPad as an Extra Display for Your Computer

With its pin-sharp screen, your iPad is great for displaying content. Normally, that'll be the content the iPad itself is displaying on its screen—but it doesn't have to be. By installing the right software, you can use your iPad as an extra display for your PC or Mac, giving yourself more screen space to work in.

 To use Air Display, your iPad and your computer must connect to the same wireless network. Normally, this is no problem, but if your computer doesn't have wireless networking capabilities, you'll need to add them.

## Buy and Install Air Display on Your iPad

First, you need to install the Air Display app on your iPad. Air Display costs $9.99 and comes from the App Store. So buy and download Air Display using either your iPad or your computer:

- **iPad**   Press the Home button to display the Home screen, then tap the App Store icon to open the App Store app. Tap the search box, type **air display**, and then tap the Air Display result in the iPad Apps area. Tap the price button, and then tap the Buy App button.
- **Computer**   In the Source pane in iTunes, double-click the iTunes Store item to open a new window to the iTunes Store. Click the Search box, type **air display**, and press ENTER or RETURN. Click the price button, and then sign in if prompted. When the download completes, sync your iPad to install the app.

# Download and Install the Windows Program or Mac Application

Next, download and install the Windows program or Mac application that you use to connect to your iPad via Air Display.

### Download the Air Display Driver on Windows or the Mac

Follow these steps:

1. Open your web browser.
2. Close all your other applications. You'll need to restart your computer to complete the installation of the Air Display driver.
3. In your web browser, select the current address in the Address box. The easiest way is to press ALT-D on Windows or ⌘-L on the Mac.
4. Type **avatron.com/d** over the selection and press ENTER or RETURN.
5. If your browser prompts you to choose whether to run or save the Air Display Setup file, click the Run button.
6. Follow through the installation routine for the software as described in the following sections.

### Install the Air Display Driver on Windows

On Windows, you use the Air Display Support Setup Wizard to install the Air Display driver. The Setup Wizard is straightforward. Here are the only points you need to know about:

- **Select Setup Language dialog box**   In this dialog box, choose your language in the drop-down list, and then click the OK button.

- **Windows Security dialog box**   This dialog box (shown here) asks you whether you want to install the Avatron display adapter. Leave the Always Trust Software From "Avatron Software, Inc." check box cleared—you don't know what Avatron will produce next. Then click the Install button.

- **Restart dialog box**   When the Air Display Support Setup Wizard prompts you to restart your PC, click the Yes button. After Windows restarts and you log back on, you'll be in business.

## Install the Air Display Driver on the Mac

On the Mac, you download a disk image file containing the Air Display Installer.

Depending on how you've configured your Mac, OS X may mount the disk image automatically for you and display a Finder window showing its contents. If this doesn't happen, click the Downloads icon on the right side of the Dock to display the Downloads stack, and then click the AirDisplayInstaller.dmg file. OS X mounts the disk image and opens a Finder window showing its contents.

Close all the applications you're running, then double-click the Air Display Installer.pkg file to launch the Air Display Installer. Click the Continue button and follow through the installation routine. It's all normal—you accept the license agreement, and so on—until you reach the dialog box (shown here) warning you that you must restart your Mac when the software finishes installing.

Click the Continue Installation button and let the installer roll. When the Install Air Display dialog box shows the message "The installation was successful," click the Restart button to restart your Mac. After your Mac restarts and you log back in, you can start using Air Display.

## Connect Your iPad and Your Computer to the Same Wireless Network

Next, make sure your iPad and your computer are connected to the same wireless network:

- **iPad**   Press the Home button to display the Home screen, then tap the Settings icon to display the Settings screen. Tap the Wi-Fi button in the left column, and then tap the network in the Choose A Network list. If the network is secured (as most are), enter the password or other security information.
- **Windows**   Click the wireless icon in the notification area to display the pop-up panel of wireless networks. Click the network's name, and then click the Connect button that appears. If the network is secured, enter the password or other security information.
- **Mac**   Click the Wi-Fi icon (in Mountain Lion or Lion) or the AirPort icon (in Snow Leopard) at the right end of the menu bar to display the Wi-Fi menu. Click the network's name to connect to it. If the network is secured, enter the required information.

## Connect Your PC to Your iPad via Air Display

To connect your PC to your iPad via Air Display, follow these steps:

1. On your iPad, launch the Air Display app. Stay on the setup screen that shows your iPad's IP address.
2. On your PC, click the Air Display icon in the notification area to display the pop-up menu (shown here).

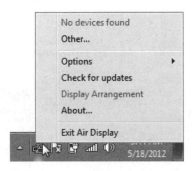

3. If your iPad appears, click it. Otherwise, click the Other item to display the Connect To Other Device dialog box (shown here), type the IP address in the text box, and then click the OK button.

4. Click the Air Display icon in the notification area to display the pop-up menu again, and then click Display Arrangement to display the Display Arrangement dialog box (see Figure 2-1).
5. Drag the monitors to the appropriate positions.
6. Click the OK button.

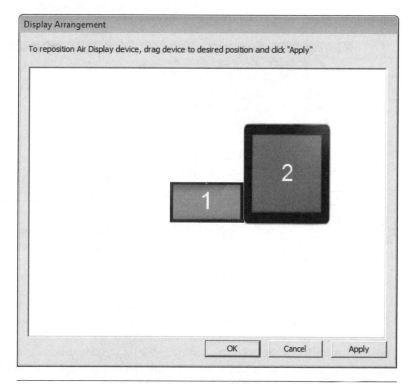

**FIGURE 2-1**    In the Display Arrangement dialog box, drag the monitors to the appropriate positions to reflect their physical locations.

You can now use your iPad as an extra monitor for your PC. When you are ready to disconnect your iPad, click the Air Display icon in the notification area, click the iPad's name or IP address on the pop-up menu, and then click the Disconnect item on the submenu.

# Connect Your Mac to Your iPad via Air Display

To connect your Mac to your iPad via Air Display, follow these steps:

1. On your iPad, launch the Air Display app. Stay on the setup screen that shows your iPad's IP address.

## DOUBLE GEEKERY

### Choose Settings for Air Display

To control how Air Display behaves, you can choose settings in the Settings app. Tap the Settings icon on the Home screen, then tap the Air Display button in the Apps list to display the Air Display screen (shown here).

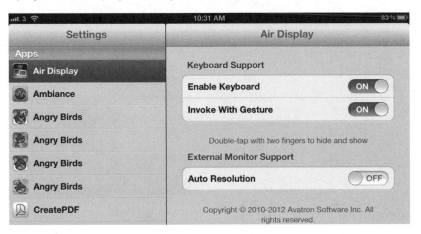

You can then choose the following settings:

- **Enable Keyboard**   Set this switch to the On position if you want to be able to use the iPad's keyboard. This is sometimes useful, but if you're using a hardware keyboard with your computer, you may prefer to set this switch to the Off position.
- **Invoke With Gesture**   Set this switch to the On position if you want to be able to summon up the keyboard by using a gesture. Set this switch to the Off position if you don't want to pop up the keyboard unintentionally.
- **Auto Resolution**   Set this switch to the On position if you want Air Display to set the resolution automatically.

2. On your Mac, choose Apple | System Preferences to display the System Preferences window.
3. In the Other category, click the Air Display icon to display the Air Display pane (see Figure 2-2).
4. Make sure the On/Off switch on the left side is set to the On position.
5. At the bottom of the pane, select the Show Air Display In Menu Bar check box so that you will be able to control Air Display from the menu bar. This is the easiest way of controlling it.

If you don't want to use high resolutions on your iPad, click the Settings tab to display the Settings pane, then clear the Use Retina Resolutions When Available check box. Using high resolutions on the iPad tends to make everything look too small on the iPad when you're using it as an extra display unless your Mac is using the HiDPI high-resolution feature on its own screen.

6. Open the Device pop-up menu, and then click the entry for your iPad. Your Mac connects to your iPad and starts using its screen as an extra desktop.

If your iPad doesn't appear on the Device pop-up menu, click the Connect To Other item to display the Connect dialog box. Type the IP address shown on the iPad's screen into the Enter IP Address Displayed On Air Display Device text box, and then click the OK button.

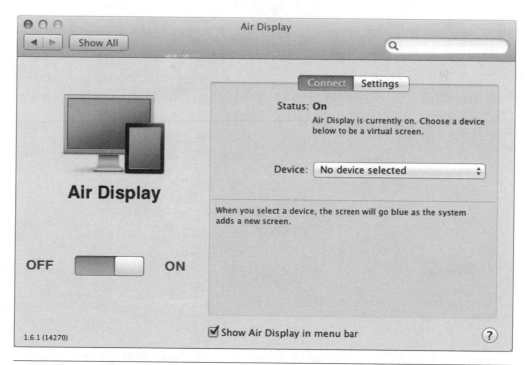

**FIGURE 2-2**    On the Mac, use the Air Display pane in System Preferences to configure Air Display and connect to your iPad.

7. Still in the System Preferences app, choose View | Displays to open the Displays preferences pane. You'll see a Displays preferences pane on each display. The Displays preferences pane on your Mac's primary display has the Arrangement tab as well as the Display tab and the Color tab.

8. Click the Arrangement tab to bring it to the front (see Figure 2-3).

9. Drag the icon for your iPad's display so that it's positioned in the appropriate place relative to your Mac's other displays. For example, if you will position your iPad to the left of your Mac's display, position the iPad's icon to the left of the icon for the Mac's display.

10. Click the Close button (the red button at the left end of the title bar) to close the System Preferences window and quit System Preferences.

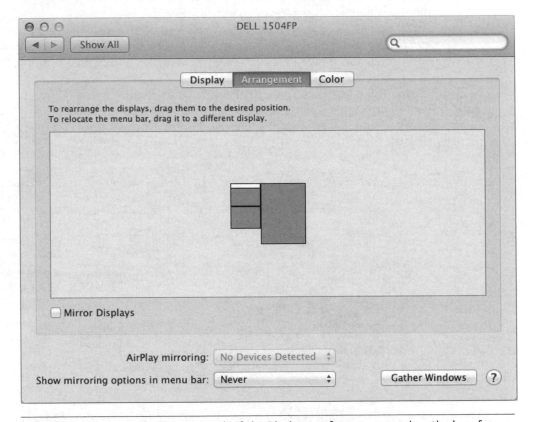

**FIGURE 2-3** On the Arrangement tab of the Displays preferences pane, drag the icon for your iPad's display to a position corresponding to its physical position.

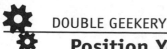

DOUBLE GEEKERY

# Position Your iPad as an Extra Monitor

If you find your iPad works well as an extra monitor, get a means of positioning it so you can use it best.

If you have a case with a built-in stand, that'll do in a pinch. But if you want to be able to position your iPad in exactly the right position for working with your computer's monitor, consider more flexible alternatives such as these:

- **WALLPORT**   The WALLPORT from Tablet WALLPORT (www.tabletwallport.com) is an aluminum mount for mounting the iPad either on a wall or on a 100mm VESA mount. That means you can mount your iPad on a regular monitor stand, should you happen to have a spare one. Even better, you can mount the iPad on a multi-monitor mounting arm, which lets you position it exactly where it's needed. The WALLPORT costs $39.95.

- **Wallee**   The Wallee—or the Wallee Modular iPad System, to give the product its full name—from Tethertools (www.tethertools.com/plugging-in/wallee-ipad-modular-case/) consists of an iPad case and modular accessories for mounting the iPad (and case) quickly on tripods, light stands, arms, and other photographic kit. The Wallee Case alone costs $39.95, but you'll probably need the Connect Kit ($119.90), which includes the case and a connect bracket.

You can now use your iPad as an extra display. When you are ready to disconnect your iPad, click the Air Display icon on the menu bar, and then click Turn Air Display Off, as shown here.

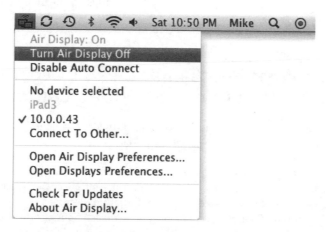

 You can also click No Device Selected on the Air Display menu to stop using Air Display for now but leave it running.

# Project 13: Put Your Videos and DVDs on Your iPad

With its bright, high-resolution screen, your iPad is great for watching video wherever you go—provided you have files of the videos and movies you want to watch.

Apple's iTunes Store provides a wide selection of video content, including TV series and full-length movies, and you can buy or download video in iPad-compatible formats from various other sites online.

But if you enjoy watching video on your iPad, you'll almost certainly want to put your own video content on it. You may also want to rip files from your own DVDs so that you can watch them on your iPad. This project shows you how to do so.

## Create iPad-Friendly Video Files from Your Digital Video Camera

If you make your own movies with a digital video camera, you can easily put them on the iPad. To do so, you use an application such as Windows Movie Maker (Windows) or iMovie (Mac) to capture the video from your digital video camera and turn it into a home movie.

Video formats are confusing at best—but the iPad and iTunes make the process of getting suitable video files as easy as possible. The iPad can play videos in the MP4 format up to 2.5 Mbps (megabits per second) or the H.264 format up to 1080p. Programs designed to create video files suitable for the iPad typically give you a choice between the MP4 format and the H.264 format. As a point of reference, VHS video quality is around 2 Mbps, while DVD is about 8 Mbps.

### DOUBLE GEEKERY

## Learn What You Can and Can't Legally Do with Other People's Video Content

Before you start putting your videos and DVDs on the iPad, it's a good idea to know the bare essentials about copyright and decryption:

- If you created the video (for example, it's a home video or DVD), you hold the copyright to it, and you can do what you want with it—put it on the iPad, release it worldwide, or whatever. The only exceptions are if what you recorded is subject to someone else's copyright or if you're infringing on your subjects' rights (for example, to privacy).
- If someone has supplied you with a legally created video file that you can put on your iPad, you're fine doing so. For example, if you download a video from the iTunes Store, you don't need to worry about legalities.
- If you own a copy of a commercial DVD, you need permission to rip (extract) it from the DVD and convert it to a format the iPad can play. Even decrypting the DVD in an unauthorized way (such as creating a file rather than simply playing the DVD) is technically illegal.

## Create iPad-Friendly Video Files Using Windows Live Movie Maker or Windows Movie Maker

Unlike the last few versions of Windows, Windows 7 doesn't include Windows Movie Maker, the Windows program for editing videos. But you can download the nearest equivalent, Windows Live Movie Maker, from the Windows Live website (http://explore.live.com/windows-live-movie-maker?os = other).

 When you install Windows Live Movie Maker, the Windows Live Essentials installer encourages you to install all the Windows Live Essentials programs—Messenger, Photo Gallery, Mail, Writer, Family Safety, and several others. If you don't want the full set, click the Choose The Programs You Want To Install button on the What Do You Want To Install? screen, and then select only the programs you actually want.

Windows Live Movie Maker can't export video files in an iPad-friendly format, so what you need to do is export the video file in the WMV format, and then convert it using another application, such as Full Video Converter Free (discussed later in this chapter).

Similarly, the versions of Windows Movie Maker included with Windows Vista and Windows XP can't export video files in an iPad-friendly format, so what you need to do is export the video file in a standard format (such as AVI) that you can then convert using another application.

**Create a WMV File from Windows Live Movie Maker**    To create a WMV file from Windows Live Movie Maker, open the project and follow these steps:

1. Click the unnamed tab at the left end of the Ribbon to display its menu, and then click the Save Movie item to display the Save Movie panel.
2. In the Common Settings section, click For Computer. The Save Movie dialog box opens.
3. Type the name for the movie, choose the folder in which to store it, and then click the Save button.

Now that you've created a WMV file, use a converter program such as Full Video Converter Free (discussed later in this chapter) to convert it to a format that the iPad can play.

**Create an AVI File from Windows Movie Maker on Windows Vista**    To save a movie as an AVI file from Windows Movie Maker on Windows Vista, follow these steps:

1. With your movie open in Windows Movie Maker, choose File | Publish Movie (or press CTRL-P) to launch the Publish Movie Wizard. The Wizard displays the Where Do You Want To Publish Your Movie? screen.
2. Select the This Computer item in the list box, and then click the Next button. The Wizard displays the Name The Movie You Are Publishing screen.
3. Type the name for the movie, choose the folder in which to store it, and then click the Next button. The Wizard displays the Choose The Settings For Your Movie screen (see Figure 2-4).

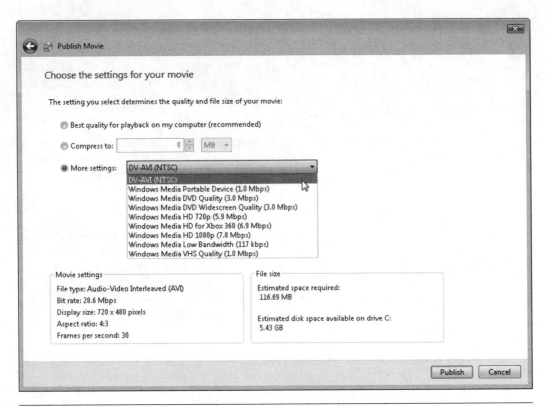

**FIGURE 2-4** On the Choose The Settings For Your Movie screen, select the More Settings option button, and then pick the DV-AVI item in the drop-down list.

4. Select the More Settings option button, and then select the DV-AVI item in the drop-down list.

 The DV-AVI item appears as DV-AVI (NTSC) or DV-AVI (PAL), depending on whether you've chosen the NTSC option button or the PAL option button on the Advanced tab of the Options dialog box. NTSC is the video format used in most of North America; PAL's stronghold is Europe.

5. Click the Publish button to export the movie in this format. When Windows Movie Maker finishes exporting the file, it displays the Your Movie Has Been Published screen.
6. Clear the Play Movie When I Click Finish check box if you don't want to watch the movie immediately in Windows Media Player. Often, it's a good idea to check that the movie has come out okay.
7. Click the Finish button.

Now that you've created an AVI file, use a converter program such as Full Video Converter Free (discussed later in this chapter) to convert it to a format that works on the iPad.

**Create an AVI File from Windows Movie Maker on Windows XP** To save a movie as an AVI file from Windows Movie Maker on Windows XP, follow these steps:

1. Choose File | Save Movie File to launch the Save Movie Wizard. The Wizard displays its Movie Location screen.
2. Select the My Computer item, and then click the Next button. The Wizard displays the Saved Movie File screen.
3. Enter the name and choose the folder for the movie, and then click the Next button. The Wizard displays the Movie Setting screen (shown in Figure 2-5 with options selected).
4. Click the Show More Choices link to display the Best Fit To File Size option button and the Other Settings option button.
5. Select the Other Settings option button, and then select the DV-AVI item in the drop-down list.

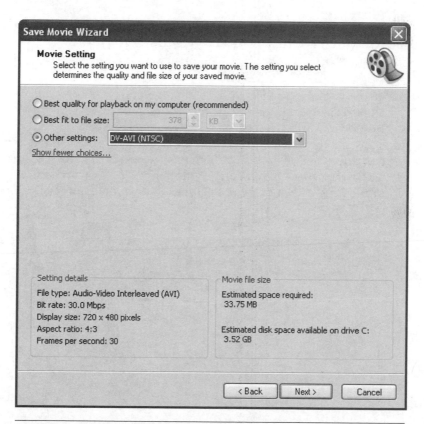

**FIGURE 2-5** Click the Show More Choices link to make the Other Settings option button available, then select the Other Settings option button and pick the DV-AVI item from the drop-down list.

The DV-AVI item appears as DV-AVI (NTSC) or DV-AVI (PAL), depending on whether you've chosen the NTSC option button or the PAL option button on the Advanced tab of the Options dialog box. NTSC is the video format used in most of North America; PAL's stronghold is Europe.

6. Click the Next button to save the movie in this format. The Wizard displays the Completing The Save Movie Wizard screen.
7. Clear the Play Movie When I Click Finish check box if you don't want to test the movie immediately in Windows Media Player. Usually, it's a good idea to make sure the movie has come out right.
8. Click the Finish button.

Now that you've created an AVI file, use a converter program such as Full Video Converter Free (discussed later in this chapter) to convert it to a format that works on the iPad.

## Create iPad-Friendly Video Files Using iMovie

To use iMovie to create video files that will play on the iPad, follow these steps:

1. With the movie open in iMovie, choose Share | iTunes to display the Publish Your Project To iTunes sheet (see Figure 2-6).
2. In the Sizes area, select the check box for each size you want to create. The dots show the devices for which that size is suitable. For example, if you want to play the video files on an iPad at high quality, select the HD 720p check box.
3. Click the Publish button, and then wait while iMovie creates the compressed file or files and adds it or them to iTunes. iMovie then automatically displays iTunes.

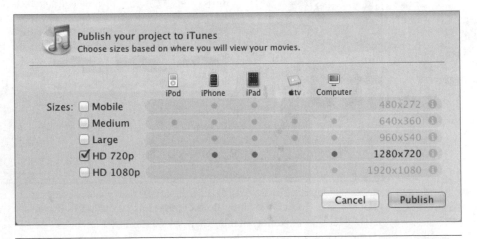

**FIGURE 2-6**   On the Publish Your Project To iTunes sheet in iMovie, choose which sizes of file you want to create—for example, HD 720p for the iPad.

4. Click the Movies item in the Source list, and you'll see the movies you just created. Double-click a file to play it, or simply drag it to the iPad to load it immediately.

# Create iPad-Friendly Video Files from Your Existing Video Files

If you have existing video files (for example, files in the AVI format or QuickTime movies), you can convert them to iPad format in several ways.

The easiest way is by using the capabilities built into iTunes—but unfortunately, these work only for some video files. You can also use QuickTime Pro, which can convert files from most known formats but which costs $30.

A free solution for converting the files is HandBrake, an application you can download from the Internet. HandBrake can open files in many video formats and convert them to other formats, including MP4 format. Even better, you can specify the output size and quality, so you can choose the best balance between video quality and compact file size.

DOUBLE GEEKERY

## Learn About Other Tools for Converting Video Files to MP4 Files

HandBrake is a great tool for converting video files from various formats to MP4 files. But if you have files that HandBrake can't convert, you may need to use other tools. Here are two possibilities:

- **Full Video Converter Free**  Full Video Converter Free is a freeware Windows program you can download from Top 10 Download (www.top10download.com) and other sites. When you install the program, make sure you decline any extra options such as adding a toolbar, changing your default search engine, or changing your home page.
- **Zamzar**  Zamzar (www.zamzar.com) is an online file conversion tool. For low volumes of files, the conversion is free (though it may take a while), but you must provide a valid e-mail address. For higher volumes of files or to get higher priority, you can sign up for a paid account.

You can find various other free programs online for converting video files. If you're looking for such programs, check carefully that what you're about to download is actually free rather than a crippled version that requires you to pay before you can convert files.

## Create iPad-Friendly Video Files Using iTunes

To create a video file for the iPad using iTunes, follow these steps:

1. Add the video file to your iTunes library in either of these ways:
   - Open iTunes if it's not running. Open a Windows Explorer window (Windows) or a Finder window (Mac) to the folder that contains the video file. Arrange the windows so that you can see both the file and iTunes. Drag the file to the Library item in iTunes.
   - In iTunes, choose File | Add To Library, use the Add To Library dialog box to select the file, and then click the Open button (Windows) or the Choose button (Mac).
2. Select the movie in the iTunes window, and then choose Advanced | Create iPad Or iPod Version.

   If the Create iPad Or iPod Version command isn't available for the file, or if iTunes gives you an error message, you'll know that iTunes can't convert the file.

## Create iPad-Friendly Video Files Using QuickTime

QuickTime, Apple's multimedia software for OS X and Windows, comes in two versions: QuickTime Player (the free version) and QuickTime Pro, which costs $29.99.

**Create iPad-Friendly Video Files Using QuickTime Player on the Mac** On OS X, QuickTime Player is included in a standard installation of the operating system; and if you've somehow managed to uninstall it, it'll automatically install itself again if you install iTunes. The Mac version of QuickTime Player includes file conversions, which you can access by using the Share menu. For example, follow these steps:

1. Open QuickTime Player from Launchpad, the Dock, or the Applications folder.
2. Choose File | Open File, select the file in the Open dialog box, and then click the Open button.
3. Choose Share | iTunes to display the Save Your Movie To iTunes dialog box (see Figure 2-7).
4. Select the iPad, iPhone 4 & Apple TV option button.
5. Click the Share button. QuickTime converts the file.

**Create iPad-Friendly Video Files Using QuickTime Pro on Windows** On Windows, you install QuickTime Player when you install iTunes, because QuickTime provides much of the multimedia functionality for iTunes. The "Player" name isn't entirely accurate, because QuickTime provides encoding services as well as decoding services to iTunes—but QuickTime Player on the PC doesn't allow you to create most formats of video files until you buy QuickTime Pro.

**FIGURE 2-7**   On the Mac, you can use QuickTime Player to convert video files to formats suitable for the iPad.

 QuickTime Pro for Windows gets rave reviews from some users but wretched reviews from others. If you are thinking of buying QuickTime Pro for Windows, read the latest reviews for it at the Apple Store (http://store.apple.com) first.

QuickTime Player for Windows is a crippled version of QuickTime Pro, so when you buy QuickTime Pro from the Apple Store, all you get is a registration code to unlock the hidden functionality. To apply the registration code, choose Edit | Preferences | Register In Windows to display the Register tab of the QuickTime Settings dialog box. On the Mac, choose QuickTime Player | Registration to display the Register tab of the QuickTime dialog box.

 When you register QuickTime Pro, you must enter your registration name in the Registered To text box in exactly the same format as Apple has decided to use it. For example, if you've used the name John P. Smith to register QuickTime Pro, and Apple has decided to address the registration to *Mr. John P. Smith*, you must use **Mr. John P. Smith** as the registration name. If you try to use **John P. Smith**, registration fails, even if this is exactly the way you gave your name when registering.

To create an iPad-friendly video file from QuickTime Pro, follow these steps:

1. Open the file in QuickTime Pro, and then choose File | Export to display the Save Exported File As dialog box.
2. Specify the filename and folder as usual, and then choose Movie To iPad in the Export drop-down list. Leave the Default Settings item selected in the Use drop-down list.
3. Click the Save button to start exporting the video file.

## Create iPad-Friendly Video Files Using HandBrake

One of the best tools for converting video files from one format to another and creating video files that will work on the iPad is HandBrake. In this section, you learn how to download, install, and launch HandBrake; choose suitable settings; and convert video files to iPad-friendly formats.

**Download, Install, and Launch HandBrake**   First, install HandBrake on your PC or Mac. Follow these steps:

1. Open your web browser and go to the Download page on the HandBrake website (http://handbrake.fr/downloads.php).
2. Click the appropriate download link under the Mac OS heading or the Windows heading.
3. When the download finishes, install the application as usual:
   - **Windows**   Click the Run button to launch the HandBrake Setup Wizard, accept the license agreement and the default settings, and then wait while the Wizard installs HandBrake.
   - **Mac**   If OS X doesn't automatically open a Finder window showing the contents of the HandBrake disk image, click the Downloads icon on the Dock, and then click the HandBrake disk image file. In the Finder window, drag the HandBrake icon to the Applications folder. When you launch HandBrake, you'll need to accept the license agreement.
4. Now that you've installed HandBrake, launch it:
   - **Windows**   Choose Start | All Programs | HandBrake | HandBrake.
   - **Mac**   Click the Launchpad icon on the Dock, and then click the HandBrake icon. If your version of OS X doesn't have Launchpad, click the desktop, choose Go | Applications, and then double-click the HandBrake icon in the Applications folder.

DOUBLE GEEKERY

## Find Out Whether Your Version of Windows Is 32-Bit or 64-Bit

HandBrake comes in different versions for Windows—a 64-bit version and a 32-bit version. You'll likely need the 32-bit version, because at this writing most Windows PCs run 32-bit versions of Windows; if you're lucky enough to have a PC running 64-bit Windows, you'll probably know about it.

Sixty-four-bit versions of Windows XP are rare, especially nowadays, so you'll only really need to check on Windows 7 or Windows Vista. To check, press WINDOWS KEY–BREAK to display the System window (on Windows 7 or Windows Vista) or the System Properties dialog box (on Windows XP). Then look at the System Type readout in the System section to see if it says 32-Bit Operating System or 64-Bit Operating System.

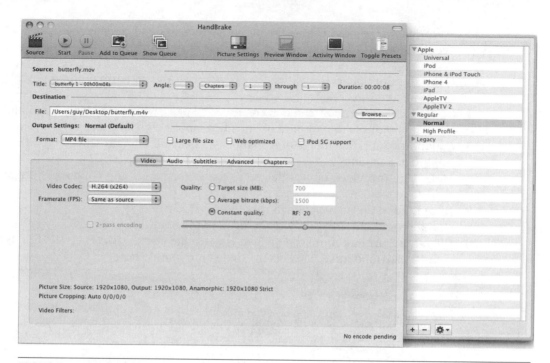

**FIGURE 2-8** The Presets pane on the right side of the HandBrake window includes an iPad preset.

Figure 2-8 shows the HandBrake window with a file loaded and the Presets pane open on the right.

 This section shows HandBrake on the Mac. On Windows, HandBrake is almost exactly the same, but I'll point out the differences you need to know about.

## Convert Video Files to MP4 Files Using HandBrake

With HandBrake open, you're ready to start converting files. Follow these steps:

1. Display the Open dialog box:
   - **Windows** Click the Source drop-down button on the toolbar, and then click Video File. You can also press CTRL-O.
   - **Mac** Click the Source button on the toolbar.
2. Click the file you want, and then click the Open button. HandBrake reads the file and then displays its details.
3. In the File box in the Destination area, specify the folder and filename to use for the converted file. You can either type in the folder path or click the Browse button and select it in the dialog box that opens.
4. If the Presets pane isn't displayed, click the Toggle Presets button on the toolbar to display it. Then click the iPad preset.

On Windows, you can choose the output picture size and cropping by using the controls on the Picture tab in the lower part of the window.

5. Open the Container drop-down list on Windows or the Format pop-up menu on the Mac, and then choose MP4 File.
6. Select the Large File Size check box if you're okay with a relatively large file size. This reduces the amount of encoding, so it's worth experimenting with, depending on how much storage your iPad has and how much video you're hoping to pack into it.
7. Make sure the Video tab is selected in the lower part of the window. If not, click the Video tab.
8. In the Video Codec drop-down list, choose H.264 (x264).
9. In the Framerate (FPS) drop-down list, choose Same As Source.
10. Click the Start button on the toolbar. HandBrake starts converting the file. When it finishes, HandBrake displays the dialog box shown here.

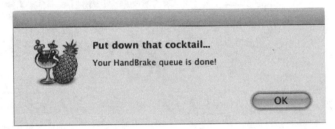

# Create Video Files from Your DVDs

If you have DVDs, you'll probably want to put them on the iPad so that you can watch them without a DVD player. This section gives you an overview of how to create suitable files, first on Windows, and then on the Mac.

 Because ripping commercial DVDs without specific permission is a violation of copyright law, there are no DVD ripping programs from major companies. You can find commercial programs, shareware programs, and freeware programs on the Internet—but keep your wits firmly about you, as some programs are a threat to your computer through being poorly programmed, while others include unwanted components such as adware or spyware. Always read reviews of any DVD ripper you're considering before you download and install it—and certainly before you pay for it. As usual on the Internet, if something seems too good to be true, it most likely *is* too good to be true.

Before you start ripping, make sure that your discs don't contain computer-friendly versions of their contents. At this writing, some Blu-ray Discs include such versions, which are licensed for you to load on your computer and your lifestyle devices (such as your iPad).

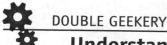

DOUBLE GEEKERY

## Understand What DVD Titles and Chapters Are

Each DVD is split up into titles and chapters:

- **Title**    A *title* is one of the recorded tracks on the DVD.
- **Chapter**    The *chapters* are the bookmarks within the titles—for example, if you press the Next button on your remote, your DVD player skips to the start of the next chapter.

# Rip DVDs with DVDFab HD Decrypter on Your PC

In this section, we'll install DVDFab HD Decrypter on your PC and use it to rip DVDs. DVDFab HD Decrypter is shareware that you can try for 30 days, which gives you plenty of time to decide whether it does what you want. After that, you're supposed to pay to register it.

## Install DVDFab HD Decrypter on Your PC

To download and install DVDFab HD Decrypter on your PC, open your web browser and go to the DVDFab HD Decrypter page on the DVDFab.com website (www.dvdfab .com/hd-decrypter.htm). Click the Download button, click the Run button in the File Download – Security Warning dialog box, and then click the Run button in the Internet Explorer – Security Warning dialog box (shown here).

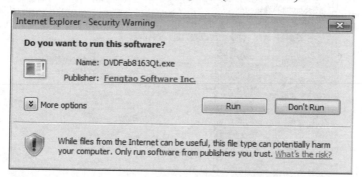

The installer then runs. Follow through the installation as usual. There are three points worth noting:

- In the Select Setup Language dialog box, choose your language, and then click the OK button.
- On the Select Additional Tasks screen (shown next), clear the Create A Desktop Icon check box if you don't want to create a desktop icon for DVDFab HD Decrypter. Similarly, clear the Create A Quick Launch Icon check box if you don't want to create an icon on the Quick Launch toolbar.

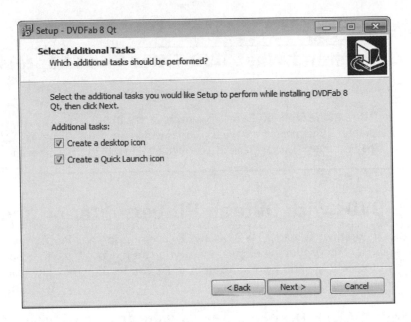

- On the Completing The DVDFab 8 Qt Setup Wizard screen (shown here), select the Yes, Restart The Computer Now option button if you're okay with restarting immediately. Otherwise, select the No, I Will Restart The Computer Later option button and restart at your convenience.

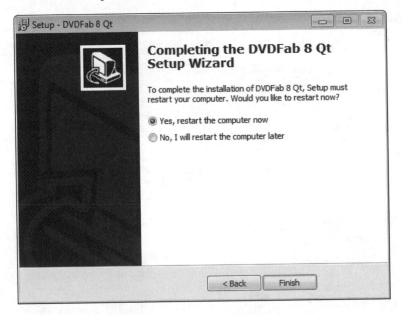

## Rip a DVD with DVDFab HD Decrypter

After restarting your PC, log in as usual. You'll then be ready to rip a DVD with DVDFab HD Decrypter. Follow these steps:

1. Launch DVDFab HD Decrypter from the Start menu (choose Start | All Programs | DVDFab 8 Qt | DVDFab 8 Qt), the desktop shortcut, or the Quick Launch toolbar.
2. Insert a DVD in your PC's DVD drive, and wait while DVDFab HD Decrypter identifies its contents.
3. Click the DVD Ripper button in the left pane of the DVDFab window to display the DVD ripping options (see Figure 2-9).
4. Click the iPad option to select it.
5. In the Target text box, enter the folder in which to store the ripped file. You can type in the path; you can click the button with the folder icon, and use the Please Choose A Folder dialog box to select the folder; or you can click the drop-down button and use a folder you've used before.

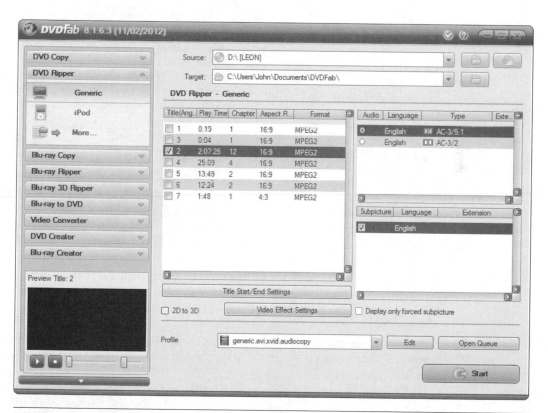

**FIGURE 2-9**  Click the DVD Ripper button in the left pane to display the DVD ripping options, then click the iPad option.

6. In the list of titles in the center of the window, select the check box for the DVD title you want to rip. Normally, you'll want the DVD's main title, which you can pick out easily by its length—it's the length of the movie.

7. If you want to rip only some chapters from the title you've chosen, click the Title Start/End Settings button to display the Title Start/End Settings dialog box (shown here). Choose the chapters by using the Start drop-down list and the End drop-down list, and then click the OK button.

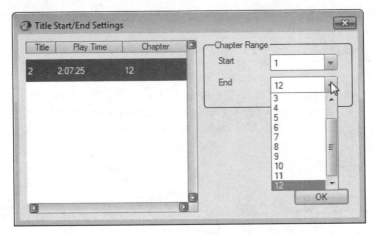

8. Click the Start button to start ripping. When DVDFab HD Decrypter finishes ripping the file, it opens a Windows Explorer window to the folder containing the file.

## Rip DVDs with HandBrake on Your Mac

The best tool for ripping DVDs on the Mac is HandBrake, which you met earlier in this project. To rip DVDs with HandBrake, you must install VLC, a DVD- and video-playing application (free; www.videolan.org). This is because HandBrake uses VLC's DVD-decryption capabilities; without VLC, HandBrake cannot decrypt DVDs.

Once you've installed VLC, you can rip DVDs like this:

1. Run HandBrake as usual. For example, click the Launchpad icon on the Dock and then click the HandBrake icon, or open a Finder window to your Applications folder and then double-click the HandBrake icon.

2. Click the Source button on the toolbar to display the Open dialog box.

3. Click the DVD in the Source list on the left, and then click the Open button. HandBrake scans the DVD, which may take several minutes, and then displays its details (see Figure 2-10).

4. In the Title pop-up menu, choose which title to rip. To rip a movie from a DVD, you'll want the main title. Usually, you can easily distinguish the main title by its length—it'll be as long as the movie (for example, two hours).

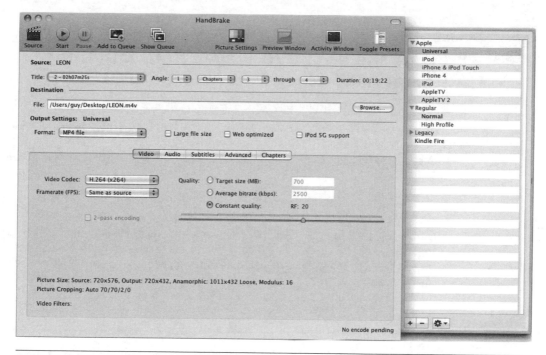

**FIGURE 2-10**  HandBrake scans the DVD and displays its details. You can then choose which title and chapters to rip.

5. Optionally, choose which chapters to rip from the movie by using the Chapters pop-up menus. For example, if you want chapters 1 through 10, choose 1 in the first pop-up menu, and then choose 10 in the second pop-up menu.

 If the DVD offers multiple angles, open the Angle pop-up menu and choose the angle you want.

6. In the Destination box, enter the folder and filename to use for the video file. You can type the path and filename if you want, but it's usually easier to click the Browse button, use the Save dialog box that opens to specify the folder and filename, and then click the Save button.

7. If the Presets pane isn't displayed on the right side of the HandBrake window, click the Toggle Presets button to display it.

8. Click the iPad preset. The settings in the lower part of the window change to the settings for the preset.

9. In the Output Settings area, select MP4 File in the Format pop-up menu.

10. Select the Large File Size check box if you're okay with a large file size.

11. Clear the Web Optimized check box.

12. Clear the iPod 5G Support check box unless you need to be able to play the video on an iPod video (fifth-generation iPod) as well.

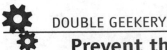

**DOUBLE GEEKERY**

## Prevent the OS X DVD Player from Running Automatically When You Insert a DVD

When you insert a movie DVD, OS X automatically launches DVD Player, switches it to full screen, and starts the movie playing. This behavior is great for when you want to watch a movie, but not so great when you want to rip it.

To prevent DVD Player from running automatically when you insert a DVD, follow these steps:

1. Choose Apple | System Preferences to open System Preferences.
2. In the Hardware section, click the CDs & DVDs item.
3. In the When You Insert A Video DVD drop-down list, you can choose Ignore if you want to be able to choose freely which application to use each time. If you always want to use the same application, choose Open Other Application, use the resulting Open dialog box to select the application, and then click the Choose button.
4. Choose System Preferences | Quit System Preferences or press ⌘-Q to close System Preferences.

---

13. In the lower part of the HandBrake window, choose suitable settings on the Video tab. These are the settings that work best for video files you'll play on the iPad:
    - **Video Codec**   Choose H.264 (x264).
    - **Framerate (FPS)**   Choose Same As Source.
    - **Quality**   Select the Constant Quality option button, and then drag the slider to the position you find gives you the quality you want. You'll need to experiment with this setting by creating video files at different qualities and seeing which look good enough on your iPad (or on the TV or screen you connect your iPad to).
14. Click the Start button on the toolbar to start ripping.

# Project 14: Watch Video from Your iPad on Your TV

Once you've loaded your video files onto your iPad, you're ready to watch them anywhere. Watching on your iPad's screen works fine when you yourself are the whole audience, but when you need to share your videos with other people, you'll likely want a bigger screen. Often, the easiest solution is to play video from your iPad to a TV.

## Connect Your iPad to the TV

To play videos from your iPad on a TV, you need a suitable cable or adapter. Look first at the Apple Digital AV Adapter, Apple Composite AV Cable, and Apple Component AV Cable on the Apple Store (http://store.apple.com) and establish which one your TV needs. Then decide between buying the Apple version of the adapter or cable or a third-party equivalent.

When you have the adapter or cable, connect it to your iPad's Dock Connector port and to the appropriate inputs on your TV.

## Play Back a Video or Movie on the TV

After connecting your iPad to the TV, you can play back a video or movie on the TV by simply starting playback on the iPad as usual.

When you start playback, your iPad displays a prompt telling you that the output is going to the TV.

 If the TV isn't showing the video, you'll need to fiddle with the AV buttons to make sure it's using the right input.

When you finish watching the video, disconnect the cable from the TV.

# Project 15: Share Your Photos with All Your Devices Using Photo Stream

Being able to take high-quality photos anywhere with your iPad's built-in camera is great. But what's even better is being able to use the Photo Stream feature to make those photos appear on your computer and your other iOS devices (for example, your iPhone) automatically.

In this section, I'll show you how to set up and use Photo Stream.

## Understand What Photo Stream Is and What It Does

Photo Stream is part of Apple's iCloud service, so to use it you must have an iCloud account. Given that you've got an iPad, you've probably set up an iCloud account already; if not, you can set one up inside a couple of minutes.

Once you've set it up, Photo Stream automatically syncs up to 1000 of your latest photos among your iOS devices and your computers. Photo Stream stores each new photo on iCloud for 30 days, so if you connect each iOS device to a wireless network several times a week, you'll soon have each new photo on each device.

On your iPad (or your iPod touch, or your iPhone), Photo Stream includes the photos in your Camera Roll folder. The Camera Roll contains not only the photos you take using the Camera app but also photos you save from e-mail messages, multimedia messages, or web pages.

Photo Stream works with any device running iOS 5—any iPad, the iPhone (3GS, 4, or 4S), or the iPod touch (third-generation or later). It works with iPhoto or Aperture on the Mac and with the Pictures Library on Windows 7 or Windows Vista.

## Set Up Photo Stream on Your iPad

To set up Photo Stream on your iPad, follow these steps:

1. Press the Home button to display the Home screen.
2. Tap the Settings icon to display the Settings screen.
3. Tap the Photos button in the left column to display the Photos screen (shown in Figure 2-11).
4. Tap the Photo Stream switch and move it to the On position.

 When you set the Photo Stream switch to the On position, your iPad prompts you to sign into iCloud if you're not currently signed in.

## Set Up Photo Stream on Your iPhone or iPod touch

To set up Photo Stream on your iPhone or iPod touch, follow these steps:

1. Press the Home button to display the Home screen.
2. Tap the Settings icon to display the Settings screen.

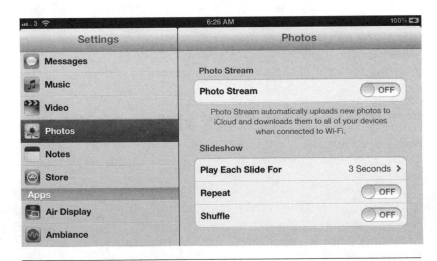

**FIGURE 2-11** Tap the Photos button on the Settings screen to display the Photos screen, and then move the Photo Stream switch to the On position.

3. Tap the Photos button to display the Photos screen.
4. Tap the Photo Stream switch and move it to the On position.

 When you set the Photo Stream switch to the On position, your iPhone or iPod touch prompts you to sign into iCloud if you're not currently signed in.

# Set Up Photo Stream on Your PC

If you have a PC running Windows 7 or Windows Vista, you can set up Photo Stream to sync your photos automatically. To do so, you install the iCloud Control Panel, then log in to your iCloud account and turn on Photo Stream. You can also change the default folders that iCloud uses:

- **Download folder** The My Photo Stream folder in your Pictures\Photo Stream\ folder—for example, C:\Users\Chris\Pictures\Photo Stream\My Photo Stream\ if your user account is named Chris
- **Upload folder** The Upload folder in your Pictures\Photo Stream\ folder—for example, C:\Users\Chris\Pictures\Photo Stream\Uploads\ if your user account is named Chris

To set up Photo Stream on your PC, follow these steps:

1. If you don't already have iTunes on your PC, download the latest version from www.apple.com/itunes/ and install it. You must be running iTunes 10.5 or a later version to use iCloud and Photo Stream.
2. Chose Start | All Programs | Apple Software Update to run the Apple Software Update program, which checks for updated versions of iTunes and new components you need. Figure 2-12 shows Apple Software Update ready to download and install updates.
3. Select the check box for each item you need to install. For example, in Figure 2-12, I've selected the check box for a new version of iTunes, the check box for a new version of QuickTime, and the check box for the iCloud Control Panel. I've refused the Safari 5 web browser.

 QuickTime is an Apple program that iTunes uses for playing back audio and video. To use iTunes, you must install QuickTime on your computer. So if Apple Software Update offers you a new version of QuickTime, download and install it.

4. Click the Install Items button to download and install the items you've chosen. You may need to accept one or more end user license agreements to proceed.

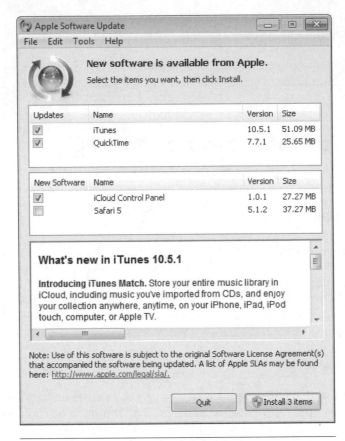

**FIGURE 2-12**    Run Apple Software Update to check for a
new version of iTunes and for any other components you need.

**5.** Restart your PC if Apple Software Update prompts you to do so (as shown here), and then log back in.

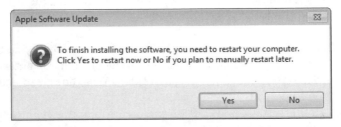

**6.** Click the Start button to open the Start menu.

7. Type **icloud** in the Search box, and then click the iCloud result that appears. The iCloud sign-in dialog box opens, as shown here.

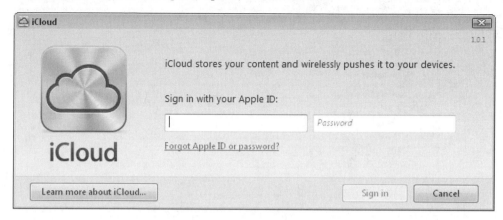

8. Type your Apple ID in the Sign In With Your Apple ID text box and your password in the Password text box.
9. Click the Sign In button. The iCloud dialog box shown in Figure 2-13 appears.
10. Select the Photo Stream check box to turn on Photo Stream.
11. If you want to verify or change the default Download folder or Upload folder, click the Options button to the right of the Photo Stream check box to display the Photo Stream Options dialog box (shown here).

12. Click the Change button on the Download Folder line, select the folder you want in the Browse For Folder dialog box, and then click the OK button.
13. Click the Change button on the Upload Folder line, select the folder you want in the Browse For Folder dialog box, and then click the OK button.
14. Click the OK button to close the Photo Stream Options dialog box and return to the iCloud dialog box.
15. Click the Apply button to apply your changes.
16. Click the Close button to close the iCloud dialog box. The Close button appears in place of the Cancel button when you click the Apply button.

**FIGURE 2-13** In this iCloud dialog box, select the check box for each iCloud feature you want to use.

Now make sure that Photo Stream is working. Follow these steps:

1. Choose Start | Pictures to open a Windows Explorer window showing your Pictures folder.
2. Double-click the Photo Stream folder to open it.
3. Double-click the My Photo Stream folder to open it.
4. Check that the photos from your Photo Stream appear in the folder.
5. Add to the Upload folder any photos that you want to upload to your Photo Stream.

## Set Up Photo Stream on Your Mac

To set up Photo Stream on your Mac, follow these steps:

1. Choose Apple | System Preferences to display the System Preferences window.
2. In the Internet & Wireless section, click the Mail, Contacts & Calendars icon to display the Mail, Contacts & Calendars screen (shown in Figure 2-14 with an iCloud account selected).
3. In the accounts list on the left, click your iCloud account to display its controls.

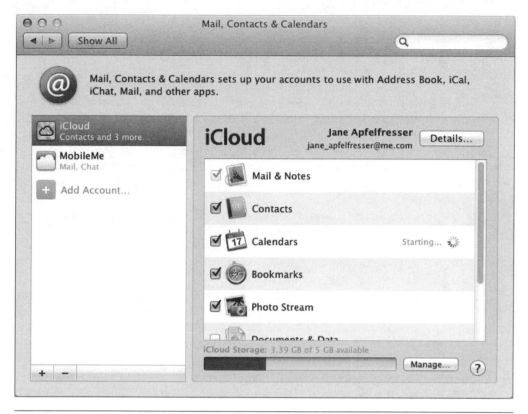

**FIGURE 2-14**  To turn on Photo Stream on your Mac, select the Photo Stream check box in the iCloud pane of the Mail, Contacts & Calendars screen in System Preferences.

 If you haven't yet set up your iCloud account on your Mac, click the Add Account button in the left column of the Mail, Contacts & Calendars screen. Then click the iCloud button to display the iCloud dialog box, type your Apple ID and password, and then click the Sign In button. In the Automatically Set Up iCloud dialog box that opens, click the OK button if you want to use the automatic setup process; click the Manual Setup button if you want to make all the choices yourself. Your iCloud account then appears in the accounts list on the left on the Mail, Contacts & Calendars screen.

4. Select the Photo Stream check box.
5. Choose System Preferences | Quit System Preferences or press ⌘-Q to quit System Preferences.

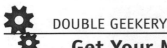

## Get Your Mac Ready for iCloud

Your Mac must be running Lion or Mountain Lion in order to make the most of iCloud. Earlier versions, including Snow Leopard (OS X 10.6), can't use all iCloud's features.

To get your Mac ready for iCloud, first make sure your Mac is running OS X Lion 10.7.2 or a later version. The easiest way to check is to choose Apple | About This Mac, and then look at the Version readout in the About This Mac dialog box. If your Mac has an earlier version of Lion, click the Software Update button in the About This Mac dialog box, and then follow the prompts to download and install the latest updates.

Second, update iTunes to the latest version. If you just updated Lion or Mountain Lion and accepted all updates offered, you've already updated iTunes. If not, choose Apple | Software Update to run Software Update, and then install any iTunes update offered, together with any other updates your Mac would benefit from. (Usually, it's a good idea to install all the updates.)

Once you've made these updates, you can set up your iCloud account in the iCloud pane of the Mail, Contacts & Calendars screen in System Preferences.

---

Now that you've set your Mac to use Photo Stream, it automatically downloads the photos that are currently in your Photo Stream. To see the photos, launch iPhoto, click the Photo Stream item in the Recent category in the Source list, and then click the Turn On Photo Stream button.

When you import photos from your camera or from an SD card into your iPhoto library, iPhoto automatically uploads the photos to Photo Stream, so they appear on your iOS devices and other computers that use Photo Stream.

To add other photos to your Photo Stream, select the photos in iPhoto, click the Share button in the lower-right corner of the iPhoto window, and then click Photo Stream on the pop-up panel.

# Project 16: Use Your iPad as an In-Car Video System

If you drive your car, the road and its hogs probably give you all the visual entertainment you need—and you certainly shouldn't be using your iPad at the wheel when you're busy drinking your coffee and applying your nail polish.

But your passengers may well need extra entertainment—and the iPad is a great way to give them personalized entertainment programs and keep them off your back until you reach your destination.

In a pinch, a passenger can simply hold the iPad—no extra equipment required. But for that airline in-seat entertainment touch, you'll probably want to get a car headrest mount holder like the one shown in Figure 2-15.

**FIGURE 2-15**   An inexpensive car headrest mount holder like this is all you need to mount a iPad on the rear of a headrest to keep a rear-seat passenger entertained.

 When choosing a car headrest mount holder, make sure it's large and strong enough to hold the iPad snugly and firmly. Normally, it's best to get an iPad-specific holder rather than one that works for other tablets, such as the Samsung Galaxy Tab and the Kindle Fire—that way, you can be sure it'll fit. And get a model robust enough to hold the iPad still even as you thunder along dilapidated highways. Some mounts are pretty feeble. You can improve them with duct tape, but ideally you'll buy a holder that's strong enough in the first place.

Once you've gotten your car headrest mount holder, mounting the iPad takes only a minute or two. Now your passenger can plug in her headphones, set her preferred movie playing, and you'll be ready to roll.

# Project 17: Take Time-Lapse Movies or Shoot Video at Different Frame Rates

Your iPad's camera takes high-definition video at 30 frames per second at a resolution of 1920 × 1080 pixels. This resolution is called 1080p.

This quality is high enough for capturing broadcast-quality video, so you'll want to make the most of it—for example, posting your edited video clips on YouTube or making them into movies using iMovie either right there on your iPad or on your Mac.

But if you're serious about capturing video and making movies, you'll probably want to go beyond what the Camera app can do. You can do so by installing a third-party app that gives you control over how the camera shoots video: choosing the resolution, setting the frame rate, locking the focus or exposure, and so on.

In this project, we'll look at how you can change the frame rate to make time-lapse movies and to shoot footage that will appear to run at higher speed. For example, if you shoot video at 15 frames per second but play it back at normal speed, everything will seem to happen twice as fast. And if you take a time-lapse video of a sunrise at a single frame per second, each minute of real time will be compressed into two seconds of video when you play it back.

## Get FiLMiC Pro

At this writing, the best app for adding capabilities to your iPad's camera is FiLMiC Pro, which costs $3.99. FiLMiC Pro gives you control over the camera's frame rate, exposure, white balance, resolution, and other settings.

Your first move is to get FiLMiC Pro. Follow these steps:

1. Activate the iTunes window.
2. Double-click the iTunes Store item in the Source list on the left to open a window showing the iTunes Store.
3. Type **filmic pro** into the Search box and press ENTER or RETURN.
4. Click the appropriate search result to display the app's page.
5. Click the button to buy the app, and then confirm the purchase.

 You can also get FiLMiC Pro by using the iTunes Store on your iPad if you prefer.

After iTunes downloads the app, sync your iPad to install it. Depending on your sync settings, you may need to select the app's check box on the Apps screen in iTunes to install it on the iPad.

## Launch FiLMiC Pro

After installing FiLMiC Pro, tap its icon on the Home screen to run it. FiLMiC Pro displays whatever the camera is seeing, as shown in Figure 2-16.

The interface is pretty straightforward to use. For example, you tap the focus reticle and drag it to the area of the screen where you want to focus; similarly, you tap the exposure reticle and move it to the area of the screen on which to meter the exposure.

## Adjust the Frame Rate

To adjust the frame rate, follow these steps:

1. Tap the Settings button on the FiLMiC Pro screen to display the Settings screen (shown on the left in Figure 2-17).

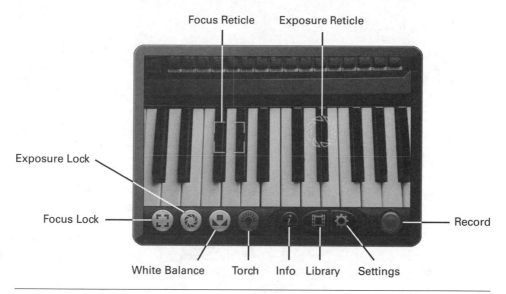

FIGURE 2-16   FiLMiC Pro provides separate reticles for focusing and exposure. You can also adjust the white balance and the frame rate.

2. Tap the FPS button to display the Frame Rate screen (shown on the right in Figure 2-17).
3. Tap the frame rate you want. Your choices range from the iPad's top speed, 30 fps, all the way down to a single frame per second, 1 fps.
4. Tap the Settings button to return to the Settings screen.
5. Tap the Done button to return to the camera.

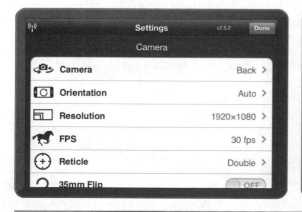 

FIGURE 2-17   On the Settings screen (left), tap the FPS button to display the Frame Rate screen (right), and then tap the frame rate you want to use.

## Shoot Your Video

With the frame rate set the way you want it, you're now ready to shoot your video. Mount your iPad on a tripod as discussed in the nearby sidebar, line up your subject, and then tap the Record button.

DOUBLE GEEKERY

### Mount Your iPad on a Tripod

Your iPad is designed for handheld use, and you'll probably want to use it that way most of the time. But when you're shooting video, you'll often do better to use a tripod.

As you know, the iPad doesn't have a tripod mount built in, so you need to provide one in order to use the iPad with a tripod. You can either get a tripod with a built-in mount designed especially for the iPad or get a tripod mount that is designed to enable you to mount the iPad on any standard tripod.

If you put the search term **iPad tripod** into eBay or Amazon, you'll find various tripods designed for the iPad. The less expensive ones tend to be flimsy and designed only for indoor use, whereas the sturdier ones tend to be uncomfortably expensive.

Depending on your needs, you may find that an iPad-specific tripod does the job. But if you're going to use your iPad seriously as a camera, you'll probably find that it makes sense to buy an iPad holder that mounts on a regular tripod thread so that you can use any normal camera tripod—a table-top model, a rugged full-size tripod, a car-window mount, or whatever you need.

Here are five examples of tripod mounts for the iPad:

- **Grifiti Nootle iPad Tripod Mount**   The Grifiti Nootle iPad Tripod Mount (around $25; Amazon and other online stores) is a snug-fitting frame made of ABS plastic that connects to a standard tripod mount.
- **Delkin Fat Gecko iPad Mount**   The Delkin Fat Gecko iPad Mount (around $25; Amazon and other online stores) is a four-point holder that connects to a standard tripod mount. You can also connect it to other Fat Gecko holders, which include suction cups for sticking to flat surfaces.
- **iPad Movie Mount**   The iPad Movie Mount (around $70; www.makayama.com/moviemount.html or online stores such as Amazon) is a case with a built-in frame that enables you to not only mount your iPad on a tripod but also mount extra lenses, lights, and microphones on the iPad for filming. You can even attach an optical viewfinder that'll let you shoot video more comfortably in bright conditions that make your iPad's screen hard to see.
- **iPad 3 Tripod Mount G7 Pro**   The iPad 3 Tripod Mount G7 Pro (around $80; http://ishotmounts.com and some online stores) is a four-point frame that grips the iPad and lets you secure it to a standard tripod. This item's key point of differentiation from other tripod mounts is that you can use it with most iPad cases, including thick cases such as the Griffin Military case. iShot Mounts also makes the G8 Pro, a mount for securing a bare (caseless) iPad to a tripod head. The G8 costs around $14 and is available from Amazon and other online stores.

- **Wallee Case and Wallee Connect**    The Wallee Case ($39.95; www.tethertools.com and major online stores) is a snap-on case with an X-shaped locking slot on the back. The Wallee Connect ($79.95) is a bracket for mounting an iPad wearing a Wallee Case to a tripod. You can get other mounting devices for stands (for example, music stands) or clamps.

The next illustration shows the iPad mounted on a full-size tripod using an iPad Movie Mount.

# Project 18: Adapt or Build a Steadicam to Stabilize Your iPad for Shooting Video

Your iPad shoots high-definition video, and it gives great results for its size. But it has a problem when your subject matter is moving.

Whereas a full-scale video camera uses a mechanical shutter to create separate video frames, your iPad uses a *rolling shutter*, which takes several milliseconds to create each frame. The rolling shutter is not good at capturing movement, because a fast-moving subject can move while a frame is being captured. This results in blurred video.

Blur also occurs when you (the cameraperson) move the iPad while capturing video. When you're shooting from a stationary position, you can keep the iPad still by using a tripod, as described in the Double Geekery sidebar in the previous project.

But when you're moving, you need to use a device to stabilize the iPad and damp down your movements so that the video you shoot appears smoother.

Such video-camera stabilization devices are usually called Steadicams. You can buy Steadicam rigs for small devices such as the iPhone, but at this writing, there aren't any designed for the iPad.

If you already have a Steadicam, you can adapt it to fit your iPad, as described in the first part of this project. If you don't have a Steadicam, you can build a DIY one from scratch with surprisingly little effort. See the second part of this project for detailed instructions.

## Mount Your iPad on an Existing Steadicam

If you already have a Steadicam, you should be able to mount your iPad on it with little trouble.

 If you don't have a Steadicam, you can buy a modest one for $100 or less. At this writing, the best bet is the Lensse MidX Camera Stabilizer, which you can find on Amazon or eBay for around $100, or the Lensse MidPro Camera Support Stabilizer (around $120).

For most Steadicams, all you need is a tripod bracket, as discussed in the Double Geekery sidebar in the previous project. Screw the tripod bracket onto the Steadicam, mount your iPad in the bracket, and see if the balance is okay.

If the Steadicam is built for a camera much heavier than the iPad, you may need to adjust the weighting or even add weight at the top of the Steadicam to get the balance right.

## Build a DIY Steadicam for Your iPad

If you don't have a Steadicam, and you don't want to buy one, you can build yourself one inside a couple of hours largely from items you probably have around your home or yard—although there's one thing you'll probably need to buy.

This section shows you how to build a Steadicam from an old bike wheel.

 This Steadicam is inspired by one created by Thomas Johnson for the iPhone. To see Johnson's Steadicam, go to YouTube and search for **thomasumjohnson.**

### Get the Things You Need for the Steadicam

Here's what you'll need to build the Steadicam:

- **Bike wheel**   A wheel from a kid's bike is best—for example, an 18- or 20-inch wheel. You can use a full-size (26- or 27-inch) bike wheel if you want, but the result is bigger than you'll probably want unless you need to be able to mount lights and a hefty microphone on the Steadicam as well.

- **Tripod bracket**   You need a tripod bracket to mount your iPad on the top of the Steadicam. The Steadicam has a standard tripod screw at the top, so you can use the same tripod bracket as for attaching the iPad to your tripod.
- **Tripod head**   To enable you to point the iPad at the angle you want, you'll need a tripod head.
- **Gimbal or universal joint**   To damp your movement, the Steadicam needs a joint that can turn freely in two directions. The best thing is a brass gimbal made by Lensse. You can pick these up on eBay from $15 upward. Alternatively, you can use a universal joint such as those made by Traxxas for its Slash radio-controlled cars.

 A *gimbal* is a device that can turn freely in two or three directions to keep an instrument level. Most gimbal designs involve several rings that pivot at right angles to each other.

- **Counterweight**   To get the balance right, the Steadicam needs a counterweight at the bottom. This can be very basic—for example, a couple of pieces of scrap metal. I used a couple of small weight plates from a dumbbell set. The weight you need will depend on the other items you use for the Steadicam, but typically it'll be in the range of two to five pounds total.
- **Tools**   You'll need a modest number of bike-repair and metalworking tools:
  - Hacksaw
  - Metal file
  - Tire levers
  - Spoke wrench
  - Standard wrenches
  - Screwdriver (bonus points for electric)
  - Reamer

**DOUBLE GEEKERY**

## Build Your Own Gimbal from Scrap or Pipe

The gimbal is the most expensive part of the DIY Steadicam, and you may balk at the price—especially given that you can buy an inexpensive Steadicam (which includes a gimbal) instead for three or four times as much.

If so, you can make your own gimbal using a design such as that shown here.

As you can see, what you need are three metal or plastic rings of sizes that will fit inside each other, and bolts to secure them. Because you won't put serious weight on the gimbal, the rings can be of lightweight material—for example, strong jar lids or plastic pipes. Mount the smallest ring on the middle ring with two bolts north and south so that it can turn freely, and then mount the middle ring on the larger ring with two bolts east and west so that it can turn freely in a different dimension.

## Build the Steadicam

To build the Steadicam, follow these steps:

1. If the bike wheel has a tire on it, take the tire off.
2. Unscrew the axle and take it out. Keep it—you'll use it later.
3. Remove the axle housing and keep that too.
4. Remove the protective strip that covers the ends of the spokes where they connect to the rim of the wheel.
5. Undo each spoke and remove the hub.

Undo each spoke by turning its fastener with the spoke wrench until the spoke itself is clear of (below) the screw slot at the top of the fastener. Then use the screwdriver to unscrew the fastener. An electric screwdriver will save you time and effort here. To prevent the hub from hanging, leave a spoke attached at each side—north, south, east, and west, as it were—until you've removed all the other spokes.

6. Saw the rim into two pieces:

Look at the join in the wheel rim and see if you can pull it apart. Some rims are easy to separate, but others are joined so tightly that sawing the rim is easier.

- The piece you'll use for the Steadicam needs to be more than half of the circle, so that there's some overlap at the top for mounting the camera and at the bottom for mounting the counterweight.
- Usually, you'll want at least 210° of the 360° in a circle—enough to make a C shape (see the illustration).
- You can either eyeball the measurement—it doesn't have to be exact—or count spoke holes. If you're counting spoke holes, divide the total number of spoke holes by 0.58 (the decimal for 21/36, or 210/360). For example, if the wheel has 48 spokes, you'll want 28 spoke holes on the longer section. If the wheel has 36 spokes, you'll want 21 spoke holes on the larger section. If the wheel has 24 spokes, you'll want 14 spoke holes on the larger section.

In many rims, the spoke holes are off center on alternate sides. This is fine for attaching the handle and the counterweight, but you'll probably find it easier to attach the tripod head to the valve hole, which is centered in the rim. So when you cut, have the valve hole just below the cut at the top of the C shape.

- If in doubt, cut a longer section than you need. You can easily cut it shorter.

7. File down the edges of the cut rim.
8. If necessary, use a metal reamer to ream out the valve hole to enable the bolt securing the tripod head to go through it.
9. Attach the tripod head to the valve hole with a bolt, as shown in the illustration.

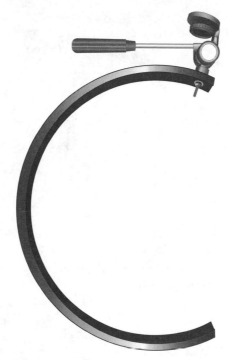

10. Ream out a spoke hole a little way back from the tripod head at the top of the C so that the end of the axle will pass through it.
11. Attach one end of the axle to the hole in the rim, so that the main part of the axle is on the inside of the C, as shown in the illustration.

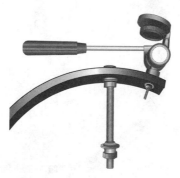

12. Attach the gimbal or universal joint to the free end of the axle.

**13.** Attach the hub (or whatever you're using as the handle) to the gimbal or universal joint, as shown in the illustration.

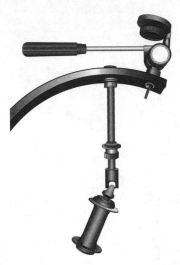

**14.** Attach the counterweight to the bottom of the C shape, as shown in the next illustration. If you're using a weight plate, mount it flat so that it will act as a crude stand for the Steadicam.

Now mount the iPad in the tripod bracket and screw it onto the top of the tripod head (see Figure 2-18). You've now got a Steadicam rig that'll stabilize the video you shoot on your iPad while you're moving. You're ready to start making movies on location.

# Project 19: View Your Webcam on Your iPad

If you use a webcam to keep tabs on what's happening at home when you're away, you can tap into the webcam from your iPad to stay on top of things no matter where you happen to be.

You can also turn your iPad into a network webcam that you can monitor from any other computer on your network. We'll look at how to do this toward the end of this project.

## Decide Which Software to Get

To view your PC's or Mac's webcam on your iPad, you need two software applications:

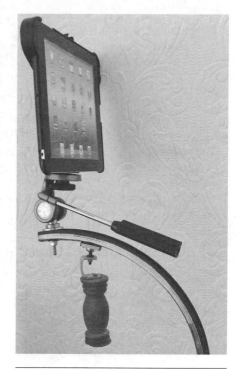

**FIGURE 2-18**    With your iPad mounted on your DIY Steadicam rig, you're ready to start shooting pro-quality video.

- **PC or Mac application**    On your PC or Mac, you run an application that will shunt the video signal out across your local network or the Internet to where your iPad can receive it.
- **iPad app**    On your iPad, you run an app that can connect to the video stream your PC or Mac is providing, and display the pictures to you.

In this section, we'll look at an iPad app that has companion software for both Windows and the Mac: Air Cam Live Video. The full version of Air Cam Live Video costs $7.99, but there's a free version called Air Cam Live Video (Lite) that you'll probably want to try first.

If you need to monitor only a webcam connected to a Windows PC, look also at JumiCam. Start with JumiCam Lite, which is free but limited to your local network, and see how well it works for your needs. If you need extra features, such as reaching across the Internet to monitor your webcam, upgrade to the full version, JumiCam ($4.99).

# Get and Set Up the Software on Your PC or Mac

First, download and install the desktop software needed: Air Cam Live Video for Windows or Air Cam for the Mac.

## Download the Software for Your PC or Mac

Open your web browser and go to the Air Cam Live Video for iOS page on the Senstic website (www.senstic.com/iphone/aircam/aircam.aspx). Then click the Download Air Cam Live Video For Windows XP/Vista/7 link or the Download Air Cam Live Video For Mac OS X link, as appropriate.

## Install and Run the Air Cam Live Video for Windows Program

When downloading the AirCamSetup.msi file, choose the option to run it (or to save it and run it, depending on your browser). When the Air Cam Setup Wizard runs, follow through its prompts. You'll need to install some codecs (*coder*/*deco*der software) unless your PC already has them, so the installation process has multiple steps, and you need to make some decisions.

These are the key points in the installation:

- Close Internet Explorer before you run the installation.
- The Select Installation Folder screen lets you choose to install Air Cam in a different folder than the default folder (a Senstic\Air Cam\ folder inside your Program Files folder), but normally you're safe sticking with the default folder.
- On Windows 7 or Windows Vista, you will need to click the Yes button in the User Account Control dialog box (shown here) to continue with the installation. Make sure the User Account Control dialog box gives the program name Air Cam Installer.

- When the installer displays the Additional Packages dialog box (shown next), click the Get K-Lite button to open a browser window to a site that provides the K-Lite pack of codecs. Follow the links to download the K-Lite pack and then install it. At this point, the Air Cam Installer is still running, but it's in the background.

 When downloading the K-Lite codec pack, be sure to click the correct link. The web page may contain tempting Download buttons for other software the web hosts would like you to try.

- When the Setup – K-Lite Codec Pack installer runs, you'll get another User Account Control dialog box, this time for the K-Lite Codec Pack. You'll need to click the Yes button in this dialog box to proceed with the installation.
- On the initial screen of the Setup – K-Lite Codec Pack installer (shown here), click the Simple Mode option button. Click the Next button and go through the next several configuration screens. You'll probably want to accept the default settings here.

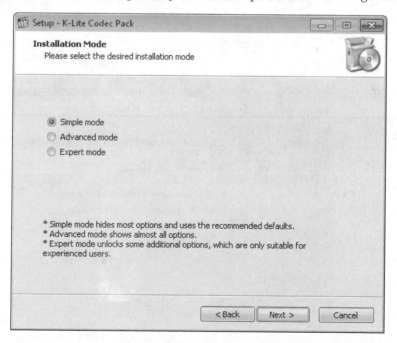

- On the Additional Options screen of the Setup – K-Lite Codec Pack installer (shown next), select the "No Thanks. I Don't Want Any Of The Above" check box to prevent the installer from burdening your PC with the StartNow Toolbar, setting your home page to StartNow, and making Yahoo! your default search engine.

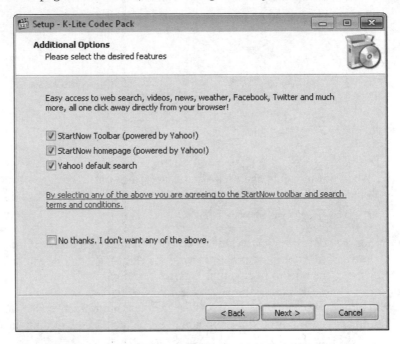

- When you reach the Ready To Install screen, click the Install button.
- When the Done! screen (shown here) appears, make sure all the check boxes are cleared, and then click the Finish button. The K-Lite Codec Pack installer closes.

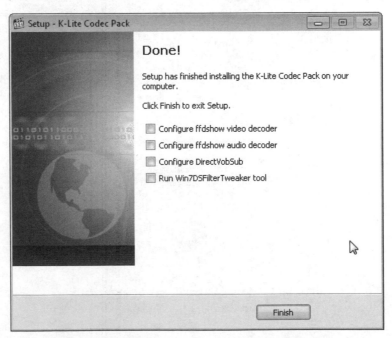

- Back in the Additional Packages dialog box, click the Install Bonjour button to install Apple's Bonjour networking protocol. The Bonjour Print Services installer then starts and displays its Welcome screen (shown here). Click the Next button and go through the screens for accepting the license agreement and reading information about Bonjour.

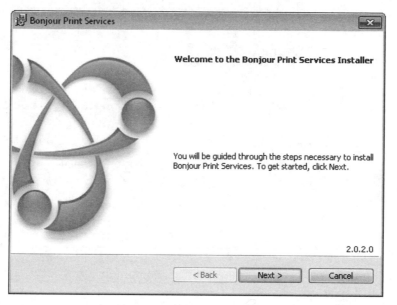

 If the Install Bonjour button in the Additional Packages dialog box is dimmed and unavailable, your PC already has Bonjour for Windows installed, so you don't need to install it. Go ahead and click the Exit button to close the Additional Packages dialog box.

- On the Installation Options screen (shown next), clear the Create Bonjour Printer Wizard Desktop Shortcut check box unless you want a shortcut for the Bonjour Printer Wizard on your desktop. Clear the Automatically Update Bonjour Print Services And Other Apple Software check box if you don't want the Apple Software Update service to check automatically for updates.

(You may prefer to check manually for updates at times that suit you.) Then click the Install button.

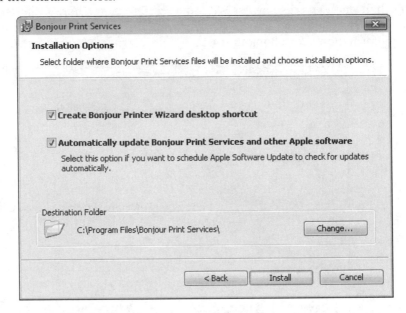

- When the Congratulations screen of the Bonjour Print Services installer appears, click the Finish button.
- At this point, you'll see the Air Cam Installer window again. Click the Close button, and you're finally done with the installation.

After installing Air Cam Live Video, run it by choosing Start | All Programs | Senstic | Air Cam | Air Cam Live Video.

If Windows displays a User Account Control dialog box, check that the program name is Air Cam for Windows, and then click the Yes button.

You can now enter your access information and configure the webcam as described in the section "Configure Air Cam Live Video or Air Cam," later in this project.

## Install and Run the Air Cam Application on OS X

After downloading the Air Cam application for OS X, install it like this:

1. Click the Downloads icon on the Dock to display a stack showing your downloaded files, and then click the Air Cam.pkg.zip file. OS X unzips the file and displays a Finder window showing the Downloads folder with the Air Cam .pkg file selected.
2. Double-click the Air Cam.pkg file to launch the Air Cam for Mac installer.
3. Click the Continue button to display the Installation Type screen. Here, you can click the Customize button to display the Customize screen if you want to prevent the installer from installing the AirCamLauncher app, but normally you'll be best off accepting the Standard install.

4. Click the Install button to run the installation, and then type your password (or an administrator's password) in the Authenticate dialog box.
5. When the installer shows the "The installation was successful" screen, click the Close button.
6. In the Finder window, click Applications in the sidebar to display the Applications folder.
7. Double-click the Air Cam icon to launch Air Cam.

## Configure Air Cam Live Video or Air Cam

The first time you start Air Cam Live Video (on Windows) or Air Cam (on the Mac), the program displays the Enter Access Information dialog box. This dialog box (the Mac version appears in the next illustration) prompts you to enter an e-mail address and password for accessing Air Cam Live Video or Air Cam from another computer. This is what you'll need to access Air Cam Live Video or Air Cam from your iPad.

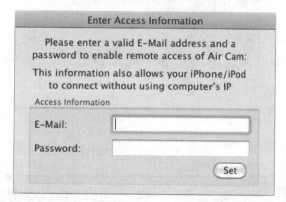

Type text that looks like an e-mail address in the E-Mail box—you don't need to enter a real e-mail address, and you may prefer not to enter a real address for security reasons. For example, enter *notmyname@example.com*.

Then click in the Password box and type the password you will use to connect your iPad to Air Cam Live Video or Air Cam. Make this a strong password—at least six characters; including upper- and lowercase letters; including at least one number and at least one symbol; and not a real word in any language.

Click the Done button (on Windows) or the Set button (on the Mac) to close the Enter Access Information dialog box. You'll then see the Air Cam Live Video window (on Windows) or the Air Cam window (on the Mac). The left screen in Figure 2-19 shows the Air Cam Live Video window; the right screen in Figure 2-19 shows the Air Cam window.

Aim the webcam (or the computer, if the webcam is built in) so that the picture shows what you want to watch. Then click the Options button to display the Air Cam

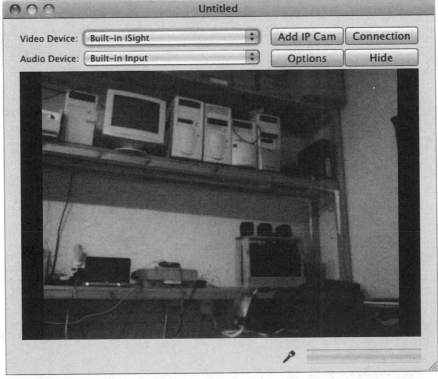

**FIGURE 2-19**   The Air Cam Live Video window (top) shows what your PC's webcam is seeing. The Air Cam window (bottom) shows the webcam's view on your Mac.

Options dialog box. On the six screens in this dialog box, you can set up Air Cam Live Video (on Windows) or Air Cam (on the Mac) to work the way you prefer:

- **Webcam**   This screen (shown here) shows options you'll want to set (or at least verify) to get Air Cam Live Video or Air Cam working correctly: You can set the resolution, flip the webcam's picture vertically or horizontally, turn on the display of the time stamp or the camera's name, and turn on Night Vision mode (for use in low light).

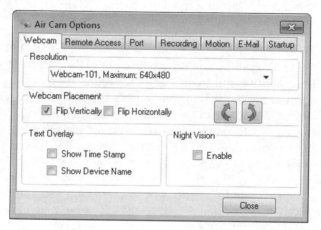

- **Remote Access**   On this screen, you can change the e-mail address and password you're using for remote access. You can also set up port forwarding by using the Auto-Config feature for Universal Plug and Play.
- **Port**   On this screen, you can change the default TCP listener port. The standard setting is port 1726.
- **Recording**   On this screen, you can select the folder to which the program saves recorded video files. (You can start and stop recording from your iPad once you connect.)
- **Motion**   On this screen, you can configure motion-detection settings. You can adjust the sensitivity level by clicking the Low option button, the Medium option button, or the High option button. You can choose what Air Cam Live Video or Air Cam should do when it detects movement: send you an e-mail, send you a push notification, or start recording automatically.
- **E-Mail**   On this screen, you can set up the e-mail account to which the program should send notifications.
- **Startup**   On this screen (which appears only on Windows), you can choose to run Air Cam Live Video automatically at startup, and you can make the program start up in hidden mode (so that you see only an icon in the notification area rather than a window showing what the webcam is seeing).

Click the Close button when you finish choosing options in the Air Cam Options dialog box. Air Cam Live Video is now running, and you can connect to it from your iPad as described later in this project.

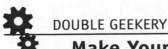

DOUBLE GEEKERY

## Make Your Internet Router Pass Requests from Your iPad to Air Cam

To connect Air Cam on your iPad to Air Cam Live Video (on Windows) or Air Cam (on the Mac) across the Internet, you need to set your Internet router to pass incoming requests for Air Cam to your PC or Mac. To do this, you set the router to forward traffic on the appropriate port. The default port is TCP port 1726.

If your Internet router supports the Universal Plug and Play (UPnP) standard, you can do this automatically by clicking the Auto-Config (UPnP) button on the Remote Access screen in the Air Cam Options dialog box. Many Internet routers support UPnP, so you'll probably want to try this approach first.

If this doesn't work, go into your router's configuration screens and make sure UPnP is turned on, and then try again. You may find that UPnP is turned off as a security measure. (Or you may have turned it off yourself.)

If your Internet router doesn't support UPnP, or if it does but you prefer to leave UPnP turned off, you can set up the port forwarding yourself. Go into your router's configuration screens, find the screen for port forwarding (or port redirection), and set up a rule to forward TCP port 1726 to your PC or Mac. For best results, you may need to give your PC or Mac a fixed IP address rather than have your Internet router allocate an address via DHCP.

# Get and Set Up Air Cam Live Video on Your iPad

Now that you've got Air Cam Live Video running on your PC or Air Cam running on your Mac, your next move is to install Air Cam Live Video on your iPad and set it up to connect to your PC or Mac.

Activate the iTunes window, and then double-click the iTunes Store item in the Source list on the left to open a window showing the iTunes Store. Type **air cam** into the Search box, press ENTER or RETURN, and then click the appropriate search result. On the app's page, click the button to download the Lite version for free or the Buy button to buy the full version.

 You can also get Air Cam by using the iTunes Store on your iPad if you prefer.

After iTunes downloads the app, sync your iPad to install it. Depending on your sync settings, you may need to select the app's check box on the Apps screen in iTunes to install it on the iPad.

After installing Air Cam, tap its icon on the Home screen to run it. If Air Cam displays the Please Turn Off Bluetooth dialog box (shown next), look at the right side of the status bar at the top of the screen to see if the Bluetooth icon appears.

At this writing, Air Cam displays the Please Turn Off Bluetooth dialog box whether Bluetooth is on or off, not just when Bluetooth is on (as you'd expect).

If the Bluetooth icon doesn't appear on the status bar, tap the Skip This button. But if the Bluetooth icon does appear, follow these steps to turn off Bluetooth:

1. Press the Home button to display the Home screen.
2. Tap the Settings icon to display the Settings screen.
3. Tap the General button to display the General screen.
4. Tap the Bluetooth button to display the Bluetooth screen.
5. Tap the Bluetooth switch and move it to the Off position.
6. Tap the General button to go back to the General screen.

Now press the Home button twice in quick succession to display the app-switching bar, and tap the Air Cam button on it to switch back to Air Cam. Tap the OK button in the Please Turn Off Bluetooth dialog box.

## Connect to the Webcam from Your iPad

Next, you see the Connection screen (shown here), which lists the webcams you can connect to—maybe just the webcam you set up.

Tap the webcam you want to view. If the webcam has a password (as is usually the case), Air Cam displays the Authentication screen (shown next) prompting you to enter it.

Type the password, and then move the Remember It switch to the On position or the Off position, as appropriate. Saving the password will make future access to the webcam quicker, so you'll probably want to save it, unless doing so is too much of a security risk.

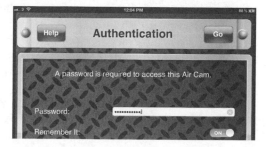

Tap the Go button at the upper-right corner of the window or the Go button on the keyboard to connect to the webcam.

Its video appears on the screen, as shown in Figure 2-20. In portrait orientation, you can use the controls to change Air Cam's settings, adjust the picture, take snapshots and recordings, and sync audio and video.

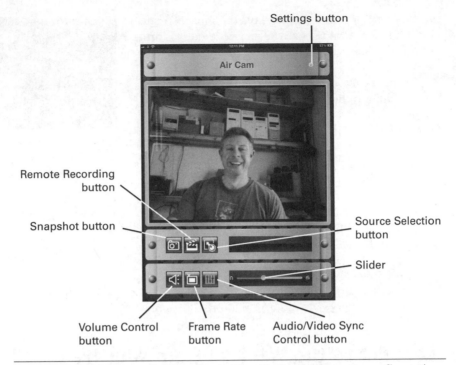

Settings button

Air Cam

Remote Recording
button

Snapshot button

Source Selection
button

Slider

Volume Control
button

Frame Rate
button

Audio/Video Sync
Control button

**FIGURE 2-20** In portrait view, you can use Air Cam's buttons to configure the app itself and the video and audio it receives.

- **Settings**   Tap this button to display the Settings screen, which gives you access to Air Cam's options.
- **Snapshot**   Tap this button to take a snapshot of the screen.
- **Remote Recording**   Tap this button to start making a recording of the video.
- **Source Selection**   Tap this button to change video source.
- **Volume Control**   Tap this button to adjust the volume using the slider that appears on the right side of the screen.
- **Frame Rate**   Tap this button to adjust the frame rate using the slider that appears on the right side of the screen.
- **Audio/Video Sync Control**   Tap this button to adjust the audio/video sync using the slider that appears on the right side of the screen.

Air Cam is easy to control on your iPad, but it appears to lack a command for shutting off the connection to a webcam you've been viewing. You can press the Home button to display the Home screen, but that leaves Air Cam running in the background. So to shut down the connection, and to shut down the app, you need to force quit Air Cam like this:

1. Press the Home button to display the Home screen.
2. Press the Home button twice in quick succession to display the app-switching bar.

3. Tap and hold the Air Cam button until a red circle containing a – sign appears at the upper-left corner of each app's icon in the app-switching bar.

4. Tap the – button for Air Cam to close the app.

### DOUBLE GEEKERY

# Turn Your iPad into a Network Webcam

As you know, your iPad has not one but two video cameras built in, together with a wireless network interface. So it's fully equipped to act as a network webcam itself if you need it to.

If you keep your iPad with you at all times, you can use it to broadcast what you're doing so that others can watch it in their web browsers. If you don't mind parking your iPad elsewhere for a while—perhaps using a tripod, as discussed in the Double Geekery sidebar in Project 17, earlier in this chapter—you can use it to keep tabs on what's happening there. For example, you can set up your iPad as a baby monitor, check on what your dogs actually do while you're out, or rig the iPad to keep watch over your desk at work to see who's disappearing your donuts.

You can broadcast either on your local network or across the Internet, and tap into it with just about any web browser.

To use your iPad as a network webcam, get the app ipCam – Mobile IP Camera ($2.99) from the App Store. Launch the app, and you'll see the Preview screen, which shows what the rear-facing camera is seeing, as in the image shown here.

Next, tap the Options button at the bottom to display the Options screen (shown on the left in the next illustration). Here you can set up the camera:

- **Camera**   Tap the Back button or the Front button to switch cameras.

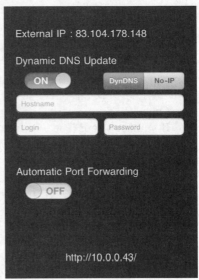

- **Image Size**   Drag the slider along the Small–Medium–Large scale to set the image size you want. Large images work fine over a local network, but if you're monitoring across the Internet, you'll normally want to use the Medium size.
- **Image Quality**   Drag the slider along the Low–High scale to set the image quality.
- **4:3 Crop**   Move this switch to the On position if you want to crop the picture to a 4:3 aspect ratio. Set this switch to the Off position if you want to see the iPad's picture unchanged.
- **Timestamp**   If you want to see the date and time superimposed on the iPad's picture, set this switch to the On position.
- **Listening Port**   If necessary, change the number in this text box from the default (80) to a different port number. You may need to use a different port when accessing your iPad across the Internet via a router.
- **Security**   If you want to secure the connection, type the login name in the Login box and the password in the Password box.
- **Audio**   Move this switch to the On position if you want to receive the iPad's audio along with the pictures. Getting the audio increases the amount of data transmitted, but it can be a great help in working out what's going on.

When you finish choosing settings on the Options screen, tap the Advanced button at the bottom of the screen to display the Advanced screen (shown on the right in the previous illustration). This screen contains three items:

- **External IP**   This readout shows the external IP address your network is using. This is the address at which you will be able to connect to the iPad across the Internet from outside your network. You may need to change the settings on your Internet router to enable computers to access your iPad across the Internet.

- **Dynamic DNS Update**   If your Internet provider uses dynamic IP addresses rather than static IP addresses, you can use either the DynDNS service or the No-IP service to provide the IP address when it changes. To use dynamic DNS, move this switch to the On position. In the controls that appear when the switch is in the On position, tap the DynDNS tab or the No-IP tab, as appropriate, and then fill in the fields.
- **Automatic Port Forwarding**   To use automatic port forwarding, move this switch to the On position. Automatic port forwarding lets ipCam tell your Internet router where to send an incoming request for ipCam from the Internet. To use automatic port forwarding, your Internet router must support either Universal Plug and Play (UPnP) or NAT-PMP.

When you've set your iPad up to monitor, open a web browser and go to the IP shown at the bottom of the ipCam window. You'll see the control screen, as shown on the left in the following illustration.

Click the JPEG Video link in the Web Browser Links area, and you will see a video feed from the iPad, as shown on the right in the illustration. Click the MJPEG Video link in the Web Browser Links area, and you can get an audio feed along with the video feed. To use audio, you will need to have set the Audio switch on the Options screen to the On position.

When using ipCam, you'll normally want to plug your iPad into the USB Power Adapter to make sure you don't run through the battery.

# 3 iPad as Your Main Computer Geekery

Up till now, you've pretty much needed a full-size computer—PC or Mac, desktop or laptop—to get serious computing done. But your iPad is now so powerful, so capable, and so well equipped with features and apps that you can use it as your main computer.

This chapter shows you the moves you'll need to make to turn your iPad into your main computer. We'll start by connecting a hardware keyboard to your iPad so that you can enter text at top speed. Then, for those times when you don't have the hardware keyboard at hand, we'll cover pro tricks for entering text quickly and accurately using the onscreen keyboards, which hide plenty of secrets most people miss. Those two projects will put you in good shape for the next topic: how to create business documents—Word documents, Excel spreadsheets, PowerPoint presentations, and PDF files—on your iPad wherever you are.

After that, I'll show you how to use your iPad first as a portable drive for your computer and then as a file server for your home network. Both these moves let you not only take your vital files with you wherever you go but also access them from any computer you're using.

At the end of the chapter, you'll learn how to develop power-user e-mail skills with the Mail app and how to give presentations directly from your iPad.

Let's get started.

## Project 20: Connect a Bluetooth Keyboard or Other Hardware Keyboard to Your iPad

Your iPad's onscreen keyboards are as good as Apple can make them, and the Dictation feature can be a great help in writing reminders, notes, e-mails, and text messages without needing to get your fingers dirty (or clean).

But when you need to enter serious amounts of text on your iPad, there's no substitute for a hardware keyboard. By connecting a keyboard via either Bluetooth or the Dock Connector port, you enable yourself to enter text at full speed in any app that requires it—Mail, Notes, the iWork apps, Documents To Go, or whatever.

### Connect and Use the Apple iPad Keyboard Dock

The easiest way to make your iPad more like a laptop is to use the Apple iPad Keyboard Dock accessory, which connects a hardware keyboard via the Dock Connector port. The iPad Keyboard Dock is customized for the iPad, so it includes hardware keys for iPad-specific actions such as returning to the Home screen, locking the iPad, changing the screen brightness, and adjusting the playback volume. The iPad Keyboard Dock also contains an audio-out port for piping audio out of your iPad at a standard volume, so you can easily leave your speakers connected.

This is all great, but the iPad Keyboard Dock does have a couple of downsides:

- Because of the port's position, the iPad has to remain in portrait orientation, which isn't great for some apps—but given that you'll be able to enter text much faster, you may be willing to make the sacrifice.
- You'll normally need to remove the iPad from its case in order to use the iPad Keyboard Dock. If you use a case you can easily slip off, this is no big deal, but it can be a problem for tight-fitting cases or heavy-duty cases.

To connect your iPad to the iPad Keyboard Dock, simply place the iPad on the iPad Keyboard Dock so that the Dock Connector engages. You can then start typing.

# Connect and Use a Bluetooth Keyboard

Before you can connect your Bluetooth keyboard to your iPad, you must do two things:

- **Turn on Bluetooth**  To save power, your iPad keeps Bluetooth turned off until you need it.
- **Pair the keyboard with your iPad**  Pairing is a one-time procedure that introduces the keyboard to your iPad and sets them up to work together. Pairing helps ensure that only approved Bluetooth devices can connect to your iPad.

## Turn On Bluetooth

To open the Bluetooth screen in the Settings app and turn on Bluetooth, follow these steps:

1. Tap the General button on the Settings screen to display the General screen.
2. Tap the Bluetooth button to display the Bluetooth screen (shown here).

3. Tap the Bluetooth switch and move it to the On position.

## Pair Your Bluetooth Keyboard

To pair your Bluetooth keyboard, follow these steps:

1. Turn Bluetooth on, as described in the previous section.
2. Put the Bluetooth keyboard into Pairing mode. How you do this depends on the keyboard, but it usually involves a magic press on the power button—for example, pressing and holding the power button until red and blue lights start flashing.
3. When the keyboard's button appears in the Devices list, showing Not Paired (as shown next), tap the button to connect the keyboard.

4. Your iPad then prompts you to type on the keyboard a pairing code, as shown here. Type the code and press ENTER or RETURN, and the keyboard and iPad establish the pairing.

After pairing the keyboard, your iPad connects it automatically (as shown here), on the assumption that you want to use the keyboard you're pairing. For subsequent use, connect the keyboard as described in the section "Connect Your Bluetooth Keyboard Again," a little later in this chapter.

### Disconnect Your Bluetooth Keyboard

To disconnect your Bluetooth keyboard from your iPad, turn it off. Your iPad then shows the keyboard as Not Connected in the Devices list on the Bluetooth screen.

You can also disconnect the keyboard by turning off Bluetooth on your iPad.

 When you're not using Bluetooth, turn it off to save power and extend your iPad's battery life.

### Connect Your Bluetooth Keyboard Again

After you have paired your Bluetooth keyboard, you can quickly connect it to your iPad again by moving it within Bluetooth range of your iPad and turning it on. As long as your iPad's Bluetooth is turned on, the iPad connects to the keyboard, and you can start using it within a few seconds.

### Make Your iPad Forget Your Bluetooth Keyboard

When you no longer need to use your Bluetooth keyboard with your iPad, you can tell your iPad to forget it. Follow these steps:

1. On the Bluetooth screen, tap the keyboard's > button to display the control screen for the keyboard. This illustration shows an example.

2. Tap the Forget This Device button. Your iPad displays a confirmation dialog box, as shown here.

3. Tap the OK button. Your iPad forgets the device, and then displays the Bluetooth screen again.

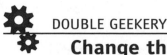

DOUBLE GEEKERY

# Change the Keyboard Layout for a Bluetooth Keyboard

Connecting a Bluetooth keyboard to your iPad is a great way to enter text quickly. And if you're used to a different layout on the keyboard, such as a European layout or the optimized Dvorak layout, you can switch the keyboard to use that layout.

If you need to use a different keyboard layout than the one you currently get on either the onscreen keyboard or an external keyboard you've connected, follow these steps to change the keyboard layout:

1. Press the Home button to display the Home screen.
2. Tap the Settings icon to display the Settings screen.
3. Tap the General button to display the General screen.
4. Scroll down to the bottom of the screen.
5. Tap the Keyboard button to display the Keyboard screen (shown on the left in this illustration).

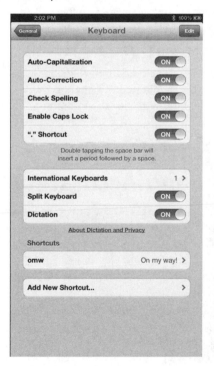

6. Tap the International Keyboards button to display the Keyboards screen, shown here with a single keyboard added.

7. Tap the top button. This button's name depends on which keyboard you're using—for example, English. The screen for the keyboard appears. The right screen in the illustration with step 5 in this sidebar shows an example.
8. In the Choose A Software Keyboard Layout box, tap the layout you want for the onscreen keyboard—for example, QWERTY.
9. In the Choose A Hardware Keyboard Layout box, tap the button for the keyboard layout you want for your external keyboard—for example, Dvorak.
10. Tap the Keyboards button to return to the Keyboards screen.
11. Tap the Keyboard button to return to the Keyboard screen.

---

From the Keyboards screen, you can also add a new keyboard by tapping the Add New Keyboard button. But if you simply need to change the keyboard you're using with the iPad, change the existing one rather than adding another keyboard.

# Project 21: Learn Pro Tricks for Entering Text Quickly and Accurately

When you're not using a hardware keyboard, you'll want to make the most of the iPad's onscreen keyboards. You can enter text quickly and accurately using these keyboards, provided you know their secrets. And when you prefer to speak your mind, you can use the Dictation feature instead.

At first glance, your iPad's main onscreen keyboard could hardly be simpler to use:

- Tap in a text field or in a document to summon the keyboard.
- Tap the letter you want to type.
- Tap either Shift key to get an uppercase letter.
- Tap the .?123 button to display the keyboard containing numbers and common symbols.
- From the numbers and common symbols keyboard, tap the # + = button to display the keyboard containing brackets, braces, comic-book expletive characters (#%^&!), and so on.

- Tap the ABC button when you need the letter keys again.
- Tap the microphone button if you want to start dictating.

But the onscreen keyboards also have a bunch of hidden tricks that can save you taps, time, and trouble. Read on...

 If you've connected a hardware keyboard, as described in the previous project, you'll need to disconnect it to make the onscreen keyboards available again. If the keyboard is connected via the Dock Connector, disconnect it physically. If the keyboard is connected via Bluetooth, turn off Bluetooth.

## Enter an Accented or Alternate Character

Tap and hold the base character until a pop-up panel appears, and then tap the character you want. For example, tap and hold the E until the panel shown here appears, and then tap the character needed.

## Enter an En Dash (–) or an Em Dash (—)

Tap and hold the hyphen key, and then tap the en dash (–) or em dash (—) on the pop-up panel. An *en dash* is a dash the width of an N character in the font, and an *em dash* is a dash the width of an M character, which is substantially wider.

From this pop-up panel, you can also enter a bullet instead of having to go to the # + = screen.

## Type a Period Quickly

To type a period quickly, tap the spacebar twice in quick succession.

If this doesn't work, you need to turn this feature on. See the section "Turn On All the Automatic Correction Features," coming right up.

## Enter Domains Other Than .com

When you're using Safari, the onscreen keyboard has a .com button you can tap to enter the .com domain easily. To enter other widely used domains, tap and hold the .com button, and then tap the domain on the pop-up panel (shown here).

## Enter the Domain for an E-mail Address

To enter the domain for an e-mail address, tap and hold the . (period) key, and then tap the domain on the pop-up panel (shown here).

## Enter Punctuation and Switch Straight Back to the Letter Keyboard

Often, you'll need to enter a single punctuation character, and then go back to typing letters. To do this, tap the .?123 button, but don't remove your finger from the screen. Slide your finger across to the punctuation key, and then take your finger off the screen. The iPad enters the character and displays the letter keyboard again.

## Keep Typing and Let Automatic Correction Fix Your Typos

Your iPad's automatic correction features (discussed next) sort out many typos. So if you find you've made a typo halfway through a word, you're usually better off to keep typing and accept the automatic correction (as shown here) than to go back and fix the typo.

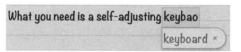

## Turn On All the Automatic Correction Features

Your iPad has a handful of automatic correction features to help you enter text faster and more accurately. To open the Keyboard screen and choose settings, follow these steps:

1. Press the Home button to display the Home screen.
2. Tap the Settings icon to display the Settings screen.
3. Tap the General button to display the General screen.
4. Scroll down to the bottom of the screen.
5. Tap the Keyboard button to display the Keyboard screen (shown on the left in Figure 3-1).
6. Set the Auto-Capitalization switch to the On position if you want your iPad to automatically capitalize the first word of a new sentence or a new paragraph.
7. Set the Auto-Correction switch to the On position if you want to use automatic corrections and text shortcuts. These are usually helpful.
8. Set the Check Spelling switch to the On position if you want the iPad to check your spelling and query apparently misspelled words.
9. Set the Enable Caps Lock switch to the On position if you want to be able to turn on Caps Lock by double-tapping the Shift button. This is usually helpful unless you find yourself turning on Caps Lock by accident.
10. Set the "." Shortcut switch to the On position if you want to be able to type a period by tapping the spacebar twice, as described earlier in this chapter. This shortcut is usually helpful.
11. Leave the Keyboard screen displayed so that you can set up text shortcuts, as described in a moment.

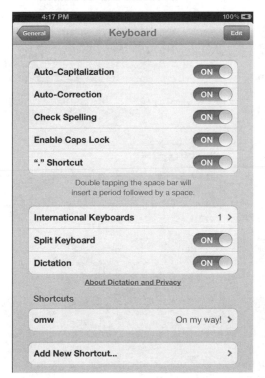 

**FIGURE 3-1**    On the Keyboard screen in Settings (left), tap the Add New Shortcut button to start creating a new shortcut. On the Shortcut screen (right), type the phrase and the shortcut, and then tap the Save button.

## Turn on the Split Keyboard and Dictation

If you want to use the split keyboard, move the Split Keyboard switch on the Keyboard screen to the On position. See the sidebar below titled "Thumb-Type with the Split Keyboard" for details on the split keyboard.

Similarly, if you want to dictate text, move the Dictation switch on the Keyboard screen to the On position.

### DOUBLE GEEKERY

## Thumb-Type with the Split Keyboard

When you're holding your iPad and typing, summon up the split keyboard so that you can type easily with your thumbs.

To switch to the split keyboard, first tap in a text field or in a document to display the regular keyboard. Then tap the Hide Keyboard button in the lower-right corner and drag its handle up to switch to the split keyboard, as shown here.

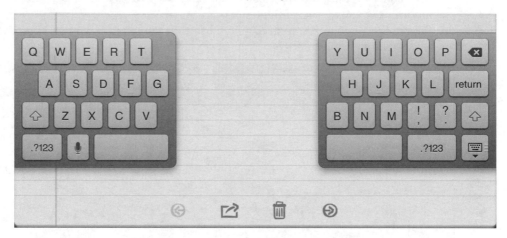

You can also tap and hold the Hide Keyboard button to display the pop-up menu, and then tap the Split button, as shown here.

After displaying the split keyboard, you can drag it up or down the screen by using the handle on the Hide Keyboard button.

If the handle doesn't appear on the Hide Keyboard button, the split keyboard isn't available. That means you need to turn it on in the Settings app, as described in the main text. Go to the Keyboard screen and move the Split Keyboard switch to the On position.

The split keyboard is easy to use: Once you've displayed it, tap the keys as usual. But you can also use the six invisible keys, which are useful if you're used to reaching across with your opposite hand to type the central characters.

When you finish using the split keyboard, tap and hold the Hide Keyboard button, and then tap the Dock And Merge button on the pop-up menu.

Instead of splitting the keyboard, you can simply undock it and then position it wherever on the screen you find most comfortable. To undock the keyboard, tap and hold the Hide Keyboard button, and then tap the Undock button on the pop-up menu. Then grab the handle on the Hide Keyboard button and drag the keyboard up to where you want it.

## Create Text Shortcuts

If you've used Microsoft Word or another word processor, you're no doubt familiar with the AutoCorrect feature, which automatically fixes typos and expands shortcuts you've defined (for example, expanding **myadd** to your full mailing address). Your iPad has a similar feature, and you can speed up your typing by defining shortcuts like this:

1. Press the Home button to display the Home screen.
2. Tap the Settings icon to display the Settings screen.
3. Tap the General button to display the General screen.
4. Scroll down to the bottom of the screen.
5. Tap the Keyboard button to display the Keyboard screen.
6. At the bottom of the screen, tap the Add New Shortcut button to display the Shortcut screen (shown on the right in Figure 3-1).
7. Type the replacement word or phrase in the Phrase box.
8. Type the shortcut in the Shortcut box.
9. Tap the Save button.
10. Repeat steps 6–9 for each other shortcut you want to create.
11. When you've finished creating shortcuts and choosing keyboard settings, tap the Keyboard button to go back to the Keyboard screen.

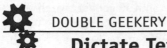

**DOUBLE GEEKERY**

# Dictate Text into Your Documents

I'm sure you know that your iPad's Dictation feature can be a great way to enter text on your iPad quickly and accurately. But you can greatly boost your speed and accuracy by using the terms that the recognition engine knows best.

To dictate text, you simply position the insertion point in the note, e-mail message, or other document you're writing, tap the microphone button on the keyboard, and then say the words you want Dictation to write down for you. When you stop speaking, Dictation processes your input and then writes down the text that the servers in the Apple data center have understood.

To insert punctuation, just say the punctuation word in the stream of text. You don't need to warn Dictation that you're about to use a punctuation term. These are the punctuation terms you can use:

- "Period" or "full stop"
- "Comma"
- "Semicolon"
- "Colon"
- "Exclamation point" or "exclamation mark"
- "Inverted exclamation mark" (¡)
- "Question mark"
- "Inverted question mark" (¿)

- "Hyphen" (-)
- "Dash" or "en dash" (–)
- "Em dash" (—)
- "Underscore" (_)
- "Open parenthesis" and "close parenthesis"
- "Open bracket" and "close bracket"
- "Ampersand" (&)
- "Asterisk" (*)

Here is a list of symbols you can tell Dictation to enter:

- "At sign" (@)
- "Copyright sign" (©)
- "Registered sign" (®)
- "Pound sign" or "hash mark" (#)
- "Dollar sign" ($)
- "Cent sign" (¢)
- "Euro sign" (€)
- "Pound sterling sign" (£)

- "Yen sign" (¥)
- "Percent sign" (%)
- "Greater-than sign" (>) and "less-than sign" (<)
- "Forward slash" (/) and "backslash" (\)
- "Vertical bar" ( | )
- "Caret" (^)

To tell Dictation how to format and lay out text, use these commands:

- **"New line"**   This gives a single line, with no blank line between paragraphs.
- **"New paragraph"**   This gives two lines, so you get a blank line between paragraphs.
- **"Cap"**   This makes Dictation apply an initial capital to the following word. For example, "cap cheese" produces *Cheese*.
- **"No caps"**   This prevents Dictation from applying an initial capital to a word that would normally get one. For example, "he's no caps Russian" produces *he's russian*.

- **"Caps on" and "Caps off"**    "Caps on" turns Caps Lock on, making everything you dictate all caps until you say "caps off."
- **"No caps on" and "No caps off"**    "No caps on" locks caps off, making everything you dictate all lowercase until you say "no caps off," after which normal capitalization resumes.
- **"Open quotes" and "Close quotes"**    For example, "open quotes cap hello exclamation point close quotes she said period" produces *"Hello!" she said*.
- **"Spacebar"**    This forces Dictation to insert a space between words that it would otherwise put a hyphen between. For example, "this document is up spacebar to spacebar date" produces *this document is up to date* (instead of *up-to-date*).
- **"No space"**    This prevents Dictation from inserting a space between words. For example, if you needed to enter the product name *BovineEmulator*, you could say "cap bovine no space cap emulator." You can also say "no space on" to turn on no-spacing until you say "no space off" to turn it off again.
- **"Dot"**    This puts a period between two words—for example, "Amazon dot com" produces *Amazon.com*.
- **"Point"**    This puts a period between numbers—for example, "two point five times as likely to succeed" gives *2.5 times as likely to succeed*.

Finally, you can also enter the most common emoticons by saying "smiley face," "frown face," and "wink face."

# Project 22: Create and Share Business Documents with Your iPad

If you're using your iPad as your main computer, you'll likely need to create business documents on it. In this project, I'll show you how to create and edit essential types of business documents—everything from killer memos and coldly calculating spreadsheets through drop-dead presentations and professional PDF files.

Even if you create your business documents on your iPad, you probably won't want to keep them there. So I'll walk you through the different means you can use to share documents between your iPad and your PC or Mac. You can copy documents back and forth using iTunes' File Sharing feature, attach documents to e-mail messages, transfer documents by using third-party apps, or share documents using iCloud.

## Create Business Documents on Your iPad

In this section, we'll look quickly at the main apps for creating business documents on the iPad: word-processing documents, spreadsheets, presentations, and PDF files.

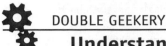

## Understand Why Your iPad Can View Office Documents but Not Edit Them

Your iPad's operating system has built-in viewers for major file types, including the following:

- **PDF files**   Reflowable PDFs work well on your iPad because it can reflow them to fit the screen, but non-reflowable ones tend to mean you need to either strain to view them at a too-small size or zoom in and scroll back and forth.
- **Word documents**   Your iPad can display both the older .doc format and the newer .docx format used by Word 2007/2008 and later versions.
- **Excel workbooks**   Your iPad can display both the older .xls format and the newer .xlsx format used by Excel 2007/2008 and later versions.
- **PowerPoint presentations**   Your iPad can display both the older .ppt format and the newer .pptx format used by PowerPoint 2007/2008 and later versions.
- **Rich Text Format**   Your iPad can display RTF documents with all their formatting.
- **Plain text**   Your iPad can display plain text documents with no problems.
- **HTML**   Your iPad can display files created in the HyperText Markup Language.

Various apps can access these viewers—for example, if you receive a Word document attached to an e-mail message, Mail can open the document in a viewer so you can see its contents. But you have to buy third-party apps to edit these document types.

Given that Microsoft Office not only dominates the Windows market for Office documents but also has a hefty chunk of the Mac market, it's most likely you'll need to create your business documents in the Word, Excel, and PowerPoint formats—so we'll start there. Next, we'll cover creating documents in the Pages, Numbers, and Keynote formats used by the apps in Apple's iWork suite. Finally, we'll look at how to create PDF files.

## Create Documents in the Microsoft Office File Formats

To create documents in the Microsoft Office file formats on your iPad, you have four main choices:

- **Documents To Go**   The basic version of Documents To Go can create Word documents and Excel spreadsheets and view PowerPoint presentations and iWork files. The advanced version, Documents To Go Premium, adds creating and editing PowerPoint presentations to the list. Figure 3-2 shows Documents To Go at work on a Word document.
- **Quickoffice**   The basic version of Quickoffice can create Word documents and Excel spreadsheets. The pro version, Quickoffice Pro, can create and edit PowerPoint presentations as well. Figure 3-3 shows Quickoffice Pro creating a presentation.
- **Google Docs**   If you have an account with Google Docs (http://docs.google .com), you can log into it using Safari or another web browser on your iPad, and

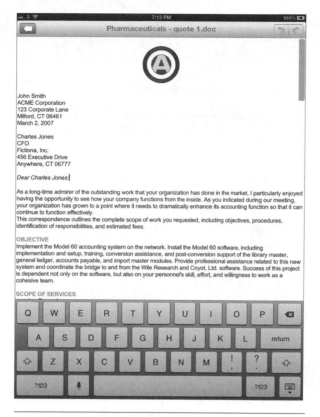

**FIGURE 3-2**   Documents To Go Premium can create and edit Word documents, Excel spreadsheets, and PowerPoint presentations.

then create word-processing documents, spreadsheets, and presentations in it. The interface is awkward because you have only a small amount of space when you're using the onscreen keyboard, but it's workable enough if you have a good Internet connection.

- **iWork**   Pages, Numbers, and Keynote (discussed in the next section) can export files in the corresponding Microsoft Office formats. For example, from Numbers, you can export a spreadsheet in the Microsoft Excel format. See the next sidebar "Convert Your iWork Files to the Microsoft Office Formats" for details.

 Documents To Go and Quickoffice are impressive apps, but they enable you to use only the most widely used formatting and objects (such as tables and shapes) when creating documents, spreadsheets, and presentations. Because of these limitations, and because the iPad's screen offers only a modest amount of space to work in, you will normally do best to finish your documents on a computer rather than on the iPad.

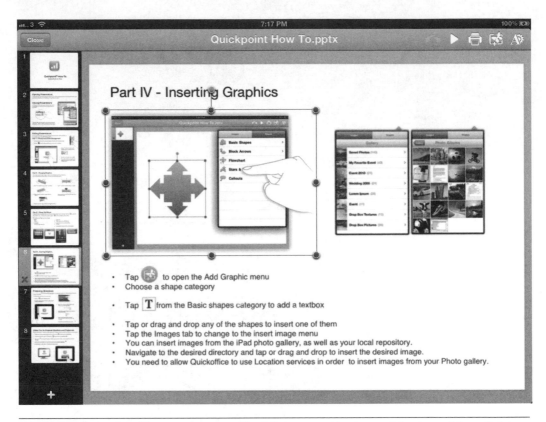

**FIGURE 3-3** Quickoffice Pro can create Word documents, Excel spreadsheets, and PowerPoint presentations.

## DOUBLE GEEKERY

# Convert Your iWork Files to the Microsoft Office Formats

The three iWork apps—Pages, Numbers, and Keynote—are great for working on the iPad. But if you or your colleagues use Microsoft Office on your computers, you'll need to convert the iWork files you create to their Office equivalents. To convert the files, you use the Share And Print feature in the iWork apps.

To convert a file using the Share And Print feature, follow these steps on your iPad:

1. Open the app to which the document belongs. I'll use Pages for this example.
2. If the app launches with a document open other than the document you want to convert, tap the Documents button, the Spreadsheets button, or the Presentations button in the upper-left corner of the screen to go back to the Document Manager screen. This is the screen that shows the contents of the Documents folder, the Spreadsheets folder, or the Presentations folder.
3. Tap the document you want to convert. The app opens the document.

4. Tap the Tools button (the button with the wrench icon in the upper-right corner of the screen) to display the Tools screen (shown on the left in this illustration).

5. Tap the Share And Print button to display the Share And Print screen (shown on the right in the illustration).

6. Tap the Email Document button or the Send To iTunes button, as appropriate. Your iPad displays a screen for choosing the format of the document. The next illustration shows the Email Document screen, which Pages displays when you choose to e-mail a document. The Email Spreadsheet screen in Numbers, the Email Presentation screen in Keynote, and the Choose Format screen (for sending to iTunes) offer similar choices.

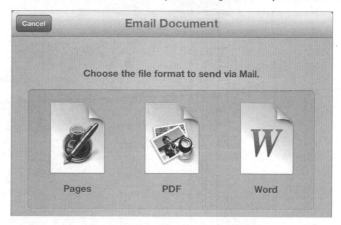

7. Tap the format to use for the exported file:
   - **Native format**   Tap the Pages button, the Numbers button, or the Keynote button to keep the document in its native format.
   - **PDF**   Tap the PDF button to create a Portable Document Format file for viewing on any computer (but not for editing).
   - **Office format**   Tap the Word button (from Pages), the Excel button (from Numbers), or the PowerPoint button (from Keynote).

8. The app exports the file in the format you chose, and then displays the document again.

## Create Documents in the iWork File Formats

If you need to create documents in the iWork file formats on your iPad, look no farther than Apple's iWork apps. These apps are the iPad versions of the full-scale OS X applications:

- **Pages**  Pages is an app for creating word-processing and layout documents. Figure 3-4 shows Pages working on a document.
- **Numbers**  Numbers is an app for creating spreadsheets. Figure 3-5 shows a spreadsheet open in Numbers.
- **Keynote**  Keynote is an app for creating and editing presentations. Figure 3-6 shows Keynote.

## Create PDF Files

Creating documents, spreadsheets, or presentations is helpful, but sometimes you may need to create PDF files on your iPad so that you can give your clients fully laid out documents that they can't change.

**FIGURE 3-4**  Use the Pages app to create and edit word-processing documents on your iPad.

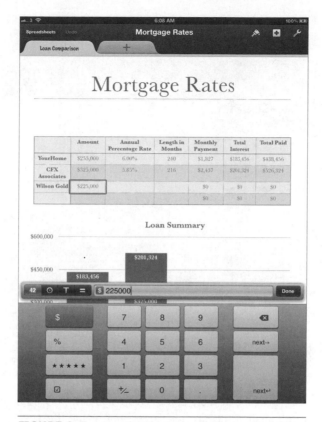

**FIGURE 3-5**   Use the Numbers app to create and edit spreadsheets.

 If you're using Pages, Numbers, or Keynote, you can create a PDF file by exporting the document. See the Double Geekery sidebar "Convert Your iWork Files to the Microsoft Office Formats" earlier in the chapter for details.

When you need to create PDF files, try these two apps:

- **Adobe CreatePDF**   CreatePDF from Adobe, the company behind the PDF file format, enables you to take a document from a file-storage area and turn it into a PDF file. CreatePDF is a little clumsy, because it doesn't have a file browser for picking the document from which to create the PDF file: Instead, you have to start from the file-storage area of the app the document is in, and then use the Open In command to open it in CreatePDF. But once you've picked the document, the conversion to PDF runs smoothly.
- **Save2PDF**   Save2PDF is an app for creating and manipulating PDF files. Save2PDF's features include merging two or more PDF files into a single file and adding extra pages to an existing document. For example, if you have a PDF file that contains a standard contract, you can add to it an extra page that turns it into a customized version.

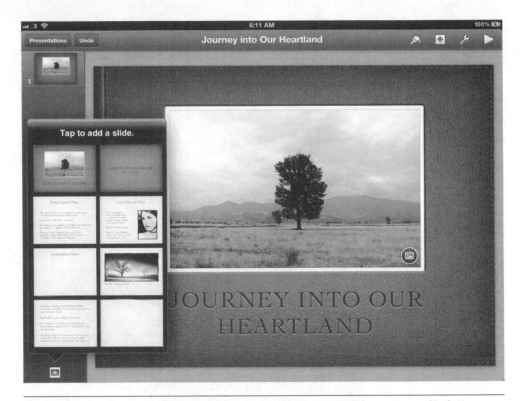

**FIGURE 3-6** Use the Keynote app to create and edit presentations on your iPad. You can export presentations in Microsoft PowerPoint format if necessary.

# Share Documents with Your PC or Mac

In this section, we'll look at how to share documents between your iPad and your computer. We'll cover iTunes' File Sharing feature, look into transferring documents via e-mail, discuss three third-party apps that can transfer documents, and finally dig into sharing documents using Apple's iCloud service.

## Share Documents Using iTunes' File Sharing

If you use iTunes rather than iCloud to sync your iPad, you can use iTunes' File Sharing feature to put documents on the iPad from your computer or copy documents from your iPad to your computer. This is the most direct way of shifting files from point A to point B.

To transfer documents by using File Sharing, follow these steps:

1. Connect your iPad to the computer as usual.
2. If the computer doesn't automatically launch or activate iTunes, launch or activate iTunes yourself.
3. In the Devices category in the Source list, click your iPad's entry to display its control screens.
4. Click the Apps tab to display your iPad's apps and files.
5. Scroll down to the File Sharing area (see Figure 3-7).
6. In the Apps list, click the app to which you want to transfer the files. The list of files for that app appears in the Documents pane to the right.
7. To add documents to the app, follow these steps:
   a. Click the Add button to display the Open dialog box.
   b. Navigate to and select the document or documents you want to add.
   c. Click the OK button (on Windows) or the Open button (on the Mac).
8. To copy documents from the app to the computer, follow these steps:
   a. Click the Save To button to display the Open dialog box.
   b. Navigate to the folder in which you want to save the document.
   c. Click the Select Folder button (on Windows) or the Open button (on the Mac).

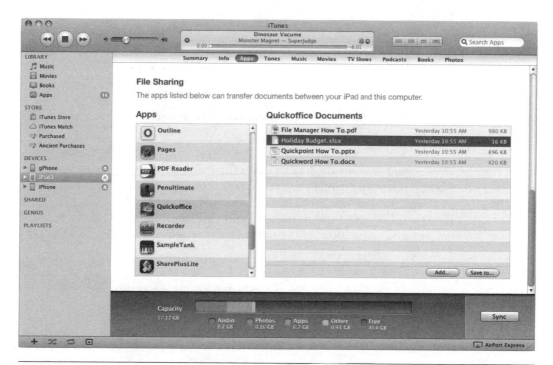

**FIGURE 3-7**  The File Sharing area on the Apps tab in the iTunes control screens for an iPad lists the apps that can transfer files to and from the iPad. Click an app to see its files.

File transfers generally run pretty quickly, as USB 2.0 can handle up to 480 megabits per second (Mbps)—but if you're transferring many large files, it'll take a while.

## Transfer Documents via E-mail

When you need to get documents onto your iPad quickly, you can simply e-mail them to an account on it. You can then open a document directly from the e-mail message into either one of the iPad's viewers or into whichever app you want to use to work on the document.

E-mail may seem like a clumsy solution to document transfer, but it's quick and effective unless the document is too big to go through e-mail servers. E-mail is especially useful when the document is on somebody else's computer rather than the computer with which you normally sync your iPad.

And you don't need me to point out that you can use Mail to send a document back after you've edited it, or send it along to the next person who needs to deal with it.

**Copy a Document from a Message to an App's Storage Area**   To get a document out of an e-mail message and into an app's storage area, follow these steps:

1. In the message list, tap the message to display its contents.
2. Tap and hold the document's button in the message until Mail displays a menu, as shown here.

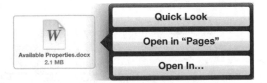

3. If you want to open the basic viewer for the document, tap the Quick Look button; normally, though, you'll do better to open the document in an app. If you want to open the document in the default app (in this example, Pages), tap the Open In "*App*" button (where *App* is the app's name). Otherwise, tap the Open In button to display the Open In menu (shown here), and then tap the app you want to use.

That's the most efficient way to copy the document from the message and get it into the app. But what you'll probably want to do often is view the contents of the document so that you can decide which app to open it in. For example, if you receive a Word document on your iPad, you may want to bring it into Pages so that you can use Pages' streamlined layout tools. But if you simply want to edit the document as a Word document, you'll do better to open the document in Documents To Go or a similar app that can maintain the Word document format.

**View a Document and Decide Which App to Open It In**   To view a document and then decide which app to open it in, follow these steps:

1. In the message list, tap the message to display its contents.
2. Tap the button for the attached document you want to open. Your iPad displays the document in the viewer.
3. Tap the action button (the button with a curving arrow in the upper-right corner of the screen) to display the menu for opening the document in the default app, opening it in another app, or printing it. This illustration shows a PDF document, for which iBooks is the default app.

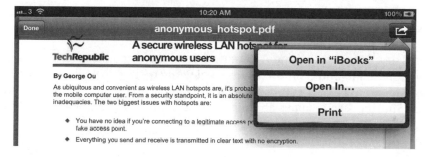

4. If you want to use the default app, tap its button to open the document in it. Otherwise, tap the Open In button to display the list of apps that can open the document. The next illustration shows an example of this list.

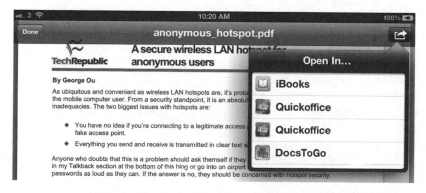

5. Tap the app in which you want to open the document.

This approach leaves the document open in the viewer in Mail. So when you go back to Mail, tap the Done button to close the viewer and return to the message.

**Delete the Document from Mail if Necessary**   Once you've opened an attached document in another app, that app stores a copy of the document in its storage area. You can now delete the e-mail message and the attached document if necessary; the copy of the document that you've added to the other app's storage area remains unaffected.

If you attach a picture to an e-mail message, the recipient can save the picture to his iPad's Photos storage area. But if you attach a music file or video file, the recipient can only play it in the viewer or add it to third-party apps that handle media file types, not add it to the iPad's Music storage area.

## Transfer Documents Using Third-Party Apps

If you need more direct or wider-ranging access to the iPad's file system than iTunes provides, you'll need to use a third-party app instead. This section introduces you to three of the most widely useful apps at this writing: Air Sharing, FileApp Pro (with or without DiskAid), and Documents To Go.

**Transfer Documents Using Air Sharing**   Air Sharing for iPad is an app for transferring documents to and from the iPad and viewing them on the device. Air Sharing enables you to connect your computer to your iPad via a wireless network connection. Air Sharing also includes abilities such as connecting to a Windows PC running a companion program, mounting remote file systems, opening and creating Zip files, and downloading files from the Web.

For instructions on connecting a PC or Mac to your iPad via Air Sharing, see Project 23, "Use Your iPad as a File Server for Your Household," later in this chapter.

**Transfer Documents Using FileApp Pro**   Like Air Sharing, FileApp Pro is an app for transferring documents to and from your iPad and for viewing documents on the devices. With FileApp Pro, you can connect to the iPad either via the USB cable (which is good for speed) or via a wireless network connection (which is good for flexibility). To connect via USB, you need to either use iTunes' File Sharing feature or run the DiskAid program from DigiDNA (www.digidna.net) on your PC or Mac. DiskAid costs $24.90 for a full version, but you can also get a free version that can copy files to apps but can't copy music, videos, messages, contacts, or other data from your iPad to your computer.

Figure 3-8 shows the Home screen in FileApp Pro, from which you can browse your local folders and set up USB sharing or Wi-Fi sharing.

You can transfer documents by using the FileApp Pro entry in the File Sharing area of the Apps tab in iTunes, but if you want to transfer many files easily and

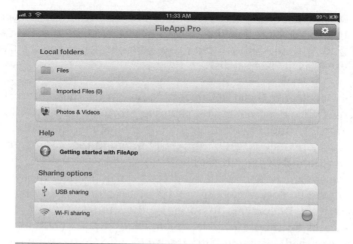

**FIGURE 3-8**    FileApp Pro lets you choose between USB and Wi-Fi connections to your iPad.

choose the folders to put them in, it's worth getting DiskAid and installing it on your computer. Once you've set up sharing on the iPad, you can connect via DiskAid and transfer files easily back and forth. Figure 3-9 shows DiskAid in action.

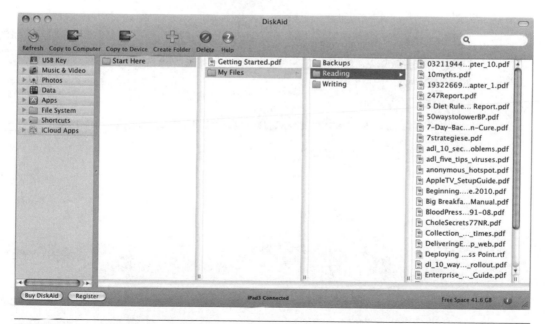

**FIGURE 3-9**    DiskAid is a companion program for FileApp Pro that makes it easy to transfer files to and from your iPad. You can also use DiskAid on its own.

DiskAid is a handy tool if you want to simply store files on your iPad—for example, to transfer them from one computer to another—rather than open the files on the iPad. With DiskAid, you can create your own folders on the iPad, enabling you to use it as an external disk.

**Transfer Documents Using Documents To Go**   If you need to work extensively with Microsoft Office documents—for example, Word documents or Excel workbooks—you'll probably find the iWork apps too cumbersome. Instead of struggling with frustrating conversions, get a third-party program that can handle the main Office file formats without having to translate them.

As discussed earlier in this chapter, the main choices for creating and editing Microsoft Office documents directly on the iPad are Documents To Go and Quickoffice. At this writing, Documents To Go seems the stronger of the two, especially as it has good features for transferring documents between your computer and your iPad.

You can load documents into Documents To Go by using the Documents To Go entry in the File Sharing area of the Apps tab in iTunes, but for regular use, download the free companion desktop program that runs on your PC or Mac to synchronize documents with the iPad. To get the program, go to the Documents To Go for iOS page on the DataViz website (www.dataviz.com/DTG_iphone.html), and then click the Download Win button or the Download Mac button. Once you've installed the program, you go through a HotSync setup process to pair your iPad with the desktop program. You can then use the desktop program to transfer files to and from your iPad (see Figure 3-10).

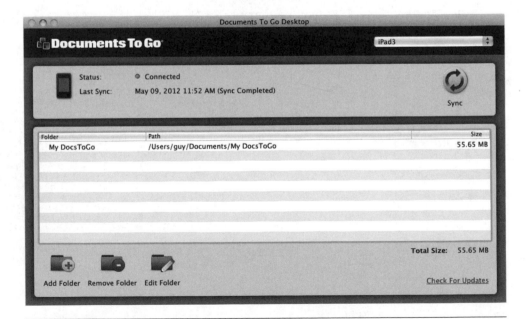

**FIGURE 3-10**   The Documents To Go desktop program runs on your computer and connects to your iPad.

Documents To Go Premium can access documents in an online storage account such as Google Docs, Box.net, Dropbox, or iDisk.

## Share Documents Using iCloud

Apple's iCloud service is a great way of sharing data among your iOS devices and your computers. You can use iCloud to sync your mail, contacts, calendars and tasks, bookmarks, and photos to both your PCs and your Macs. If you've got a Mac, you can also sync your documents and notes. In this section, we'll focus on syncing your documents. (If you're a PC user, you may want to skip this section.)

Once you've set up your iCloud account on your iPad, iCloud-enabled apps can save documents to iCloud and access them from there. Similarly, your other iOS devices or your Mac can access your iCloud account, enabling you to create and edit documents there.

**Set Up iCloud on Your iPad** To set up iCloud on your iPad, follow these steps:

1. Press the Home button to display the Home screen.
2. Tap the Settings icon to display the Settings screen.

 If you set up an iCloud account while setting up your iPad, you won't need to set it up again. But you may need to make sure the Documents & Data switch is set to the On position.

3. Tap the iCloud icon to display the iCloud screen. If you haven't yet set up an iCloud account on your iPad, the iCloud screen appears as shown on the left in Figure 3-11.
4. Tap the Apple ID button and then type your e-mail address.
5. Tap the Password button and then type your password.
6. Tap the Sign In button. Your iPad signs you into iCloud and then displays the Allow iCloud To Use The Location Of Your iPad? dialog box (shown here).
7. Tap the OK button if you want to be able to use the Find My iPad features. This is usually a good idea. If you don't want to be able to track your iPad, tap the Don't Allow button.
8. The iCloud screen then displays the settings for your account, as shown on the right in Figure 3-11.

**FIGURE 3-11** If you haven't yet set up your iCloud account, enter your details and tap the Sign In button (left). After signing in, choose which iCloud services to use.

9. Set the switches to specify which iCloud features you want to use. For example, set the Contacts switch to On if you want to store your contacts in iCloud so that you can easily sync them across all your devices.

10. Tap the Documents & Data switch to display the Documents & Data screen (shown here).

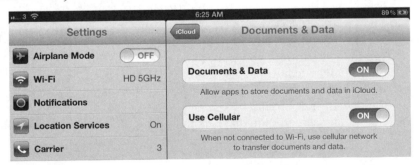

11. Tap the Documents & Data switch and move it to the On position.

12. If your iPad has cellular connectivity, move the Use Cellular switch to the On position if you want to sync your documents over the cellular network. Move the switch to the Off position if you want to sync only via Wi-Fi.

Syncing documents over the cellular network is great for keeping your data synced, but if your documents are large, you can go through your data allowance quickly. Test this setting and monitor your usage so that you know whether cellular syncing is sensible on your data plan.

13. Tap the iCloud button to return to the iCloud screen.

**Set Up iCloud on Your Mac**   To set up iCloud on your Mac, follow these steps:

1. Choose Apple | System Preferences to open the System Preferences window.
2. In the Internet & Wireless section, click the iCloud icon to display the iCloud pane (see Figure 3-12).

 If you have already signed in to iCloud, the iCloud pane in System Preferences displays the full range of controls, as shown in Figure 3-14. Go to step 8 in this list.

3. Type your Apple ID and password, and then click the Sign In button to sign in. The iCloud pane then displays the iCloud setup screen shown in Figure 3-13.
4. Select the Use iCloud For Contacts, Calendars, and Bookmarks check box if you want to store your contacts, calendars, and bookmarks in iCloud. This is usually a good idea.

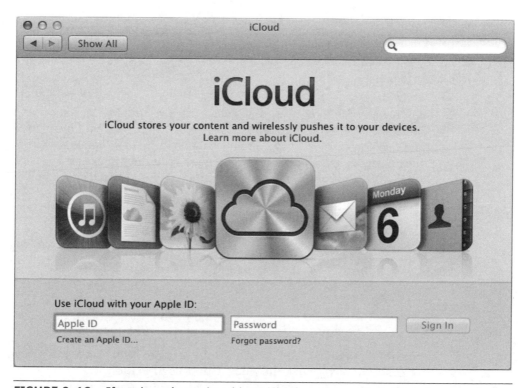

**FIGURE 3-12**   If you haven't yet signed in to iCloud, enter your Apple ID and password, and then click the Sign In button.

**FIGURE 3-13** On this iCloud screen, you'll normally want to select the Use iCloud For Contacts, Calendars, and Bookmarks check box. For a MacBook, select the Use Find My Mac check box too.

5. If you have a MacBook, be sure to select the Use Find My Mac check box so that you can locate—and if necessary erase—your MacBook if you misplace it or someone takes it. If you have an iMac, a Mac mini, or a Mac Pro, you may trust it not to wander, but Find My Mac is a good safety net in case it gets stolen.
6. Click the Next button. If you selected the Use Find My Mac check box, follow these steps:
   • In the confirmation dialog box, click the Allow button.

   • In the Allow Guests To Log In To Help Recover Your Mac If It's Lost? dialog box (shown next), click the Allow Guest Login button.

7. System Preferences sets up iCloud and displays the iCloud pane with its full set of controls (see Figure 3-14).
8. Select the check box for each item you want to sync. To share your documents via iCloud, select the Documents & Data check box.
9. Choose System Preferences | Close System Preferences to close System Preferences.

**Set an iOS App to Use iCloud**   To make your iOS apps use iCloud, you either choose an option to enable iCloud when you start using the app, or you turn iCloud on in the Settings app. For example, follow these steps to turn iCloud on for the Pages app:

1. Press the Home button to display the Home screen.
2. Tap the Settings icon to display the Settings screen.

**FIGURE 3-14**   In the iCloud pane, select the Documents & Data check box to start sharing your documents via iCloud.

3. Scroll the left column until you see the Pages app in the Apps list.
4. Tap the Pages button to display the Pages settings screen (shown here).

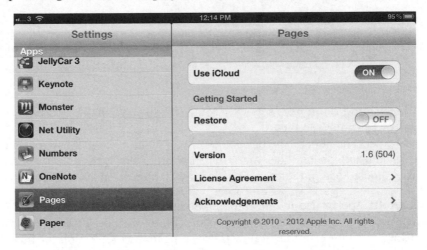

5. Tap the Use iCloud switch and move it to the On position.

**Open an iCloud Document in OS X**   After you create a document on iCloud, you can open it and work on it using your Mac. The process varies depending on the application, but here's an example using TextEdit:

1. Choose File | Open to display the Open dialog box.
2. On the left side of the title bar, click the iCloud button. Your documents and folders stored on iCloud appear (see Figure 3-15).
3. Click the document you want to open.
4. Click the Open button.

# Project 23: Use Your iPad as a Portable Drive

If you have files you need to keep with you at all times, you can store them on your iPad and use it as a portable drive. This is great both for carrying files you need to be able to access at any moment or from any computer and for making backups of your most critical files.

You can also use your iPad as a handy way to transfer large files from one computer to another.

In this section, I'll show you how to copy files to and from your iPad. We'll start with iTunes' File Sharing feature, which you use to copy files to and from the iPad's storage area for a particular app. We'll then move on to third-party programs that let you store files wherever you want in your iPad's file system.

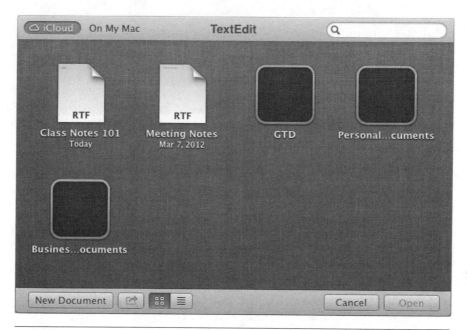

**FIGURE 3-15** Click the iCloud button on the left side of the title bar of the Open dialog box to display the documents you've stored in iCloud.

 Storing files on your iPad is a great way to keep them available to you at all times, but make sure you back them up to your computer or an online storage account as well. Otherwise, if your iPad gets lost, stolen, or merely smashed, you'll lose forever any files stored only on the iPad.

## Copy Files to Your iPad Using iTunes' File Sharing

The first way to copy files to and from your iPad is by using iTunes' File Sharing feature. File Sharing enables you to put a file into the file-storage area for a particular app rather than into a folder of your own choice. See the next sidebar "Understand the iPad's Separate Storage Areas for Documents" for an explanation of how these file-storage areas work.

To transfer documents to and from your iPad by using File Sharing, follow the instructions in the section "Share Documents Using iTunes' File Sharing" in Project 22, earlier in this chapter.

## Find a Suitable Program for Transferring Other Files to and from Your iPad

When you need full-on access to your iPad's file system, iTunes' File Sharing isn't enough. Instead, you need to use a third-party program that enables you to use your iPad as an external drive.

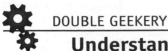

DOUBLE GEEKERY

## Understand the iPad's Separate Storage Areas for Documents

For security, the iPad's file system, iOS, gives each app a separate storage area for documents. iOS largely confines each app to its own storage area and prevents it from accessing the storage areas of other apps. This security measure both protects against malware and prevents one app from making unwanted changes to another app's data files.

For example, if you have the Pages app on your iPad, you can use File Sharing to transfer a Pages document from your Mac to your iPad. Once the Pages document is on your iPad, you can launch Pages and then open the document. But you can't open the document in another app, because it's stored in Pages' storage area.

The exception is apps that can receive incoming files, such as Mail and Safari. These apps can provide those files to other apps. For example, if you receive a Word document attached to an e-mail message on your iPad, you can choose to open that document in Pages or another app that can handle Word documents. Mail makes the document available to Pages or the app you choose.

When you open the document in Pages, your iPad copies the document to Pages' storage area. You can then use Pages to open that new copy from Pages' storage area. The original attached document remains attached to the message in Mail, and you can copy it to another app's storage area if you need to.

---

This section shows you three such programs: DiskAid, Air Sharing, and PhoneView. You can find others on the Web or in the App Store (which you can access via iTunes on your computer or via the App Store application on your iPad).

### DiskAid (Windows and OS X)

DiskAid from DigiDNA ($24.90; www.digidna.net/diskaid) is a utility that lets you mount your iPad as an external disk. Figure 3-9 (earlier in this chapter) shows DiskAid at work on a Mac.

DiskAid's toolbar buttons let you easily create folders, copy items to and from the device, and delete items from the device. But you can also simply drag files and folders from a Windows Explorer window or a Finder window to the DiskAid window to add them to the device.

 DiskAid includes a feature called TuneAid, which you can use to recover your songs from your iPad to your computer—for example, after your computer's hard drive gives up the ghost and you have to replace it.

## Air Sharing (Windows and OS X)

Air Sharing for iPad from Avatron Software (www.avatron.com), which you can buy from the App Store for $7.99, lets you access your iPad across a wireless network connection rather than the USB connection that most other programs require. Not having to connect the device to your computer is an advantage, but you get slower file transfers than via USB, and your iPad doesn't get to recharge while you're using Air Sharing unless you plug it into the Apple USB Power Adapter.

Air Sharing can also mount remote file servers (such as Dropbox) and print to some printers.

 For instructions on setting up Air Sharing on your iPad and connecting to it from your PC or Mac, see Project 24, "Use Your iPad as a File Server for Your Household," later in this chapter.

## PhoneView (OS X Only)

PhoneView (see Figure 3-16) from Ecamm Network ($19.95; www.ecamm.com/mac/phoneview) lets you access your iPad from your Mac. Ecamm provides a mostly functional trial edition, which gives you seven days to find out how well PhoneView suits your needs.

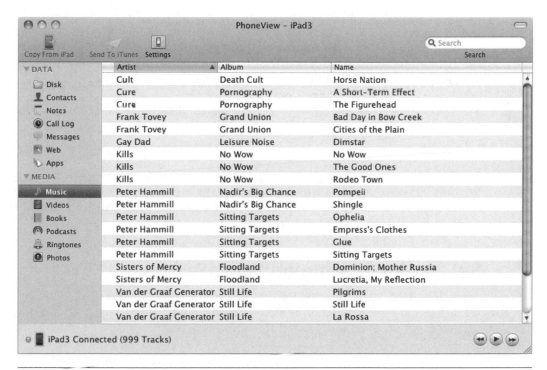

**FIGURE 3-16**   PhoneView lets you quickly access the contents of your iPad to copy, add, or delete files.

When you finish using PhoneView, quit it (for example, press ⌘-Q or choose PhoneView | Quit PhoneView). PhoneView closes its window and releases its grip on your iPad's file system.

# Project 24: Use Your iPad as a File Server for Your Household

If your household has several computers, you probably need to share files among them. You can do so by sharing folders on one computer or another, but this works well only as long as each computer that's sharing files is turned on and running properly. Many people find that they're better off with a single computer or device sharing files, acting as a file server.

 Using your iPad as a file server means that you can keep all your important files on your iPad, and take them with you wherever you go. Use your iPad as a file server only for a small group of computers. The iPad's wireless network connection transfers modest amounts of data plenty fast enough, but if you try to connect many computers to the iPad at once, you'll get poor performance.

You can pay hundreds of dollars for a computer to use as a file server, or you can buy a network attached storage (NAS) device—in effect, a modest computer configured as a server on a network. But if you don't want to spend the money, you can turn your iPad into a file server instead. All you need to do is install the right app, set it up to share files, and then connect your computers to it.

 Keep your iPad plugged in to a power source while you're using it as a server. And be sure to back up all the files you care about to avoid losing your data if you lose your iPad.

You can get various apps that let you use your iPad as a server, but at this writing the best bet is Air Sharing, which you've already met earlier in this chapter. In this section, I'll show you first how to set up Air Sharing on your iPad, and then how to connect to your shared folders using your PC or Mac.

## Set Up Air Sharing on Your iPad

After downloading Air Sharing for iPad and installing it on your iPad, either by using the App Store on your iPad or by synchronizing with iTunes, set up Air Sharing so that your computer can connect to it. Follow these steps:

1. On your iPad, launch Air Sharing by tapping its icon on the Home screen. The My Documents screen appears.

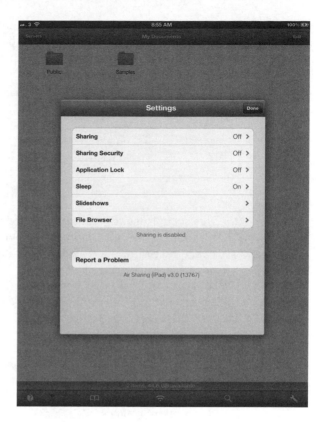

**FIGURE 3-17**  Tap the wrench icon in the lower-right corner of the My Documents screen to display the Settings screen.

2. Tap the wrench icon in the lower-right corner to display the Settings screen (shown in Figure 3-17).
3. Tap the Sharing button to display the Sharing screen (shown here).

4. Tap the Enabled switch and move it to the On position.

 After moving the Enabled switch on the Sharing screen to the On position, you can change the HTTP Port setting or the HTTPS Port setting if you need to. Normally, it's easiest to keep the default settings—port 80 for HTTP and port 443 for HTTPS. HTTP is the regular HyperText Transport Protocol, which you use for unsecured access. HTTPS is the secure version of HTTP, which you use for secure access.

5. Tap the Settings button to return to the Settings screen.
6. Tap the Sharing Security button to display the Sharing Security screen (shown here).

 This section shows you how to implement a reasonable level of security on your iPad for sharing. Air Sharing can provide not only password-free access but also public access to your iPad, but normally you're better off providing only secured access to what you're sharing.

7. Tap the Require Password switch and move it to the On position.
8. Type the username and password to use for the connection. Each user will use the same username and password.

 The username is optional—you can use only the password if you prefer. But usually it's easier to set the username as well.

9. Tap the Public Access switch and move it to the Off position unless you want to provide public access.
10. Tap the Settings button to return to the Settings screen (shown in Figure 3-18). Look at the readout at the bottom giving the Bonjour addresses and IP addresses of your iPad, and note the address you need—the non-https IP address for Windows, and the non-https Bonjour address for OS X.
11. Tap the Done button to return to the My Documents screen.

Now that you've set up Air Sharing on your iPad, you can connect to Air Sharing from your PC or Mac, as discussed next.

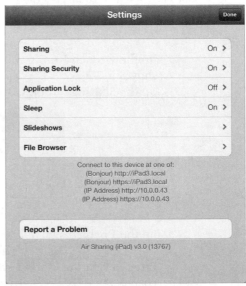

**FIGURE 3-18** The lower part of the Settings screen shows the Bonjour addresses and IP addresses for connecting to your iPad via Air Sharing.

You can also see the Bonjour addresses and IP addresses by tapping the Wi-Fi icon (the dot with two arcs above it) in the middle of the bar at the bottom of the Air Sharing screen.

## Connect to Air Sharing on Your iPad from a PC

To connect to Air Sharing on your iPad from a PC, follow these steps:

1. Choose Start | Computer to open a Computer window.
2. Click the Map Network Drive button on the toolbar to display the Map Network Drive dialog box (see Figure 3-19).
3. In the Drive drop-down list, choose the drive letter you want to map to your iPad.
4. In the Folder text box, type **http**:// and the IP address shown for your iPad—for example, **http://10.0.0.36**.
5. Select the Reconnect At Logon check box if you want Windows to automatically reconnect the drive each time you log on. Unless you plan to run Air Sharing on your iPad all the time, you're usually better off clearing this check box and establishing the connection manually when you need it.
6. Click the Finish button. Windows attempts to connect to your iPad.

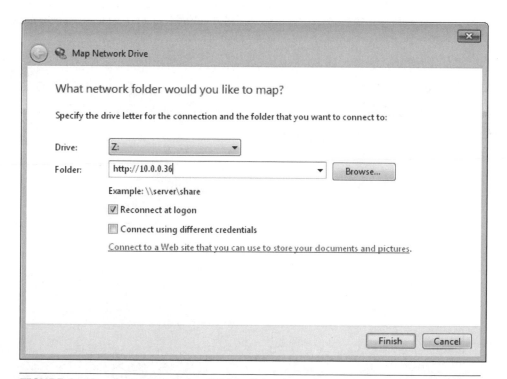

**FIGURE 3-19** In the Map Network Drive dialog box, choose the drive letter to use, and then enter your iPad's address in the Folder field.

7. If you have set a username and password on Air Sharing, Windows prompts you to enter them, as shown here.

8. Type your username and password.
9. Select the Remember My Credentials check box if you want Windows to store the username and password for future use. If you're using your own PC, this is usually a good idea.
10. Click the OK button. Windows establishes the connection to your iPad and displays a Windows Explorer window showing its contents (see Figure 3-20).

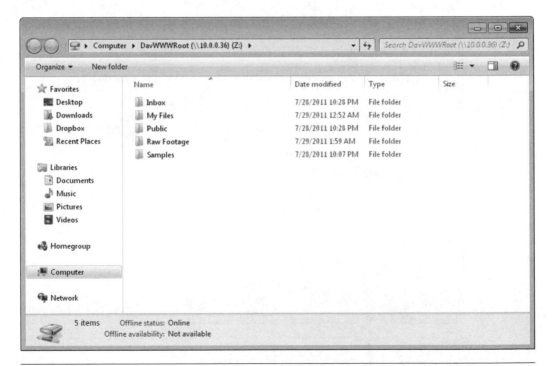

**FIGURE 3-20**   Windows opens a Windows Explorer window showing your iPad's file system.

You can now work with your iPad's file system using standard Windows Explorer techniques. For example, to create a new folder, right-click in open space in the document area, choose New | Folder from the context menu, type the name to give the folder, and then press ENTER

When you finish using your iPad from your PC, disconnect the network drive like this:

1. In the Windows Explorer window, click Computer in the address box to display the Computer window. Alternatively, choose Start | Computer to open a Computer window.
2. Right-click the drive representing your iPad, and then click Disconnect on the context menu.

## Connect to Air Sharing on Your iPad from a Mac

To connect to Air Sharing on your iPad from a Mac, follow these steps:

1. Click the desktop to activate the Finder.

DOUBLE GEEKERY

### Connect to Air Sharing from Windows XP

If your PC is running Windows XP, you must have Service Pack 3 installed in order to connect to Air Sharing. If you're not sure which Service Pack your PC is running, click the Start button, right-click the My Computer icon, click Properties on the context menu, and then look at the System readout on the General tab of the System Properties dialog box.

There's also another complication: XP can't connect to the iPad's shared directory. Instead, you must connect to a subdirectory—preferably the one you want to work in. If you use your iPad mainly with a Windows XP PC, you'll probably want to set up your iPad's file system with a subfolder that contains all your other folders.

Provided your PC has Service Pack 3 installed, connect like this:

1. Choose Start | My Computer to open a My Computer window.
2. Choose Tools | Map Network Drive to display the Map Network Drive dialog box.
3. In the Drive drop-down list, choose the drive letter you want to map.
4. In the Folder text box, type **http://**, the iPad's IP address, a forward slash, and the name of a folder—for example, **http://10.0.0.36/Files**.
5. Click the Finish button.
6. If Windows XP displays a dialog box prompting you for your username and password, enter them, and click the OK button.

2. Choose Go | Connect To Server or press ⌘-κ to display the Connect To Server dialog box (shown here).

3. In the Server Address text box, type **http://** and the Bonjour address shown for your iPad—for example, **http://ipad3.local**.

 Instead of typing the Bonjour address, you can type the IP address shown for your iPad. But given that your Mac is running Bonjour anyway, the Bonjour address is usually a better choice. This is because your iPad's Bonjour address remains the same unless you change your iPad's name, whereas if your iPad gets its IP address from a DHCP server (as is the normal setup), your iPad may get a different IP address any time it connects to the DHCP server.

4. Click the Add (+) button if you want to add your iPad to your list of servers. This is a good idea if you plan to access your iPad frequently using this Mac.
5. Click the Connect button. The Finder attempts to connect to your iPad.
6. If you have set a username and password on Air Sharing, OS X prompts you to enter them, as shown here.

7. Make sure the Registered User option button is selected.

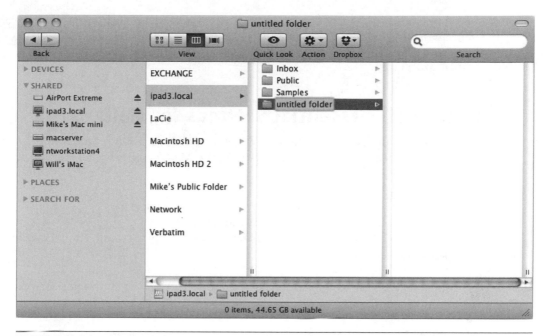

**FIGURE 3-21**  After connecting to your iPad using Air Sharing, you can work with its file system using normal Finder techniques.

8. Type your username and password.
9. Select the Remember This Password In My Keychain check box if you want your Mac to store the password for future use. When you're using your own Mac (as opposed to someone else's Mac), this is usually a good idea.
10. Click the Connect button. The Finder establishes the connection to your iPad and displays your iPad's contents in a Finder window.

You can now work with your iPad's file system using the same techniques as for any other drive. For example, CTRL-click or right-click and then click New Folder on the context menu to create a new folder. You can then type the folder's name over the default name, **untitled folder** (see Figure 3-21).

When you finish using your iPad from the Mac, click the Disconnect button in the Finder window to disconnect the drive.

# Project 25: Develop Power-User E-mail Skills with Mail

Whether you use your iPad for work, play, or both, you'll almost certainly want to work with e-mail on it. You'll be able to start using the Mail app easily enough, but you'll also find that it has plenty of power and lots of hidden secrets.

This section shows you ten ways to work faster and smarter with e-mail on your iPad—everything from saving time by batch-editing your messages to working with drafts and changing the quote level in a message. We'll start by choosing five essential settings for Mail.

# Choose Five Essential Settings for Mail

To make the Mail app behave your way, you can choose settings on the Mail, Contacts, Calendars screen. Start by opening the Mail, Contacts, Calendars screen like this:

1. Press the Home button to display the Home screen.
2. Tap the Settings icon to display the Settings screen.
3. Tap the Mail, Contacts, Calendars button to display the Mail, Contacts, Calendars screen (see Figure 3-22).

Many of the settings are straightforward, but this section shows you how to choose the five most important ones:

- Choose how many messages to show and how to preview them.
- Set your default account for sending messages.
- Get your messages pushed to your iPad.
- Protect yourself against spam images.
- Set up the signature you need.

## Choose How Many Messages to Show and How to Preview Them

At the top of the Mail box on the Mail, Contacts, Calendars screen, choose how many messages Mail should show and what kind of previews it should display for them:

- **Show**   Tap this button to display the Show screen, and then tap the button for the number of messages you want to see: 50 Recent Messages, 100 Recent Messages, 200 Recent Messages, 500 Recent Messages, or 1,000 Recent Messages. Unless you get a mass of e-mail, 50 Recent Messages is usually the best way to start. Tap the Mail, Contacts, Calendars button when you've made your choice.
- **Preview**   To choose how much of a preview of each message Mail displays, tap this button, and then tap the appropriate button on the Preview screen: None, 1 Line, 2 Lines, 3 Lines, 4 Lines, or 5 Lines. The more lines you display, the better you can identify each message from the preview—but the fewer previews you can see on the screen at once. Choose your poison. Tap the Mail, Contacts, Calendars button when you've made your choice.

 If you find Mail is slow to load, try turning off previews by tapping the None button on the Preview screen. See if this change makes an improvement you want to keep.

**FIGURE 3-22**   Open the Mail, Contacts, Calendars screen in the Settings app to choose essential settings for the Mail app.

## Set Your Default Account for Sending Messages

If you set up two or more e-mail accounts on your iPad, you need to tell Mail which is the default account to use to send messages. To specify the default account, follow these steps from the Mail, Contacts, Calendars screen:

1. Tap the Default Account button to display the Default Account screen (shown here).

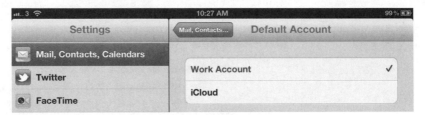

2. Tap the account you want to make the default.
3. Tap the Mail, Contacts, Calendars button to return to the Mail, Contacts, Calendars screen.

## Get Your Messages Pushed to Your iPad

To get your messages as quickly as possible, set your e-mail accounts on your iPad to use push. Using push tells the server to "push" out a message to your iPad as soon as the message arrives at the server, instead of leaving the message at the server until the Mail app checks in for mail.

 Not all e-mail providers support push. If your e-mail account doesn't offer push, you can set your iPad to check for messages at short intervals instead. This is called *fetch*. And whether you use push or fetch, you can check for messages manually at any point by tapping the Refresh button, the clockwise curling arrow in the lower-left corner of the Mail screen.

To set your iPad to use push, follow these steps:

1. Tap the Fetch New Data button on the Mail, Contacts, Calendars screen to display the Fetch New Data screen (shown in Figure 3-23).
2. Make sure the Push switch is set to the On position.
3. In the Fetch area, tap to place a check mark on the button for the fetch timing you want to use when push isn't available: Every 15 Minutes, Every 30 Minutes, Hourly, or Manually.

**FIGURE 3-23**   On the Mail, Contacts, Calendars screen, tap the Fetch New Data button to display the Fetch New Data screen, and then move the Push switch to the On position.

 If you want to choose different settings for each e-mail account, tap the Advanced button on the Fetch New Data screen. On the Advanced screen that appears, tap the account to display a screen with its name. Then, in the Select Schedule box, tap the Push button, the Fetch button, or the Manual button, putting a check mark on the method you want to use. Tap the Advanced button to go back to the Advanced screen, then tap the Fetch New Data button to return to the Fetch New Data screen.

4. Tap the Mail, Contacts, Calendars button to return to the Mail, Contacts, Calendars screen.

## Protect Yourself from Spam Images

These days, it's hard to avoid receiving at least some spam—unwanted messages. When you do, you can simply delete them. But malefactors have another trick up their sleeve: remote images, which are also called *web bugs*. By including in a message a reference to an image stored on a remote server, a spammer can learn not only when you open that message but also your IP address and approximate geographical location.

To avoid this problem, you can set the Load Remote Images switch on the Mail, Contacts, Calendars screen to the Off position. This tells Mail not to load remote images. The images then appear as placeholders in your messages. You can tap a placeholder to display its image—preferably after checking that the message is wholesome.

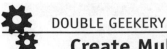

DOUBLE GEEKERY

## Create Multiple Signatures by Using Text Shortcuts

At this writing, your iPad lets you create only a single signature, which it applies to all your accounts. That means any new message you create gets the same signature. Any message you forward or reply to receives the signature too.

This works fine for some people, but if you need to be able to apply different signatures to different messages, you must take another approach.

Instead of creating a signature, go to the Signature screen and tap the Clear button to wipe out whatever signature is there. Then open the General settings screen, tap the Keyboard button to display the Keyboard screen, and set up a text shortcut for each signature or partial signature you want to be able to enter quickly. For example, create a text shortcut for your name, another for your job title, a third for your company name, and a fourth for your address. See the section "Create Text Shortcuts" earlier in this chapter for instructions on creating text shortcuts.

Once you've created your shortcuts, you can finish an e-mail message quickly with the appropriate signature by typing each shortcut needed and tapping the spacebar.

## Change Your Signature

Instead of typing a closing line and your name at the end of each message, you can have Mail add a signature for you automatically. Adding a signature can save you plenty of time and typing, especially if you need to include your business name or contact information.

Your iPad comes with the default signature of "Sent from my iPad." This is cute for the first message or two, but you'll likely want to change it before you use your iPad extensively.

To change your signature, follow these steps from the Mail, Contacts, Calendars screen:

1. Tap the Signature button to display the Signature screen (shown here).

2. If there's an existing signature you need to get rid of, tap the Clear button.
3. Type the signature you want.
4. Tap the Mail, Contacts, Calendars button to return to the Mail, Contacts, Calendars screen.

## Batch-Edit Your E-mail Messages

Instead of dealing with the e-mail messages in an inbox or folder one by one, you can use batch-editing to manipulate multiple messages at once. To use batch-editing, follow these steps:

1. Open the inbox or folder that contains the messages. The left screen in Figure 3-24 shows an example using Gmail.
2. Tap the Edit button in the upper-right corner of the screen to turn on editing mode.
3. Tap the selection button for each message you want to affect, as shown in the right screen in Figure 3-24.
4. Tap the appropriate command button. For example, tap the Move button to display the Mailboxes screen, and then tap the mailbox to which you want to move the messages.

## Send Your Electronic Business Card to Your Contacts

When you need to share your contact information with someone, send it as an electronic business card attached to an e-mail message. The recipient can then import the data straight into her address book or contact-management program without having to retype any of it.

 You can also send your electronic business card as an attachment to an instant message. Just tap the Message button in the Share Contact Using dialog box, and then address and send the instant message.

To send your electronic business card, follow these steps:

1. Press the Home button to display the Home screen.
2. Tap the Contacts icon to display the Contacts app.
3. Tap the contact record that contains the data you want to share.
4. Tap the Share Contact button. The Share Contact Using dialog box opens, as shown here.

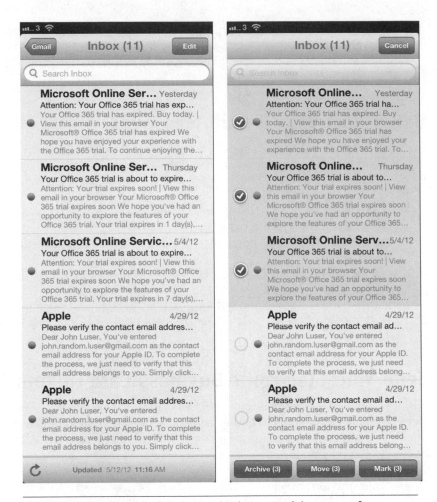

**FIGURE 3-24** Tap the Edit button in the upper-right corner of an inbox or folder (left) to turn on Edit mode. You can then tap the selection button for each message you want to affect, and then tap the appropriate command button.

5. Tap the Email button. Your iPad causes Mail to start a new message with the contact record attached.
6. Address the message, give it a title and any explanatory text needed, and then tap the Send button.

## See Where a Link in a Message Leads

As you know, a link in an e-mail message can display a different address than the one the link will actually take you to.

To see the URL to which a link in an e-mail message points, tap and hold the link until Mail displays the Actions dialog box (shown here) with a button for each action you can take with the link. The URL appears at the top. You can then tap the Open button if it's safe to open the link, tap the Copy button if you want to store the URL or share it with someone, or tap outside the dialog box to stop opening the link.

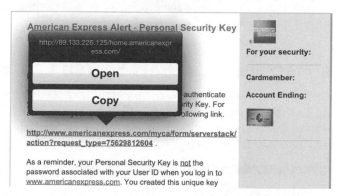

# Mark a Message as Unread or Flag It as Important

When you receive a new message, Mail places a blue dot to its left in your inbox so that you can see at a glance that it's unread. When you open the message, Mail marks the message as read, and removes the blue dot.

 Tap the iPad's status bar at the top of the screen to scroll quickly to the top of the open message.

When you're triaging your e-mail, you may want to look quickly at a message but then mark it as unread so that you can see it still needs your attention. To mark the message as unread, tap the Details button to the right of the From line to display the details; the Details button changes to a Hide button. Then tap the Mark button to the right of the message's date, and then tap the Mark As Unread button in the dialog box that opens (shown here).

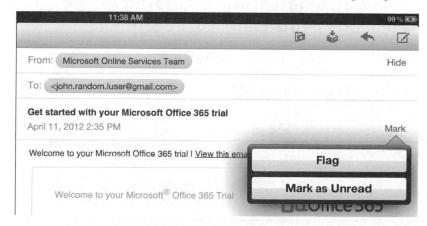

From the dialog box that opens when you tap the Mark button, you can also tap the Flag button to mark the message with a flag. Mail then displays a flag icon to the left of the message in the inbox or folder.

The flag persists until you remove it by tapping the Mark button and then tapping the Unflag button. You can use flagging for whatever purpose you choose, but its basic advantage over marking the message as unread is that the flag stays in place when you open the message for reading.

## Save a Message as a Draft So You Can Finish It Later

When you don't have time to complete an e-mail message you've started writing, save it as a draft so that you can finish it later. Tap the Cancel button, and then tap the Save Draft button in the Draft dialog box (shown here) that Mail displays. Mail saves the message in your Drafts folder. (If the Drafts folder doesn't yet exist, Mail creates it.)

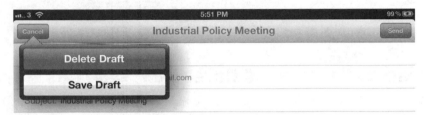

You can quickly reopen the last draft message you were working on by simply tapping and holding the Compose button in Mail. To open an older draft message, go to the Drafts mailbox for the account, and then tap the message:

1. Tap the Mailboxes button in the upper-left corner of the screen to display the Mailboxes screen.

### DOUBLE GEEKERY

## Prevent Gmail from Archiving Messages You Want to Delete

Gmail's limitless storage is a huge asset, but if you're like me, you'll want to delete some of your old messages rather than archiving them until doomsday. To stop Gmail from archiving messages, follow these steps from the Mail, Contacts, Calendars screen in the Settings app:

1. In the Accounts box, tap your Gmail account to display its control screen.
2. Tap the Archive Messages switch and move it to the Off position.
3. Tap the Done button to return to the Mail, Contacts, Calendars screen.

After you do this, Mail displays the Delete button for your Gmail account instead of the Archive button, and you can delete messages instead of archiving them.

2. In the Accounts box, tap the account you were using when you created the draft. The list of folders for that account appears.
3. Tap the Drafts button. The Drafts folder opens, showing the list of draft messages.
4. Tap the message you want to open.

## Change the Account You're Sending a Message From

If you start an e-mail message from the wrong account, you don't need to scrap the message and start again. Just tap the From field to expand the Cc/Bcc and From area, tap the From field again, and then tap the address you want to use on the list that appears (see the illustration).

## Apply Formatting to Text in a Message

If you want to make parts of a message you're composing stand out, you can apply boldface, italics, or underline (or two of those three, or all three).

To apply formatting, follow these steps:

1. Select the text you want to format. The bar containing a Cut button and a Copy button appears.
2. Tap the > button to display the next section of the bar (shown on the left in the illustration).

3. Tap the BIU button to display the Bold, Italics, Underline bar (shown on the right in the illustration).
4. Tap the Bold button, the Italics button, or the Underline button, as needed.

## Change the Quote Level in a Message

Another way to make text in a message you're writing stand out is to mark it as being indented. You can do this by selecting the text, tapping the > button on the bar that appears, tapping the Quote Level button, and then tapping the Increase button on the bar that appears (as shown here). You can also tap the Decrease button to decrease the indentation of text that's already indented.

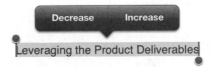

## Send a Message to a Group Without Revealing the E-mail Addresses

When you need to send an e-mail message to a group of people who don't necessarily know each other, don't put all the e-mail addresses in the To box or the Cc box, because each recipient will be able to see all the other addresses.

Instead, put your own address in the To box, and then tap the Cc/Bcc, From area to display the Bcc field. Put each e-mail address in this field, and each recipient will see only his or her own e-mail address, not those of the other Bcc recipients. (They'll also see your e-mail address, both in the To field and in the Sender field.)

# Project 26: Give Presentations Straight from Your iPad

If you travel for business, chances are you need to give presentations. If you have a laptop with you, great, because that's still the best tool for giving presentations. But if you have only your iPad, don't worry—you can give a fine presentation using it. You'll just need to do a bit more preparation and arm yourself with the right apps and cables.

In this section, we'll first run through your options for giving a presentation from your iPad, and then we'll look at how to use each of those options.

# Choose How You Will Give Your Presentation

First, choose how you will give your presentation. You have three main options:

- **Connect your iPad physically to a projector, monitor, or TV**   This approach is just like using a laptop and works well for standard presentation situations—for example, presenting to a group of people who are in the same room and looking at the same screen. The best app for giving the presentation is Apple's Keynote, which you can also use for creating and editing presentations.
- **Connect your iPad wirelessly to one or more laptops or desktops**   This approach requires no cable and enables you to send the presentation wirelessly to a web browser on one or more computers within broadcasting distance. You can't use Keynote on your iPad for this—you need to use a third-party app instead. Your presentation is limited to PDF files and photos.
- **Use your iPad as a remote control for Keynote on the Mac**   With this approach, you're using the iPad to control the presentation, but the presentation is actually running on a Mac that's connected to a projector, monitor, or TV. We'll cover these possibilities in turn in the following sections.

# Give a Presentation Using Keynote and a Projector, Monitor, or TV

In this section, we'll look at how to give a presentation using Apple's Keynote app on your iPad. You'll need to connect your iPad to the projector, monitor, or TV on which you will show the presentation.

## Add Keynote to Your iPad

The first step is to add Keynote to your iPad if you don't have it already. Go to the App Store using either your iPad or iTunes on your computer, buy Keynote (it costs $9.99), and then download and install it.

## Prepare Your Presentation

Next, prepare your presentation. Normally, you'll want to use one of these ways:

- **Create the presentation in Keynote on the Mac**   When the presentation is ready for use, you can transfer it to your iPad by using iTunes' File Sharing feature or by storing it in iCloud.
- **Create the presentation in PowerPoint on Windows or the Mac**   In this case, too, you can transfer the presentation to your iPad by using iTunes' File Sharing feature.

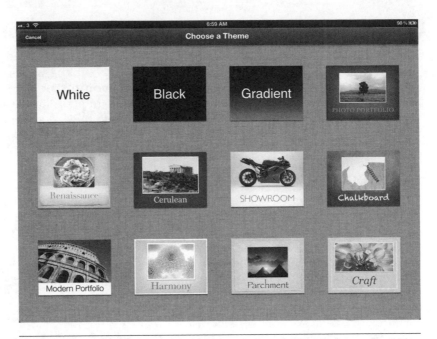

**FIGURE 3-25** On the Choose A Theme screen, tap the theme you want to base the new presentation on.

- **Create the presentation in Keynote on your iPad**   Keynote on the iPad offers strong features for creating presentations wherever you go. To start a new presentation, tap the New (+) button in the upper-left corner of the screen, tap the Create Presentation button in the pop-up panel (shown here), and then tap the theme you want on the Choose A Theme screen (see Figure 3-25).

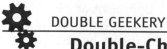

DOUBLE GEEKERY

# Double-Check Any Presentation You Import into Keynote for iPad

Always check a presentation closely after you import it into Keynote for iPad. While Keynote supports as many features the iWork team has been able to pack in, it doesn't support all the features of its older sibling Keynote for Mac, let alone all the features of PowerPoint.

Here are three examples:

- **Fonts**   When Keynote doesn't have a font that the presentation uses, Keynote substitutes a similar font. Unless you're heavily into design (or your audience is), this substitution usually makes little difference.
- **3D charts**   Keynote for iPad doesn't support 3D charts, so it converts them to 2D charts.
- **Build order**   Keynote may change the build order of objects on some slides. This can cause some entertaining surprises.

So after you import a presentation, go through it, and make sure that each slide looks okay.

## Connect Your iPad to a Projector, Monitor, or TV

If you're presenting to an audience of one, you may need only brandish your iPad at that person. But if you're going to give a conventional presentation directly from your iPad, you need to connect it to a projector, a monitor, or a TV.

To connect your iPad to a projector, monitor, or TV, you need the right kind of cable. These are the three types of cables you're most likely to need:

- **Apple Digital AV Adapter**   This short cable has a Dock Connector on one end and an HDMI port and a Dock Connector port on the other end. You plug the Dock Connector into your iPad, and then plug an HDMI cable into the other end of the cable and into your TV. You can connect your iPad's USB cable to the Dock Connector port to charge the iPad.

 If you have to choose among HDMI, VGA, and composite, choose HDMI every time, because it will give you higher quality.

- **Apple VGA Adapter**   This short cable has a Dock Connector at the iPad's end and a female VGA connector at the other end to which you connect a standard VGA cable running from the projector or monitor.

- **Apple Composite AV Adapter**   This cable has a Dock Connector on one end and three RCA plugs on the other end—red and white connectors for the audio channels, and a yellow connector for the video. The RCA end also has a USB cable for powering the iPad. Use this cable to connect to a TV that has composite video jacks.

After you connect your iPad to the output device, Keynote appears mirrored on it. So when you change the slide on your iPad, the new slide appears on the output device as well.

### Give Your Presentation on the iPad

To give your presentation on the iPad, open the presentation in Keynote, display the first slide, and then tap the Play button in the upper-right corner of the screen.

The presentation starts playing on both your iPad's screen and on the screen you've connected to your iPad. You can display the next slide by tapping anywhere on the screen or by swiping a finger from right to left across the screen. If you need to display the previous slide, swipe from left to right across the screen.

To end the presentation, place two fingers apart on the screen and pinch inward.

## Connect Your iPad Wirelessly to One or More Computers

When you can't use Keynote or establish a physical connection between your iPad and a projector, monitor, or TV, you can give a presentation wirelessly. Connecting wirelessly also enables you to give your presentation on multiple screens at once, which can be useful for lab or classroom situations.

At this writing, the best bet for presenting wirelessly like this is Air Projector, which you can get from the App Store for $2.99. Start by trying the free version, Air Projector Free, to see how it works for you, and then move to the full version if you need to.

Air Projector enables you to broadcast PDF files or photos from your iPad to a web browser on a laptop or desktop computer. You can either use that computer's screen or connect that computer to a projector for a large-screen presentation. On the computer, you simply enter in the web browser the IP address and port number that Air Projector is using on the iPad. The browser then displays the photo or PDF file you display on the iPad's screen.

## Use Your iPad as a Remote Control for Your Mac

If you're giving a presentation from a Mac, you can use your iPad as a remote control.

  At this writing, the Keynote Remote app is designed for the iPhone and iPod touch, so it occupies only a small part of the iPad's screen unless you tap the 2× button.

To do so, download and install the Keynote Remote app (which costs $0.99) from the iTunes Store. Search for "Keynote Remote," and you'll find it in moments.

Once you've installed the app, locate it—you'll find it appears as "Remote" rather than "Keynote Remote," but you can use "Keynote" when searching—and then run it. You'll see first a screen telling you that you haven't linked it to Keynote, as shown on the left in the next illustration. Tap the Link To Keynote button. Keynote Remote then automatically displays the Settings screen, shown on the right in the illustration.

 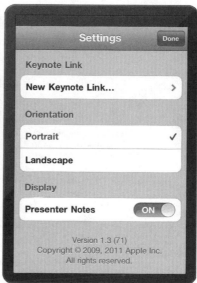

To set up the link to Keynote, follow these steps:

1. Tap the New Keynote Link button on the Settings screen. Keynote Remote displays the New Link screen, which contains a fresh passcode for linking to Keynote.
2. Launch Keynote on your Mac, or switch to Keynote if it's already running.
3. In Keynote, choose Keynote | Preferences to display the Preferences window.

4. Click the Remote tab to display its contents, as shown here. Your iPad should appear with a Link button to its right.

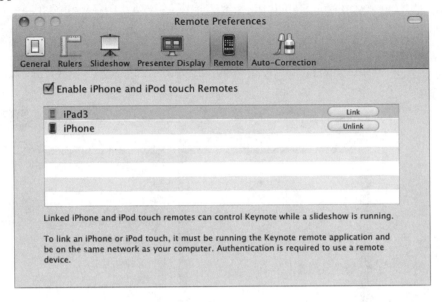

5. Make sure the Enable iPhone And iPod touch Remotes check box is selected.
6. Click your iPad's Link button to display the Add Remote For iPhone And iPod touch dialog box (shown here).

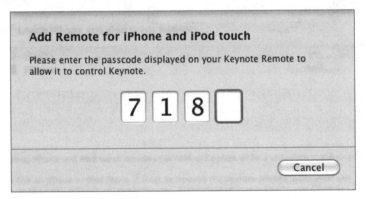

7. Type the passcode that the Remote app is displaying. Keynote checks the passcode and then closes the Add Remote For iPhone And iPod touch dialog box automatically. Your iPad then appears with an Unlink button on the Remote tab of the Preferences window.
8. Click the Close button (the red button) to close the Preferences window.

# 4 Security and Troubleshooting Geekery

In this chapter, we'll look at how to secure your iPad against theft or intrusion, how to track it down if you lose it, and how to wipe the data from your iPad if you can't recover it.

I'll also show you how to deal with problems closer to home. We'll consider your options for using your iPad safely in wet or dirty conditions and for making your iPad safe for your kids to use. We'll then look at how to troubleshoot software and hardware problems and how to restore your iPad to factory settings if its software becomes messed up or you need to sell it.

## Project 27: Secure Your iPad Against Theft or Intrusion

Packed with not only the highest technology around but also your priceless personal secrets and business intelligence, your iPad is a tempting target for thieves, who know they can readily sell it or the data it contains for a fistful of dollars. So no matter how firmly you grip your iPad in public or how well you hide it at home, you need to secure it effectively in case it goes missing (presumed stolen).

Locking your iPad in a fire- and waterproof strongbox in your bank might keep it physically safe, but it wouldn't be much use to you. Given that you likely need to keep your iPad with you all the time, securing your iPad consists of preventing other people from accessing the data on it.

There are two main ways to secure the data on your iPad:

- Set your iPad to lock itself shortly after you stop using it.
- Require a passcode to unlock the iPad. If necessary, set your iPad to wipe its data when someone enters the wrong passcode too many times in succession.

### Set Your iPad to Lock Itself Automatically

First, set your iPad's Auto-Lock feature to lock the iPad automatically a short time after you stop using it.

To set up Auto-Lock, follow these steps:

1. Press the Home button to display the Home screen.
2. Tap the Settings icon to display the Settings screen.
3. Tap the General button to display the General screen.
4. Tap the Auto-Lock button to display the Auto-Lock screen (shown in Figure 4-1).
5. Tap the button for the interval you want: 2 Minutes, 5 Minutes, 10 Minutes, 15 Minutes, or Never. The shorter the interval, the safer, so try the 2 Minutes setting and see how well it works for you.
6. Tap the General button to return to the General screen.

 You can also lock your iPad at any point by pressing the Sleep/Wake button when the iPad is unlocked. To make your iPad lock the moment you put it to sleep, set the Require Passcode setting (discussed later in this chapter) to Immediately.

## Protect Your iPad with a Passcode Lock

Next, protect your iPad with a passcode lock. The passcode is a sequence of characters that you must type each time you unlock the iPad from the lock screen. The next sidebar "Choose Between a Simple Passcode and a Complex Passcode" explains the ins and outs of passcodes.

 If your company or organization provides your iPad, an administrator may apply a configuration profile that compels you to use a passcode on the iPad. If you find you cannot change the passcode settings on your iPad, you will know that a profile is installed.

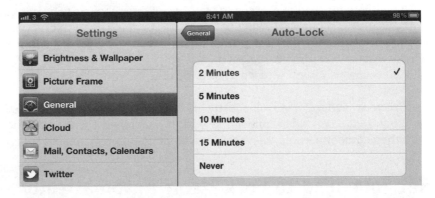

**FIGURE 4-1**   On the Auto-Lock screen, choose as short an interval as is practical for the way you use your iPad.

DOUBLE GEEKERY

# Choose Between a Simple Passcode and a Complex Passcode

You can protect your iPad with either a simple passcode or a complex passcode:

- **Simple passcode**   Four digits—for example, 1924. This is the default type, and it works well for general-purpose needs.
- **Complex passcode**   A variable number of characters and that mixes letters and other characters with digits.

A complex passcode can provide much greater security than a simple passcode:

- **You can set a longer passcode**   A longer passcode is harder to crack because it contains more characters. This is true even if the passcode consists only of numbers rather than letters and non-alphanumeric characters.
- **You can include letters**   Including letters as well as numbers greatly increases the strength of the passcode even at short lengths.
- **You can include non-alphanumeric characters**   Including non-alphanumeric characters (such as symbols—&*#$!, and so on) increases the strength of the passcode even further.

The Enter Passcode screen that prompts you for the passcodes shows whether the iPad is using a simple passcode or a complex passcode. For a simple passcode, the Enter Passcode screen displays four boxes and a numeric keypad, as shown in the left illustration. For a complex passcode, the Enter Passcode screen displays a text box and the QWERTY keyboard, as shown in the right illustration.

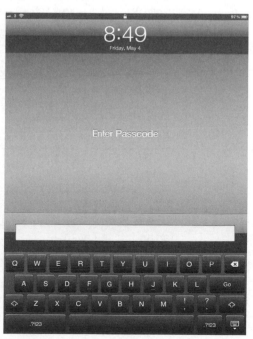

Whether you should use a simple passcode or a complex passcode depends on how much security you feel you need. Having to enter a long passcode for each unlock can make it hard to jot down quick notes and use your iPad to its full potential. Keep these points in mind when deciding which type of passcode to use:

- **A simple passcode may be strong enough with auto-erase**  Given enough time and tries, anyone can break a simple passcode by plodding through all 10,000 possible numbers until they hit the jackpot. Your iPad makes this harder by automatically disabling itself for increasing periods of time—1 minute, 5 minutes, 15 minutes, 60 minutes, and so on—as the wrong passcodes hit in sequence (see the next illustration). A determined attacker can keep entering passcodes as soon as the iPad starts accepting them again, but if you set your iPad to erase its data automatically after a handful of failed attempts to enter the passcode, your data should be pretty safe—unless you've chosen a personal number that the attacker can guess (for example, your birth year, which is a regrettably popular passcode).

- **With a complex passcode, you may not need auto-erase**  If you use a complex passcode of a certain length (say eight or more characters) and including both alphanumeric and non-alphanumeric characters, you may consider it strong enough that your iPad doesn't need auto-erase. But if your iPad's contents are highly valuable or important, you'll probably want to use auto-erase.
- **A complex passcode can be shorter than a simple passcode**  Because the Enter Passcode screen for a complex passcode gives no indication of the passcode's length, you may be able to bluff an attacker by setting a short, letters-only passcode (for example, aq) rather than a lengthy excerpt from a monkey's attempts to type *Hamlet*. A short passcode like this is easy for you to remember and type, so you can set a low number for the Maximum Number Of Failed Attempts setting as a safety net.

To set your passcode lock and (if you want) automatic wiping, follow these steps:

1. Choose Home | Settings | General to open the General screen in Settings (shown on the left in Figure 4-2).
2. Tap the Passcode Lock button to display the Passcode Lock screen (shown on the right in Figure 4-2).
3. If you want to use a simple passcode—a four-digit number—make sure the Simple Passcode switch is set to the On position. If you want to lock your iPad down more tightly by using a complex passcode, move the Simple Passcode switch to the Off position.

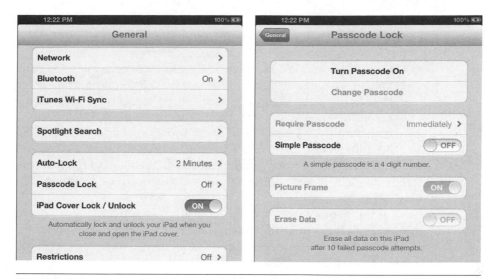

**FIGURE 4-2**  On the General screen (left), tap the Passcode Lock button to display the Passcode Lock screen (right).

4. Tap the Turn Passcode On button to display the Set Passcode screen. For a simple passcode, you'll see the Set Passcode screen shown on the left in Figure 4-3; for a complex passcode, you'll see the Set Passcode screen shown on the right in Figure 4-3.

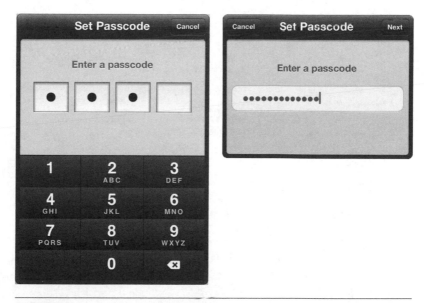

**FIGURE 4-3**  On the Set Passcode screen, enter either a simple four-digit passcode (left) or a complex passcode as long—or as short—as you like (right).

5. Tap the numbers or characters for the passcode:
   - **Simple passcode**   When you've entered four numbers, your iPad displays the Set Passcode: Re-enter Your Passcode screen automatically.
   - **Complex passcode**   Tap the .?123 button when you need to reach the keyboard with numbers and some symbols. From here, you can tap the # + = button to reach the remaining symbols, punctuation characters, and currency characters. When you've finished entering the passcode, tap the Next button to display the Set Passcode: Re-enter Your Passcode screen.

6. Tap the numbers or characters for the passcode again; for a complex passcode, tap the Done button when you finish. Your iPad displays the Passcode Lock screen again. This time, all the options are enabled, as shown in the screen on the left in Figure 4-4.

7. Look at the Require Passcode button to see how quickly the passcode requirement kicks in: Immediately, After 1 Minute, After 5 Minutes, After 15 Minutes, After 1 Hour, or After 4 Hours. If you need to change the setting, follow these steps:
   a. Tap the Require Passcode button to display the Require Passcode screen (shown on the right in Figure 4-4).
   b. Tap the button for the interval you want.
   c. Tap the Passcode Lock button to return to the Passcode Lock screen.

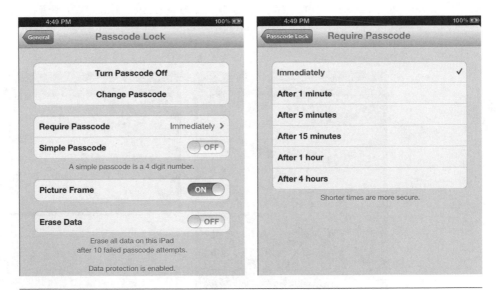

**FIGURE 4-4**   After you set a passcode, the remaining options on the Passcode Lock screen become available (left). Tap the Require Passcode button to display the Require Passcode screen (right), on which you can set the interval after which your iPad requires the passcode.

For the Require Passcode setting, the Immediately option is by far the most secure, because it locks your iPad the moment you put it to sleep or the Auto-Lock feature runs. But if you tend to put your iPad to sleep and then immediately think of something else you must note, you may find the After 1 Minute option a better choice, because it will allow you to unlock your iPad to jot down your new item.

8. If you want your iPad to erase its contents after ten failed attempts to crack the passcode, tap the Erase Data switch and move it to the On position. Then tap the Enable button in the confirmation dialog box (shown here) that appears.

# Project 28: Use Your iPad Safely in Wet or Dirty Conditions

To stay in touch with your contacts and in control of your life, you'll probably want to take your iPad with you more or less everywhere. Chances are that'll include plenty of places that are wet, dirty, or both.

Your iPad dreads water even more than it fears gravity and small children, and it's not big on dirt either—so you'll need to protect it. For most people, that means using a case.

You can find a wide variety of cases at bricks-and-mortar stores (such as the Apple Store or Best Buy) and a bewildering variety online. If you don't find what you need

 DOUBLE GEEKERY

## Don't Let the Police Connect Your iPad to a UFED

Your iPad has strong security against conventional threats—but watch out for the police.

Various police departments use devices called Universal Forensic Extraction Devices, or UFEDs. If you allow the police to connect your iPad to a UFED, the UFED can grab all of the data from your iPad, even if you have secured your iPad with a password. Most UFEDs use a physical connection to the Dock Connector, but some models have Bluetooth capability as well.

The American Civil Liberties Union is arguing that this data extraction constitutes an unreasonable search under the Fourth Amendment—but at this writing, the argument is still unresolved.

If you have the choice (and you may not have), don't let the police connect your iPad to a UFED.

among the loads of cases at major sites such as Amazon and eBay, either search the Internet or visit case manufacturers such as OtterBox (www.otterbox.com), Speck Products (www.speckproducts.com), Marware (www.marware.com), RadTech (www.radtech.us), Gumdrop Cases (www.gumdropcases.com), or DecalGirl (www.decalgirl.com).

If you need to keep your iPad dry, the first question is whether you need the case to be water-resistant or actually waterproof. You can find plenty of protective cases that are water-resistant enough for general use but that make your iPad's ports and buttons easily accessible. For example, many protective cases use rubber plugs to close cutouts for the headphone jack, camera lens, mute switch, and Dock Connector port. You can easily swing out a rubber plug when you need to use the port, switch, or lens; but when the plug is in place, it keeps rain, water splashes, or dust out of the iPad. But this arrangement is only water-resistant—it's not waterproof.

If you actually need to be able to drop your iPad in water without major sadness and expense ensuing, you need the next step—either a fully waterproof case or a bag or box you can put the iPad in to keep the water out.

Here are the two main sources of waterproof iPad cases:

- **Amazon.com**   At this writing, Amazon offers various waterproof cases including the iHip Discovery Waterproof Underwater Case (around $30), the iOttie Waterproof Skin Case (around $25), the Overboard Waterproof Protective Case (around $50), and the Aquapac Waterproof Large Whanganui (around $45). The iHip Discovery and the iOttie are tailored for the iPad, whereas the Overboard and the Aquapac are general-purpose cases that fit the iPad and similar-size tablets.

 Read the buyer reviews on Amazon.com to get a clearer idea of what a particular case is good for, how well it delivers on its promises, and what its weak points are.

- **eBay**   As you know, you can find just about anything on eBay—and that includes plenty of cases that claim to be waterproof. You can find both high-end cases, such as the Aryca WS-iP Waterproof Hard Case (around $75; look also on www.aryca.com), and low-end cases.

 Even a teaspoon of water in the wrong place can ruin your iPad, so you'll want to be sure you can trust the case you buy. This is one area where saving money by buying a no-name brand can cost you dear, so you may decide that you want to stick with a big-name brand—perhaps one that provides a guarantee. If you go for an inexpensive option, test it by putting a kitchen towel in it and giving it a good immersion before you try dunking the iPad in it.

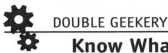
DOUBLE GEEKERY

# Know What the IPX Certifications Mean

When you're shopping for waterproof cases, you'll see certification numbers such as IPX7 and IPX8. Here, IP stands for *ingress protection*—how much protection the case provides against stuff getting in. The following list shows what the IPX ratings mean for liquid ingress protection.

| IPX Rating | Protection Against |
|---|---|
| 1 | Vertically dripping water |
| 2 | Water dripping at an angle of up to 15 degrees |
| 3 | Water spraying at an angle of up to 60 degrees |
| 4 | Water splashing from any direction |
| 5 | Water jets from any direction |
| 6 | Powerful water jets |
| 7 | Immersion up to 1 meter (approx. 3 feet) deep |
| 8 | Immersion of more than 1 meter deep |

So if you want your iPad to survive a drop into household water, IPX7 has you covered. If you're planning to take your iPad swimming or diving, you'll want IPX8, which typically means the case is hermetically sealed.

---

Fully waterproof cases are great if that's what you need, but because they're sealed, they tend to make access to the iPad's ports difficult. You can use the screen as usual through the case, and play music wirelessly by using AirPlay, but you'll typically need to remove all or part of the case in order to recharge the iPad. The bigger waterproof cases simply snap open, but those that fit more snugly can take time and effort to remove.

If you need to make your iPad fully waterproof only on special occasions, you may prefer the next type of waterproofing: instead of getting a waterproof case, get a waterproof bag or box into which you can put your iPad in its existing case (if any). If you need to use your iPad, you'll have to take it out of the case. But the priority here is keeping the iPad dry and happy.

At this writing, you can find plenty of waterproof boxes the right size for an iPhone or similar-size device, but waterproof boxes the right size for the iPad are few and far between. You may be best off getting a general-purpose box such as the Plano 1612 Deep Water Resistant Field Box (around $25; www.amazon.com and other online stores) that'll take not just your iPad but also your camera or other gear you need to keep dry.

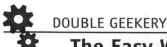

## The Easy Way to Check How Wet Your iPad Just Got

Many an iPad has taken a dive into a sink or bath, and Apple is well aware of how little water it takes to destroy an iPad. If you've read the small print, you probably know that your iPad's warranty doesn't cover liquid damage. Worse still, Apple has built in a way of checking instantly whether you've soaked your iPad.

Your iPad contains two Liquid Contact Indicators to enable a technician to tell whether water has gone into the iPad. One of the Liquid Contact Indicators is in the headphone port. The other is in the Dock Connector port. The Liquid Contact Indicators turn red when the iPad gets wet.

If you think your iPad may have gotten wet—or (let's be honest) when your iPad has gotten wet and you want to find out how badly—shine a light into first the headphone port and then the Dock Connector port. If you see red, you'll know that Apple won't be fixing or replacing your iPad.

Even so, all may not be lost. Try leaving your iPad to dry for about three days, either in a warm (but not hot) and well-ventilated place, or snuggled into a nest of desiccant packets. If you can't get desiccant packets quickly, fill several socks with dry rice, lay out a towel, and wrap your iPad in a nest of socks in the towel. When your iPad has dried out thoroughly, cross your fingers and try turning it on.

---

If your needs are more modest, experiment with sealable plastic bags and sandwich boxes. Either works well in a pinch—and you probably have enough of both in the kitchen to keep your iPad safe and dry without spending a cent.

# Project 29: Make Your iPad Safe for Your Kids to Use

If you let your kids use your iPad, use your iPad's Restrictions feature to prevent them from taking unwanted actions—anything from browsing the Web at all to setting up Mail accounts or watching adult movies. This section shows you how to set up suitable restrictions and lock them with a passcode to prevent your victims from changing them.

 If your company or organization provides your iPad, an administrator may use the restrictions to prevent you from taking unwanted actions on the iPad—for example, installing games, dallying on YouTube, or disturbing the serenity of the cube farm by dictating at the top of your voice.

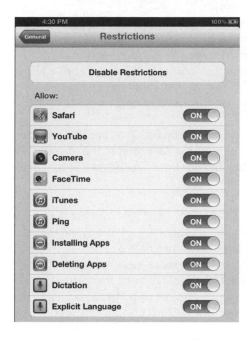

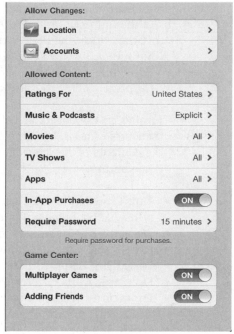

**FIGURE 4-5**   On the Restrictions screen, choose which features to allow users to use and which to restrict.

To set restrictions, follow these steps:

1. Tap the Settings button to display the Settings screen.
2. Tap the General button to display the General screen.
3. Tap the Restrictions button to display the Restrictions screen, the upper part of which is shown on the left in Figure 4-5, with the lower part shown on the right.
4. At first, the restrictions are all disabled, so they appear faded. To make them usable, tap the Enable Restrictions button at the top of the screen. Your iPad then displays the Set Passcode screen, shown here.
5. Type a four-digit passcode, and then type it again on the Set Passcode: Re-enter Your Passcode screen. Your iPad then returns you to the Restrictions screen, where the controls are enabled and ready for use.

6. In the Allow box, move each item's switch to the On position to allow the item or to the Off position to forbid the item. These are the items and a description of what they allow the user to do when set to the On position:
   - **Safari**   Allow the user to use the Safari web browser app at all.
   - **YouTube**   Allow the user to use the YouTube app.
   - **Camera**   Allow the user to use the Camera app.

Turning off the Camera app also turns off the FaceTime app, because FaceTime uses the iPad's cameras. Even if you turn off the Camera app, the user can still capture the contents of the screen by holding down the Sleep/Wake button and pressing the Home button.

   - **FaceTime**   Allow the user to use the FaceTime app for making video calls to other users of iPads, iPhones, iPod touches, and Macs.
   - **iTunes**   Allow the user to use the iTunes Store.
   - **Ping**   Allow the user to use the Ping social-networking feature.
   - **Installing Apps**   Allow the user to install apps from the App Store.
   - **Deleting Apps**   Allow the user to delete apps from the iPad.
   - **Dictation**   Allow the user to use the Dictation feature in the apps that support it.
   - **Explicit Language**   Allow the user to access the iTunes Store material that contains explicit language—for example, misogynistic or misanthropic rap songs.

Setting the Explicit Language switch on the Restrictions screen to the Off position affects only the iTunes Store. The user can still get his fill of filth on the Web unless you disallow Safari.

7. In the Allow Changes box, tap the Location button to display the Location screen, shown on the left in Figure 4-6. You can then choose the following settings:
   - **Allow Changes/Don't Allow Changes**   Tap to select the Allow Changes button, placing a check mark on it, if you want the user to be able to change the other settings on the screen. Tap to select the Don't Allow Changes button if you want to lock the other settings so that the user can't mess with them.
   - **Location Services**   If you want to turn off Location Services entirely, tap this switch and move it to the Off position. Your iPad displays a dialog box to warn you that turning off Location Services will prevent you from using the Find My iPad service. Tap the Turn Off button if you're sure you want to do this.
   - **Apps using Location Services**   In the list of apps that use Location Services, tap an app's switch and move it to the Off position if you want to prevent the app from using Location Services. For example, to prevent iMovie from using Location Services, move the iMovie switch to the Off position.

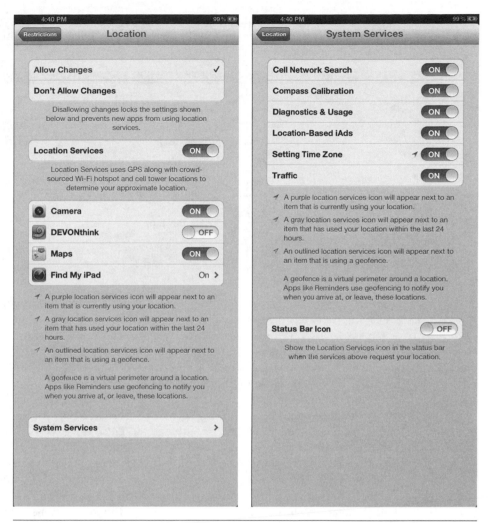

**FIGURE 4-6**   On the Location screen (left), you can either turn off Location Services altogether or restrict it to certain apps. On the System Services screen (right), choose which system services can use Location Services.

- **Find My iPad**   To control whether the Find My iPad feature is enabled, tap the Find My iPad button, and then work on the Find My iPad screen (shown next). You can then move the Find My iPad switch to the Off position if you want to turn off the Find My iPad feature. You can also move the Status Bar Icon switch to the On position if you want the iPad's status bar to display a telltale arrow showing that you're tracking this iPad's location from another computer. When you've made your choices, tap the Location button to go back to the Location screen.

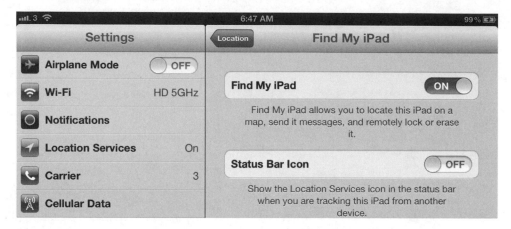

- **System Services** Tap this button to display the System Services screen (shown on the right in Figure 4-6), and then set the switches to choose which system services can use Location Services. For example, move the Location-Based iAds switch to the Off position if you want to prevent your iPad from receiving in-app ads that are based on the iPad's location. At the bottom of the System Services screen is the Status Bar Icon switch, which you can set to the On position if you want the Location Services icon to appear in the status bar when a system service requests your location from Location Services. When you've made your choices, tap the Location button to return to the Location screen.

8. Tap the Restrictions button to return to the Restrictions screen.
9. In the Allowed Content box, choose which content the user may enjoy:
   a. Make sure the Ratings For button shows the right country. If not, tap the Ratings For button, tap the country on the Ratings For screen that appears, and then tap the Restrictions button to display the Restrictions screen again.
   b. Tap the Music & Podcasts button to display the Music & Podcasts screen (the top part of which is shown here), and then move the Explicit switch to the On position or the Off position, as needed. Tap the Restrictions button to display the Restrictions screen again.

c. Tap the Movies button to display the Movies screen (shown on the left in Figure 4-7), and then tap the highest rating you'll permit—for example, PG-13. Your iPad removes the check marks from the stronger-rated items and turns their buttons red. You can't see it in the book's grayscale, but the R, NC-17, and Allow All Movies buttons have red text to indicate that they're turned off. Tap the Restrictions button to display the Restrictions screen again.

d. Tap the TV Shows button to display the TV Shows screen. This works in the same way as the Movies screen: Tap the highest rating you'll allow, and then tap the Restrictions button to display the Restrictions screen again.

e. Tap the Apps button to display the Apps screen, shown on the right in Figure 4-7. Tap the button for the oldest app rating you'll allow (for example, tap 12 +), and then tap the Restrictions button to display the Restrictions screen once more.

10. Tap the In-App Purchases switch and move it to the On position or the Off position, as needed.

 An *in-app purchase* is a purchase the user can make from the iTunes Store from within an app. For example, many apps have in-app purchases for professional versions, and many games have in-app purchases for extra levels, good for wasting a few more hours. You'll probably want to turn off in-app purchases to prevent your kids spending your money without your say-so.

11. Tap the Require Password button to display the Require Password screen, and then tap the button for the time period after which the user must enter an Apple ID to make in-app purchases: Immediately, or 15 Minutes. Tap the Restrictions button to display the Restrictions screen again.

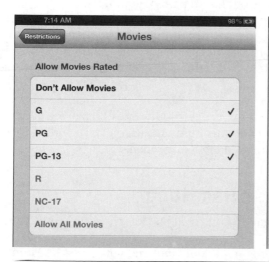 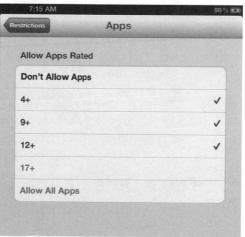

**FIGURE 4-7**   On the Movies screen (left), tap the highest rating you'll permit. On the Apps screen (right), tap the highest rating the user may run.

12. In the Game Center box at the bottom of the Restrictions screen, set the two switches to the On position or the Off position, as needed:
    - **Multiplayer Games** This switch controls whether the user can send and receive invitations to play games.
    - **Adding Friends** This switch controls whether the user can add friends in Game Center.
13. When you finish choosing restrictions, tap the General button to return to the General screen.

Now that you've implemented restrictions, your iPad is ready for your kids.

# Project 30: Troubleshoot Software and Hardware Problems

Apple has made your iPad and its operating system, iOS, as stable and reliable as possible. But even so, you may run into software and hardware problems now and then.

This project shows you five essential moves:

- **Force quit an app** When an app stops responding, you can force it to quit.
- **Restart your iPad** Restarting your iPad can clear up software and hardware problems.
- **Hardware reset** When a restart doesn't do the trick, you can perform a hardware reset. This is a restart on steroids. It doesn't affect the data or settings on the iPad.
- **Software reset** The next stage is to reset all the settings on your iPad. This move loses your custom settings but doesn't affect your data.
- **Erase all content and settings** If the software reset doesn't clear the problems, you can erase all your content and settings from your iPad. Before you do this, you need to sync your iPad or (if it won't sync) save any content that's only on the iPad. After erasing all content and settings, you sync the content and settings back to the iPad.

Beyond these five moves, there's the heaviest-duty move: restoring your iPad to factory settings. I'll show you how to do this in the next project, including how to put your iPad into Device Firmware Upgrade mode if needed.

## Force Quit an App That Has Hung

Normally, the apps you've launched on your iPad just keep running until you turn your iPad off.

For example, say you're working in the Mail app, and you press the Home button to display the Home screen so that you can launch another app. iOS doesn't close

Mail; instead, Mail keeps running in the background, where you can't see it. When you go back to Mail, either by tapping its icon on the Home screen or by using the quick switching feature, Mail will be as you left it. So if you've left a message half-written, it'll still be there for you to continue.

When you use the Home screen to switch to a different app, iOS keeps the app you were previously using suspended in the background, where you can't see it. When you go back to that app, you'll find it doing what it was doing before.

If an app stops responding, you can close it by "force quitting" it—in other words, forcing it to quit. To force quit a program, follow these steps:

1. Press the Home button twice in rapid succession to display the app-switching bar.
2. If the app you want to force quit doesn't appear on the first screen displayed of the app-switching bar, scroll left or right until you can see it.
3. Tap and hold the app's icon on the app-switching bar until the icons start to jiggle and a Close button (a red circle with a horizontal white bar across it) appears at the upper-left corner of each icon, as shown here.

4. Tap the Close button for the app.
5. Press the Home button to stop the icons jiggling.

## Restart Your iPad

If your iPad is not running stably, try restarting it. Follow these steps:

1. Hold down the Sleep/Wake button until the screen shows the message Slide To Power Off.
2. Tap the slider and drag it to the right. The iPad shuts down.
3. Wait a few seconds, and then press the Sleep/Wake button again. Hold the button down for a second or two until the Apple logo appears. The iPad then starts.

## Perform a Hardware Reset

If you're not able to restart your iPad as described in the previous section, try a hardware reset. Hold down the Sleep/Wake button and the Home button together for around ten seconds until the Apple logo appears on the screen, and then release them. The iPad then restarts.

## Perform a Software Reset

If performing a hardware reset (as described in the previous section) doesn't clear the problem, you may need to perform a software reset. This action resets the iPad's settings but doesn't erase your data from it.

To perform a software reset, follow these steps:

1. Press the Home button to display the Home screen.
2. Tap the Settings icon to display the Settings screen.
3. Tap the General button to display the General screen.
4. Scroll down to the bottom and tap the Reset button to display the Reset screen (shown here).

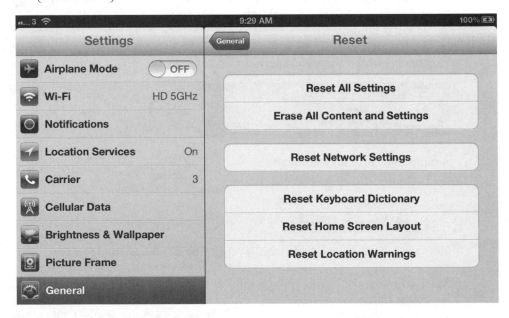

5. Tap the Reset All Settings button.
6. If you've locked your iPad with a passcode, type the passcode in the Enter Passcode dialog box that appears. If it's a complex passcode, tap the Done button.
7. If you've applied restrictions to your iPad, type the restrictions passcode in the Enter Passcode dialog box that appears.
8. Tap the Reset button in the confirmation dialog box (shown here).

Your iPad then restarts. When it is running again, tap the Settings button on the Home screen to open the Settings app, and start choosing the settings that are most important to you. For example, connect to a wireless network, set the screen brightness, and choose which notifications to receive.

## Erase the Content and Settings on Your iPad

If even the software reset doesn't fix the problem, try erasing all content and settings. Before you do so, remove any content you have created on your iPad and not yet synced—assuming the iPad is working well enough for you to do so. For example, send to yourself via e-mail any notes that you have written on the iPad and not synced to an online account, or sync the iPad to your computer to transfer any photos you have taken with its camera.

To erase the content and settings, follow these steps:

1. Press the Home button to display the Home screen.
2. Tap the Settings icon to display the Settings screen.
3. Tap the General button to display the General screen.
4. Tap the Reset item to display the Reset screen.
5. Tap the Erase All Content And Settings button.
6. If you've locked your iPad with a passcode, type the passcode in the Enter Passcode dialog box that appears. If it's a complex passcode, tap the Done button.
7. If you've applied restrictions to your iPad, type the restrictions passcode in the Enter Passcode dialog box that appears.
8. Tap the Erase button on the first confirmation screen (shown on the left in the next illustration).
9. Tap the Erase button on the second confirmation screen (shown on the right in the next illustration). (Erasure is such a serious move that the iPad makes you confirm it twice.)

After erasing all content and settings, sync the iPad to load the content and settings back onto it.

# Project 31: Restore Your iPad to Factory Settings

If your iPad's software gets really messed up, you may need to restore it to factory settings.

Restoring your iPad to factory settings wipes out all third-party apps, leaving only the built-in apps—Safari, Mail, Photos, Notes, Camera, and so on. So after restoring to factory settings, you'll need to reload all your third-party apps from your backup on your computer or from the App Store.

To restore your iPad, follow these steps:

1. Connect your iPad to your computer, and wait for it to appear in the Source list in iTunes.
2. Click the iPad's entry in the Devices category in the Source list to display the iPad control screens.
3. If the Summary screen isn't displayed already, click the Summary tab to display it.
4. Click the Restore button. iTunes displays a confirmation dialog box, as shown here, to make sure you know that you're about to erase all the data from your iPad.

 If a new version of the iPad software is available, iTunes prompts you to restore and update your iPad instead of merely restoring it. Click the Restore And Update button if you want to proceed; otherwise, click the Cancel button.

5. Click the Restore button to close the message box. iTunes wipes the iPad's contents, and then restores the software, showing you its progress while it works.
6. At the end of the restore process, iTunes restarts the iPad. iTunes displays an information message box, for ten seconds while it does so, as shown here. Either click the OK button or allow the countdown timer to close the message box automatically.

7. After the iPad restarts, it appears in the Source list in iTunes. Instead of the iPad's regular tabbed screens, the Set Up Your iPad screen appears (see Figure 4-8).

**FIGURE 4-8**   After restoring the iPad's system software, you will normally want to restore your data from backup. The alternative is to set up the iPad as a new iPad.

8. To restore your data, make sure the Restore From The Backup Of option button is selected, and verify that the correct iPad appears in the drop-down list.
9. Click the Continue button. iTunes restores your data and then restarts the iPad, displaying another countdown message box while it does so. Either click the OK button or allow the countdown timer to close the message box automatically.
10. After the iPad appears in the Source list in iTunes following the restart, you can use it as normal.

DOUBLE GEEKERY

# Secret Tricks for Recovering from Restore Failures

Sometimes, when you try to restore your iPad as described in the main text, the restore operation fails in one of these ways:

- The iPad shows the Connect To iTunes screen, but when you connect the iPad, it doesn't appear in iTunes. The Connect To iTunes screen shows the iTunes logo with a USB cable pointing toward it.
- Your iPad keeps restarting, but it doesn't get as far as the Home screen.
- Your iPad stops responding during the restore operation. The screen may show only the Apple logo or the Apple logo and a progress bar that has stopped moving.

If you run into any of these problems, try using recovery mode. Follow these steps:

1. Disconnect the USB cable from your iPad.
2. Press and hold the Sleep/Wake button on the top of the iPad until the Slide To Power Off slider appears, and then tap the slider and drag it to the right. The iPad powers off.
3. Press and hold the Home button while you plug the USB cable into the iPad's Dock Connector port. You'll see the iPad turn on.
4. Keep holding down the Home button until your iPad shows the Connect To iTunes screen, and then release the Home button.
5. Wait until iTunes displays the Recovery Mode dialog box (shown here).

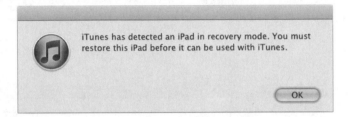

6. Click the OK button (it's the only choice). iTunes displays the Summary tab of the iPad control screens (as shown here) with only the Restore button enabled.

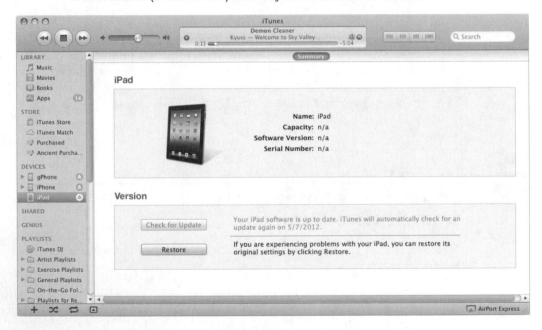

7. Click the Restore button, and then follow through the process of restoring the iPad.

# Project 32: Track Your iPad Wherever It May Roam

Your iPad's Find My iPad feature enables you to track your iPad down if you lose it or someone steals it. You can display a message on the iPad—for example, asking whoever has found the iPad to call you to arrange its return—or you can wipe the data on the iPad remotely if you decide you're not going to get it back.

To use Find My iPad, you must have an Apple ID. If you already have an iCloud account, you're all set. If you don't have an Apple ID, you can set one up in just a minute or two.

 If you apply restrictions to an iPad that someone else uses, you can use Find My iPad to track that iPad too. For example, you may want to keep tabs on where your child is, or be able to locate a tablet an employee has mislaid.

## Turn On Find My iPad

To turn on Find My iPad, follow these steps:

1. Press the Home button to display the Home screen.
2. Tap the Settings icon to display the Settings screen.
3. Tap the iCloud button to display the iCloud screen:
   - If you haven't yet set up an iCloud account on your iPad, you'll see a screen like the one shown on the left in Figure 4-9. Type your Apple ID and password, and then tap the Sign In button.

 If you don't have an Apple ID yet, tap the Get A Free Apple ID button at the bottom of the iCloud screen, and then follow through the process for setting up the iCloud account. When you've done so, use the Apple ID to sign in.

   - When you have set up your iCloud account on your iPad (and signed in), you'll see a screen like the one shown on the right in Figure 4-9.
4. Scroll down to the bottom of the screen.
5. Tap the Find My iPad switch and move it to the On position. Your iPad displays a dialog box (shown here) confirming that you want the iPad to be tracked.
6. Tap the Allow button to close the confirmation dialog box.

**FIGURE 4-9**    If you haven't yet set up iCloud on your iPad (left), enter your Apple ID and password or create a new Apple ID. After you set up iCloud, you see the available services (right).

## Locate Your iPad with Find My iPhone

After turning on Find My iPad, you can locate your iPad at any time from any computer or device that has an Internet connection. To locate your iPad with Find My iPhone, follow these steps:

1. Open your web browser—for example, Internet Explorer on Windows, Safari on a Mac (or on Windows), or Firefox on most any operating system.

 The feature for locating your iPad is named Find My iPhone because Apple debuted this feature for locating missing iPhones. At this writing, the feature also works for Macs, but it's still called Find My iPhone.

2. Go to www.icloud.com.
3. Log in using your Apple ID. The iCloud home screen appears (see Figure 4-10).

**FIGURE 4-10**   On the iCloud home screen, click the Find My iPhone icon.

4. Click the Find My iPhone icon to display the Find My iPhone screen (see Figure 4-11). If the Sign In Required dialog box appears, type your password, and then click the OK button.
5. In the My Devices list box, click the iPad or other iOS device you want to locate. As long as Find My iPad is able to track your iPad, its location appears on a map of the area it's in.

 If your iPad is your only iOS device, it will already be selected in the My Devices list box.

6. If necessary, change the map display so that you can see the location better:
   • Click the Center button (the circular icon that looks like a telescopic sight) in the upper-right corner of the Find My iPhone window to center the map on the iPad's location.
   • Click the + button to zoom in, or click the – button to zoom out.
   • Click the Standard button to display a standard map like the one shown in Figure 4-11.
   • Click the Satellite button to display a map of satellite imagery.
   • Click the Hybrid button to display the standard map's names on the satellite map.

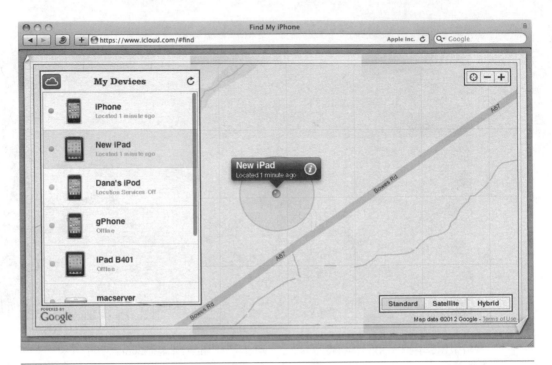

**FIGURE 4-11** On the Find My iPhone screen, go to the My Devices list box and click the iPad or other iOS device you want to locate.

7. Click the *i* button in the iPad's location button to display the Info dialog box (shown here). You can then take actions with your iPad as described in the next section.

# Project 33: Lock or Wipe Your iPad After It Gets Lost or Stolen

As you saw in the previous section, you can use the Find My iPad feature to locate your iPad when it goes missing.

Once you know your iPad's geographical location, you'll probably have a better idea of what's happened to it and what you should do. For example:

- If you realize you've left your iPad in your car or your office, you can cancel the APB and go retrieve it.
- If you can see that your iPad is following your spouse's usual route to work, you can display a message on the iPad asking him or her to pull a U-turn and give it back.
- If you detect that your iPad has entered terra incognita, you'll probably want to make sure it's locked, then display a message on it—and then wipe the iPad's data if you don't get a positive response.

In the following sections, we'll look at your options in turn.

## Lock Your iPad with a Passcode

What you'll often want to do first is lock your iPad if either you hadn't applied a passcode lock before or you suspect that the iPad may have been unlocked when whoever has it picked it up.

To lock your iPad with a passcode, follow these steps on the Find My iPhone screen:

1. Click the *i* button in the iPad's location button to display the Info dialog box.
2. Click the Remote Lock button to display the Remote Lock dialog box. If your iPad doesn't have a passcode applied, the Remote Lock dialog box appears as shown on the left here, and you follow steps 3 and 4 to lock the iPad. If the iPad does have a passcode, the Remote Lock dialog box appears as shown on the right here, with its title bar showing Info, and you simply click the Lock iPad button to lock the iPad.

3. Click the buttons for the four-digit passcode you want to apply.
4. Click the Lock button to apply the passcode to the iPad.

The passcode takes effect almost immediately—just as soon as it passes through the Internet and over the air to your iPad.

## Display a Message on Your iPad

The next capability the Find My iPad feature offers is to display a message on your iPad's screen. You can also choose whether to play a sound on the iPad to cause whoever has the iPad, or is near it, to look at its screen.

To display a message on your iPad, follow these steps on the Find My iPhone screen:

1. Click the *i* button in the iPad's location button to display the Info dialog box.
2. Click the Play Sound Or Send Message button to display the Send Message dialog box (shown here).

3. Type your message in the Message box. For example, type a message requesting the finder to call your other phone number to arrange the iPad's return.
4. If you want to play a sound, make sure the Play Sound switch is set to the On position.
5. Click the Send button to send the message and to play the sound (if you chose to do so).

## Wipe Your iPad's Contents Remotely

If you've exhausted your other options for recovering your iPad, you can wipe the data it contains to make sure nobody else can read it.

 Treat wiping your iPad's contents as a last resort, because wiping them means that you can no longer locate the iPad. Unless you're wiping the iPad for practice, or you have exceptional luck, you'll never see your iPad again.

To wipe your iPad's contents, follow these steps:

1. Click the *i* button in the iPad's location button to display the Info dialog box.
2. Click the Remote Wipe button to display the Wipe iPad screen of the Info dialog box (shown here).

3. Click the Wipe iPad button, and wave a fond farewell to your iPad.

 To wipe its data, your iPad simply deletes the key used to encrypt and decrypt the data. The key is tiny, so this deletion takes only the blink of an eye and renders the data unreadable, even though it is still on the iPad.

# 5  Cellular, Wi-Fi, and Remote Geekery

So far in this book, we've geeked out on music, photography, work, and security. Now it's time to turn our attention to your iPad's cellular capability, its Wi-Fi network connections, and its ability to control your computer remotely.

If you value connectivity enough to have paid for an iPad with cellular capability, your iPad may be locked to a particular carrier. Shotgun weddings don't always work out well in the long term, so we'll start by looking at how you can unlock your iPad from your carrier so that you can connect it to a different carrier's network instead.

After that, I'll show you how to share your iPad's Internet connection with your computers and devices, so that you can get them online no matter where you are, and how to take control of your PC or Mac from your iPad.

Finally, you'll learn how to connect your iPad to your company network across the Internet using a virtual private network (VPN), which is great for when you need to work remotely using your iPad.

## Project 34: Unlock Your iPad from Your Carrier

If you bought your iPad from a particular carrier on a contract, the iPad will be locked to that carrier's network. So you can't just eject your current SIM card (the subscriber identity module, the card that gives your iPad its cellular identity), pop in a new SIM card for another carrier, and start using that carrier's network. Instead, you need to unlock the iPad so that you can use it freely.

How you unlock your iPad depends on which country you're in, which carrier your iPad is currently locked to, and which type of contract you're on. Because unlocking has many variables, this project explains the essentials of unlocking your iPad but leaves the details up to you.

Before deciding to unlock your iPad, make sure you understand how locking works and what the consequences of unlocking may be.

### Understand Why Carriers Lock iPads on Contracts

Typically, a carrier offers locked iPads to make sure you stay with that carrier for the duration of your contract (and perhaps longer). As you know, on a contract, the carrier typically sells the iPad at a hefty discount from its headline cost, and then charges you for a monthly plan for a year or two. By the end of the contract, the carrier is ahead on the hardware cost.

If you want to avoid a long contract, you can buy an unlocked iPad, install in it a SIM card for your preferred GSM carrier's network, and use it for as long as you like. The unlocked iPad is much more expensive upfront than the locked iPad, but you can save in the long term by paying only for the usage you need rather than paying a fixed fee every month on a contract. And you can resell the iPad at any time without being tied by a contract, which is good if you want to be able to upgrade to the next iPad soon after Apple releases it.

## Understand How iPad Locking Works

So that's *why* carriers lock iPads sold on contracts—but how does the locking work?

The locking is called *SIM locking*, because it uses the SIM card. A carrier can lock an iPad to accept only SIM cards that have an approved International Mobile Subscriber Identity (IMSI). For example, the carrier can lock the iPad so that it'll work only if the SIM has the carrier's own network code. Or the carrier can use the Mobile Station Identification Number (MSIN—the SIM number) to lock the iPad so it will work only with a particular SIM card.

## Understand the Ways of Unlocking Your iPad

There are four main ways of unlocking your iPad:

- Get your carrier to unlock it for you over the air.
- Get the master code from the carrier, and then unlock the iPad yourself.

 The master code for unlocking an iPad is also sometimes called the *network code key* or the *multilock code*.

- Run software on your computer, connect the iPad, jailbreak it, and then unlock it.
- Connect your iPad to a hardware unlocking device, and unlock it.

We'll look at each of these possibilities in turn.

### Get Your Carrier to Unlock Your iPad or Give You the Master Code

As discussed earlier in this section, the easiest option for getting an unlocked iPad is simply to buy an iPad that isn't locked. This approach makes your initial purchase much more expensive, and if you already have an iPad, you probably won't want to consider it—at least, not until Apple releases the next iPad.

The next option is to get your carrier to unlock your iPad for you. If this option is open to you, take it—it's far preferable to messing around with a software unlock or hacking the SIM card.

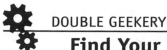

DOUBLE GEEKERY

## Find Your iPad's IMEI

To get your iPad unlocked, you may need to know the iPad's International Mobile Equipment Identity (IMEI). This is a 15-digit decimal number that's unique to your iPad.

You can find your iPad's IMEI either on the iPad itself or in iTunes with the iPad connected.

On the iPad itself, press the Home button, choose Settings | General | About, scroll down to the bottom of the second box, and then look at the IMEI readout.

In iTunes, connect your iPad and follow these steps:

1. Click the iPad's entry in the Devices category in the Source list to display the iPad's control screens.
2. If the Summary screen isn't displayed, click the Summary tab to display it.
3. In the top box, click the Serial Number readout to change the readout. With each click, iTunes displays a different item of information:
   - **Identifier (UDID)**   The Unique Device Identifier (UDID) is a 40-digit string of characters that uniquely identifies your iPad.
   - **Cellular Data Number**   The Cellular Data Number readout shows the cellular number of your iPad's SIM card.
   - **IMEI**   The 15-digit International Mobile Equipment Identity number (shown here) identifies your iPad.

   - **ICCID**   The Integrated Circuit Card ID (ICCID) is a number of up to 19 digits that works as the primary account number to identify the SIM card.

4. Click again to display your iPad's serial number.

Some carriers will not unlock iPads. Most carriers who do unlock iPads will unlock an iPad only at the end of its contract or on payment of a hefty fee. Getting your carrier to unlock the iPad is fully legal and aboveboard in all countries.

If your carrier does unlock iPads, you may have to wait until the end of the contract, you may have to pay a fee, or both. If you have to wait until the end of the contract, you may well have upgraded already to the next iPad.

Some carriers unlock the iPad over the air, which can take a day or two to implement. Other carriers give you an unlock code and instructions for how to enter it.

 In some countries, you can also find services online that unlock iPads (and other phones) for you. These services work by submitting your iPad's IMEI to Apple, just as the carrier would, and requesting an unlock. The cost varies depending on the iPad, the carrier, and the contract. Most services that are worth using aren't cheap, but they're effective. The unlocking procedure takes several days to complete.

## Use Software to Unlock Your iPad

If your carrier won't unlock your iPad, you need to take matters into your own hands. This means unlocking the iPad by jailbreaking it (as described in Chapter 6) and then using an unlocking application such as Ultrasn0w.

Apple frequently changes the security arrangements in iOS to prevent unlocking, and the developers of the unlocking software then have to develop new versions— so the exact moves you need to perform to unlock your iPad vary. But here are the general steps to follow:

1. Find the latest instructions for unlocking by visiting a site such as Redmond Pie (www.redmondpie.com) or by searching online. Make sure the instructions are for your iPad model rather than other iPads.
2. Download an unlocking tool such as Sn0wbreeze from a site such as www .idownloadblog.com/iphone-downloads/.
3. Jailbreak your iPad following the instructions in Projects 39 and 40 in Chapter 6.
4. Follow the instructions for the unlocking tool to unlock your iPad.

 Unlocking your iPad via software or hardware is legal in the United States and the United Kingdom but illegal in some countries. If in doubt whether it's legal in your country, check online.

## Use a Hardware Unlocking Device

Another way of unlocking an iPad is to use a hardware unlocking device. These devices are typically operated by companies that unlock phones as part of their business rather than something you'd buy yourself to unlock a single iPad. You take your iPad to such a service, pay (inevitably), and have the company unlock it for you.

 You can also get unlocking SIM cards for unlocking the iPad. Some work, others don't, so look for good reviews before buying. These SIM cards are specific not only to the iPad model but also to the iPad's baseband version—so make sure you get exactly the card you need. To find the baseband version, choose Settings | General | About, and then scroll down and look at the Modem Firmware number.

# Project 35: Share Your iPad's Internet Connection with Your Computers and Devices

If your iPad has cellular capability, it can not only get a high-speed Internet connection through the cellular network, but also share that connection with your computer or other devices. This capability is great for when you're on the road and need to get your computer online where no Wi-Fi connection is available. But you can also use it for home Internet access if your data plan is generous enough or if your regular connection dies.

Sharing the iPad's Internet connection used to be called *Internet tethering*, and some people still use that term. In iOS 5, the feature for sharing the Internet connection is called Personal Hotspot. You can connect up to five computers or other devices at a time using Personal Hotspot. You can connect a single computer via USB or connect multiple computers and devices via Wi-Fi or Bluetooth. In this section, we'll look at how to use USB and Wi-Fi, which are the two most useful connections.

 USB gives the fastest connection to Personal Hotspot—but it works for only one computer at a time. Wi-Fi gives good speeds and is the best choice for connecting multiple devices. Bluetooth gives slower speeds and requires pairing your iPad with the computer or device, so it is best used only when you have no other means of connection.

## Set Up Personal Hotspot

To set up Personal Hotspot on your iPad, follow these steps:

1. Press the Home button to display the Home screen.
2. Tap the Settings icon to display the Settings screen.
3. Tap the General button to display the General screen.
4. Tap the Network button to display the Network screen.

5. Tap the Personal Hotspot button to display the Personal Hotspot screen (shown here).

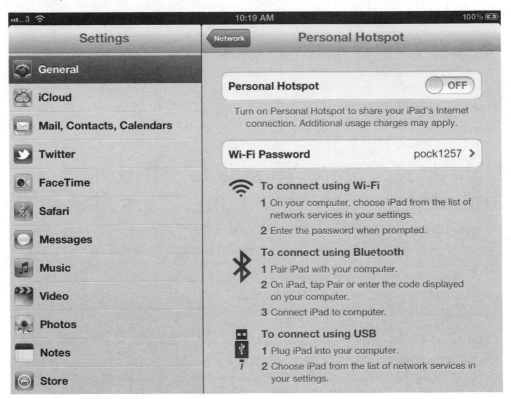

6. Tap the Personal Hotspot switch and move it to the On position. The Personal Hotspot screen shows that the network is discoverable under the name you've given your iPad.

7. If Bluetooth is turned off, your iPad displays the Bluetooth Is Off dialog box (shown here). If you want to use Bluetooth to share your Internet connection, tap the Turn On Bluetooth button. Otherwise, tap the Wi-Fi And USB Only button to confirm you're happy with Wi-Fi and USB sharing.

8. Look at the default password on the right side of the Wi-Fi Password button. If you want to change it, tap the Wi-Fi Password button, and then type the new password on the Wi-Fi Password screen. The password must be at least eight characters long. Tap the Done button to return to the Personal Hotspot screen.

9. Now that you've turned Personal Hotspot on, the Personal Hotspot appears near the top of the Settings column, under the Wi-Fi item (as shown here), giving you quick access to the settings for turning Personal Hotspot on and off.

With Personal Hotspot turned on, you can connect your computers or devices to it.

# Connect a Computer or Device to Personal Hotspot via Wi-Fi

To connect a computer or device to Personal Hotspot via Wi-Fi, you need only connect via Wi-Fi to the Personal Hotspot wireless network, just as you would connect to any other wireless network.

The Personal Hotspot wireless network has your iPad's name and uses the password that appears on the Personal Hotspot screen.

# Connect a Single Computer to Personal Hotspot via USB

Instead of connecting via Wi-Fi, you can connect a single computer to Personal Hotspot by using your iPad's USB cable.

### Connect a Windows PC to Personal Hotspot via USB

When you connect your iPad via USB to a Windows PC, and Personal Hotspot is enabled on the iPad, Windows automatically detects the iPad's Internet connection as a new network connection. The first time this happens, Windows automatically installs the driver for the connection and displays the Driver Software Installation dialog box to let you know it has done so. Click the Close button to close the dialog box.

Next, Windows displays the Set Network Location dialog box (see Figure 5-1), asking you whether this new network is a Home Network, a Work Network, or a Public Network. Normally, you'll want to click the Home Network button here.

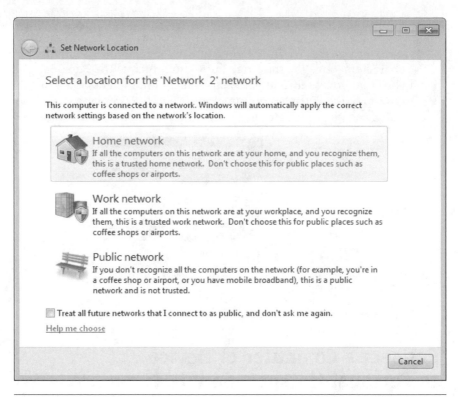

**FIGURE 5-1** In the first Set Network Location dialog box, click the Home Network button to tell Windows that the Personal Hotspot network is safe to use.

Windows then sets up the network. When it has done so, it displays another Set Network Location dialog box (see Figure 5-2) confirming the network location.

Click the Close button to close the Set Network Location dialog box. The connection is now ready for you to use.

 An easy way to check that the Internet connection is working is to open Internet Explorer and see if it can load your home page.

## Connect a Mac to Personal Hotspot via USB

When you connect your iPad via USB to a Mac, and Personal Hotspot is enabled on the iPad, the Mac automatically detects the iPad's Internet connection as a new network connection. The first time this happens, Mac OS X may automatically display the Network preferences pane in System Preferences so that you can set up the network.

Click the iPad USB interface in the left box, and then click the Apply button. Mac OS X assigns an IP address to the iPad USB interface, and then displays the details (see Figure 5-3).

Press ⌘-Q or choose System Preferences | Quit System Preferences to quit System Preferences. You can now start using the Internet connection.

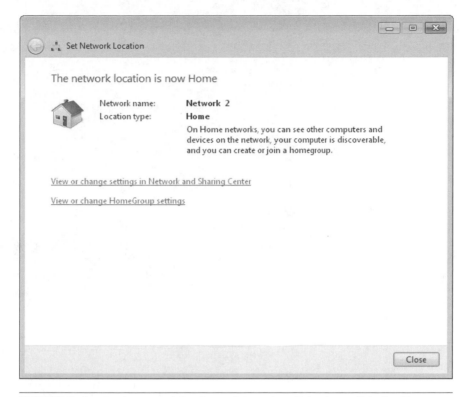

**FIGURE 5-2** In the second Set Network Location dialog box, click the Close button. You can then start using the network.

 If you want to check that the Internet connection is working, open Safari and see if your home page appears.

## Turn Off Personal Hotspot

When Personal Hotspot is on with no computers or devices connected to it, the only way to tell it's on is that the Personal Hotspot switch on the Personal Hotspot screen is in the On position.

When any computers or devices are connected to Personal Hotspot, your iPad displays a blue bar across the top of the screen, as in the two examples shown here.

**FIGURE 5-3**   Mac OS X assigns an IP address to the iPad USB interface to enable your Mac to use the iPad as a network connection.

To turn off Personal Hotspot, follow these steps:

1. Press the Home button to display the Home screen.
2. Tap the Settings icon to display the Settings screen.
3. Tap the Personal Hotspot button to display the Personal Hotspot screen.
4. Tap the Personal Hotspot switch and move it to the Off position.

# Project 36: Control Your PC or Mac from Your iPad

If you use your iPad to get work done no matter where you happen to be, you'll definitely want to make the most of your iPad's capability to control computers remotely. In this project, I'll show you how to reach out from your iPad and take control of a PC or Mac anywhere on the Internet.

First, we'll get you the remote-control software you need for your iPad. Then we'll set up your PC or Mac for remote control. After that, you'll be ready to take control of your PC or Mac from your iPad across the Internet.

## Choose Your Remote Control Technology

There are two main technologies for connecting to a computer remotely and controlling it:

- **Remote Desktop Protocol (RDP)**   RDP is Microsoft's proprietary protocol for controlling Windows PCs remotely. RDP is part of the Terminal Services feature built into the "business" versions of Windows: Windows 7 Professional, Windows 7 Ultimate, Windows 7 Enterprise, Windows Vista Business, Windows Vista Ultimate, Windows Vista Enterprise, and Windows XP Professional.

 RDP is a well-designed and effective protocol that enables you to work remotely on your PC. Given the choice between RDP and VNC for connecting to your Windows PC, choose RDP. But if you have one of the "Home" versions of Windows, you will need to use VNC instead, because these versions don't have the Remote Desktop feature.

- **Virtual Network Computing (VNC)**   VNC is a protocol originally developed by AT&T for controlling one computer from another computer. VNC is built into Mac OS X as part of the Screen Sharing feature, but you can add a VNC server to a Windows PC if you need to.

 The advantage of VNC is that VNC client applications are available for all major operating systems, so you can connect to a VNC server running on any major operating system from a VNC client running on any major operating system.

You can find plenty of RDP client apps and VNC client apps on the App Store. In this project, we'll use the apps Mocha RDP and Mocha VNC. Each works well, is comparatively inexpensive at $5.99, and has a free Lite version (supported by ads) that you can try out to see if you want to pay for the full version.

## Set Up Your PC for Remote Control

To set up your PC for remote control, follow these steps:

1. Press WINDOWS KEY–BREAK to display the System window. You can also click the Start button, right-click the Computer item to display the context menu, and then click the Properties item on it.
2. In the left column, click the Remote Settings link to display the Remote tab of the System Properties dialog box (see Figure 5-4).
3. In the Remote Desktop box, select the Allow Connections From Computers Running Any Version Of Remote Desktop (Less Secure) option button.

**FIGURE 5-4**   On the Remote tab of the System Properties dialog box, select the Allow Connections From Computers Running Any Version Of Remote Desktop (Less Secure) option button.

4. Click the Select Users button to display the Remote Desktop Users dialog box (shown here).

5. Verify that your name appears above the Add button with the message "already has access." If not, click the Add button and use the Select Users dialog box to add yourself to the list of users who can connect via Remote Desktop.
6. Click the OK button to close the Remote Desktop Users dialog box.
7. Click the OK button to close the System Properties dialog box.
8. Click the Close button (the × button) to close the System window.

# Set Up Your Mac for Remote Control

To set up your Mac for remote control, follow these steps:

1. Choose Apple | System Preferences to display the System Preferences window.
2. In the Internet & Wireless category, click the Sharing icon to display the Sharing preferences pane.
3. In the left pane, click the Screen Sharing item (but don't select its check box yet) to display the Screen Sharing options (shown in Figure 5-5).

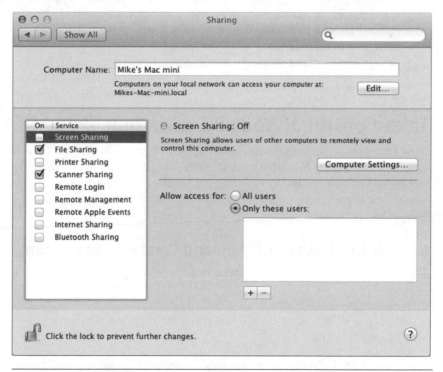

**FIGURE 5-5**   Click the Screen Sharing item in the left pane of the Sharing preferences pane to display the controls for setting up sharing.

4. Click the Computer Settings button to display the dialog box shown here.

☐ Anyone may request permission to control screen

☑ VNC viewers may control screen with password: ●●●●●●●●

Cancel    OK

5. Make sure the Anyone May Request Permission To Control Screen check box is cleared.
6. Select the VNC Viewers May Control Screen With Password check box.
7. In the text box, type the password you will use from VNC.
8. Click the OK button to close the dialog box.
9. In the Allow Access For area, select the All Users option button or the Only These Users option button, as appropriate. Normally, you will want to select the Only These Users option button, and then either leave the Administrators group in the list box (where it appears by default) or click the Add (+) button and add yourself as the user who is allowed to access the Mac via Screen Sharing.
10. Now that you have specified who may connect, select the Screen Sharing check box in the left pane.
11. Press ⌘-Q or choose System Preferences | Quit System Preferences to quit System Preferences.

# Take Control of Your PC with Your iPad

Now that you've set up your PC to accept RDP connections, you can connect to it from your iPad using the Mocha RDP app. First, you need to launch the RDP app and set up the details of the connection. Then you establish the connection and get to work. And when you finish using the connection, you disconnect from the computer or log off Windows.

## Launch the Mocha RDP App and Create a Connection

To create a connection, follow these steps:

1. Launch the RDP app from your iPad's Home screen as usual. Because you don't yet have any connections, the app displays the first Configure screen (shown here).

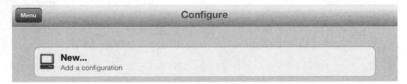

The RDP app offers many settings that you can use to adjust how the app behaves. In this section, we'll set only the essential settings, such as the computer's address and the screen resolution. When you have time, explore the other options and see which suit you.

2. Tap the New button to start creating a new configuration file. The RDP app displays the second Configure screen (shown in Figure 5-6).

The Mocha RDP screens look different in portrait orientation than in landscape orientation. In landscape orientation, the menu panel appears as a left column. You use this panel to navigate among the various screens. In portrait orientation, the menu panel is hidden until you tap the Menu button in the upper-left corner to display it. The menu panel then appears as a floating panel that disappears again when you tap a button on it.

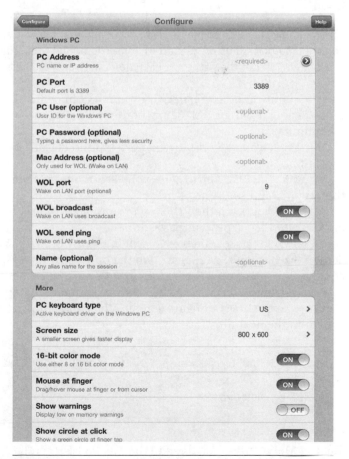

**FIGURE 5-6** On the second Configure screen, tap the > button at the right end of the PC Address button to display the Find Local Workstations screen, and then tap the name of the computer you want to connect to.

3. Tap the > button at the right end of the PC Address button to display the Find Local Workstations screen (shown here).

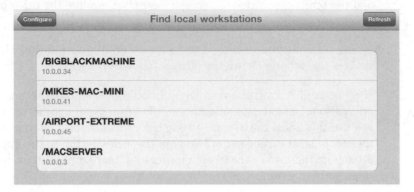

 If you know your PC's computer name or IP address, tap in the <required> placeholder on the PC Address button to place the insertion point and bring up the onscreen keyboard. You can then type the computer name or IP address.

4. Tap the name of the computer you want to connect to. The RDP app returns you to the second Configure screen, where the PC Address button now shows the computer's name.
5. If your PC is using a nonstandard port, tap the PC Port button, and then type the port number.
6. If you want the RDP app to store your username, tap the PC User button, and then type your username.
7. Similarly, if you want the RDP app to store your password, tap the PC Password button, and then type your password.
8. Scroll down to the second box, and then tap the Screen Size button. On the PC Screen Size screen that appears, tap the button for the resolution you want. You can tap the > button at the bottom to set a custom resolution.
9. When you finish choosing settings for the connection, tap the Configure button to return to the first Configure screen. The connection appears as a button, as shown in the next illustration.

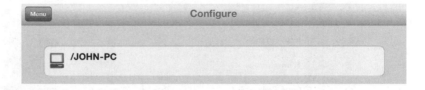

10. Tap the Menu button to return to the Mocha RDP screen.

## Connect to Your PC

From the Mocha RDP screen, follow these steps to connect to your PC:

1. In portrait orientation, tap the Menu button to display the menu panel.
2. Tap the Connect button. The Connect To screen appears, as shown here.

3. Tap the button for the computer you want to connect to. The RDP app connects to your PC.
4. If you didn't enter your username and password, the RDP app displays the Windows login screen. Tap your username to display the Password field, and then tap the keyboard icon to display the keyboard (see Figure 5-7). Type your password, and then tap the Return button to enter it.
5. The RDP app then displays your Windows Desktop (see Figure 5-8), and you can start working on it. These are the main moves you'll need:
   - **Click**  Tap with your finger.
   - **Double-click**  Double-tap.
   - **Right-click**  Tap and hold for a second.

**FIGURE 5-7**  Use the onscreen keyboard to enter your password for your PC if you didn't enter the password when configuring the RDP app.

QWERTY        Command     Menu      Enter        Zoom        Lock Screen  Hide Toolbar
Keyboard button  Keys button  button  Key button  Out button  button       button

**FIGURE 5-8**   The toolbar at the bottom of the screen in the RDP app gives you quick access to the keyboard, the menu, and the command for zooming out.

- **Zoom in**   Place your thumb and finger (or two fingers) together on the screen, and then pinch outward.
- **Zoom out**   Place your thumb and finger (or two fingers) apart on the screen, and then pinch them together.
- **Scroll**   Tap and drag your finger to move the displayed part of the screen in that direction.

## Disconnect from or Log Off Your PC

When you finish using your PC, you can either disconnect from it or log off:

- **Disconnect**   In the RDP app, tap the Menu button to display the Menu dialog box (shown next), and then tap the Disconnect item. The RDP app disconnects from your PC, but your user session keeps running. So if you connect again, you can pick up your work where you left off.

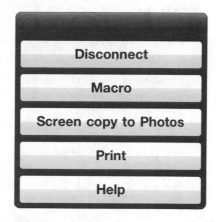

- **Log off**   In the RDP app, tap the Start button, and then tap the Log Off button. Windows closes your user session, and the RDP app closes the connection to your PC.

# Take Control of Your Mac with Your iPad

After setting your Mac to accept VNC connections, you can connect to it by using the VNC app. First, you'll launch the VNC app and specify the details of the connection. Then you can make the connection and start using your Mac. When you finish using your Mac, you can disconnect from your Mac.

 VNC uses the Mac's current screen resolution—unlike RDP, VNC cannot change the resolution for display on your iPad. Because of this limitation, you may want to change the resolution your Mac is using if you plan to use VNC extensively. You can change the resolution either while you're at your Mac or remotely after connecting via VNC.

## Set Up a Connection in Mocha VNC

To set up a connection in Mocha VNC, follow these steps:

1.  Launch the VNC app from your iPad's Home screen by tapping its icon. The app then displays the first Configure screen (shown here).

The Mocha VNC screens look different in portrait orientation than in landscape orientation. In landscape orientation, the menu panel appears as a left column. You use this panel to navigate among the various screens. In portrait orientation, the menu panel is hidden until you tap the Menu button in the upper-left corner to display it. The menu panel then appears as a floating panel that disappears again when you tap a button on it.

2. Tap the New button to start creating a new configuration file. The VNC app displays the second Configure screen (see Figure 5-9).

The VNC app has many settings for configuring your VNC sessions—for example, choosing which Mac keyboard driver the app uses or controlling whether movements detected by the iPad's accelerometers scroll the screen in VNC. In this section, we'll set only those settings needed to establish a connection. When you have time, explore the other options and see which you find useful.

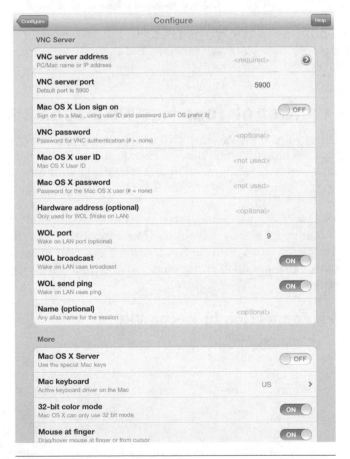

**FIGURE 5-9** On the second Configure screen, tap the > button at the right end of the VNC Server Address button to display the Find Local Workstations screen, and then tap the name of the computer you want to connect to.

3. Tap the > button at the right end of the VNC Server Address button to display the Find Local Workstations screen (shown here).

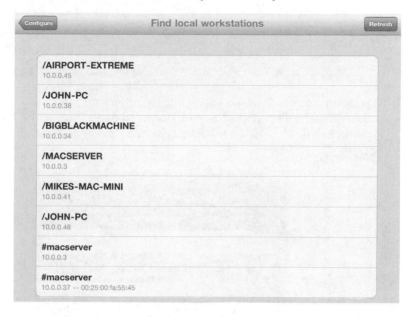

If you know your Mac's IP address or computer name, tap in the "<required>" placeholder on the VNC Server Address button to place the insertion point and bring up the onscreen keyboard. You can then type the IP address or computer name.

4. Optionally, tap the VNC Password field on the second Configure screen and type the password if you want to store it in the connection. If you prefer not to store the password for security reasons, you can provide it when you make the connection.

If you're connecting to a Mac that runs Lion (OS X 10.7) or Mountain Lion (OS X 10.8), you can log in to the Mac remotely instead of merely connecting via Screen Sharing. To do this, tap the Mac OS X Lion Sign On switch and move it to the On position, and then tap the Mac OS X User field and type your username. You can also provide your password by tapping the Mac OS X Password field and typing, or you can wait and provide it when you try to connect to the Mac.

5. Tap the Configure button to return to the first Configure screen.
6. Tap the Menu button to return to the Mocha VNC screen.

## Connect to Your Mac

From the Mocha VNC screen, follow these steps to connect to your Mac:

1. If you're using VNC in portrait orientation, tap the Menu button to display the menu panel.

2. Tap the Connect button to display the Connect To screen (shown here).

3. Tap the button for the Mac you want to connect to.
4. If the VNC app displays the Server Password dialog box or the Mac User Password dialog box (shown here), type your password, and then tap the OK button.

The app then displays your Mac's desktop, with the toolbar at the bottom overlaid on it (see Figure 5-10). You can then start using the apps on your Mac.

## End the Connection to Your Mac

To disconnect from your Mac, tap the Menu button, and then tap the Disconnect button on the Menu screen (shown here).

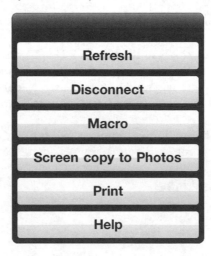

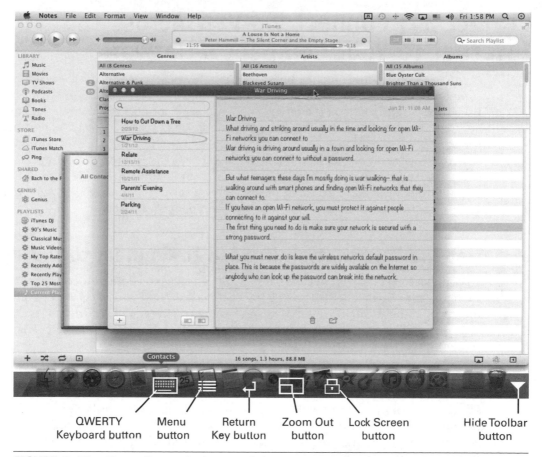

QWERTY        Menu        Return        Zoom Out        Lock Screen        Hide Toolbar
Keyboard button        button        Key button        button        button        button

**FIGURE 5-10**   The toolbar at the bottom of the screen in the VNC app gives you quick access to the keyboard, the menu, and the command for zooming out.

---

DOUBLE GEEKERY

# Control Your iPad from Your PC or Mac

At this point, you may be wondering if you can control your iPad from your PC or Mac.

The answer is: Yes, you can. But you need to jailbreak your iPad first. We'll look at how to control your iPad from your computer in Project 46 in Chapter 6.

---

# Project 37: Connect via VPN Across the Internet to Your Company's Network

If you use an iPad for company business, you may need to connect the iPad to your company's network so that you can grab your e-mail or your data from Microsoft Exchange. When you're in the office, you'll probably connect via a wireless network, but when you're out of the office, you can connect across the Internet using a virtual private network, or VPN.

A VPN uses an insecure public network (such as the Internet) to connect securely to a secure private network (such as your company's network). A VPN acts as a secure "pipe" through the insecure Internet, providing a secure connection between your computer (in this case, your iPad) and your company's VPN server.

## Get the Information Needed to Connect to the VPN

To connect to a VPN, you need to know various pieces of configuration information, such as your username, the server's Internet address, and your password or other means of authentication. You also need to know which type of security to use: Layer 2 Tunneling Protocol (L2TP), Point-to-Point Tunneling Protocol (PPTP), or IP Security (IPSec).

Your company's network administrator will provide this information. The administrator may provide it as a written list, which you enter manually in your iPad, as described a little later in this chapter. But it's easy to get one or more items wrong, so usually an administrator will use the iPhone Configuration Utility (a tool Apple provides for administering the iPad, iPhone, and iPod touch) to create a file called a *configuration profile* that you then install on your iPad and that does the work for you. We'll start with this easier approach.

 If you're the administrator, you'll find the iPhone Configuration Utility here: www .apple.com/support/iphone/enterprise. There are versions for both Windows and Mac OS X.

## Set Up a VPN by Using a Configuration Profile

To set up a VPN on your iPad by using a configuration profile, all you need to do is get the configuration profile onto your iPad. Normally, the administrator will either put the configuration profile on your iPad directly by connecting it to his or her computer via USB or distribute the configuration profile in one of these ways:

- **Via e-mail**   This is an easy way of distributing configuration profiles as long as the administrator knows your e-mail account. But if the configuration profile is for a corporate e-mail account as well as for the VPN, you'll need to use another e-mail account (because the iPad won't yet be able to access your corporate account).

- **Via a website**   The administrator can place the configuration profile on a website from which you can download it using the iPad. Typically this will be an internal corporate website or at least a password-protected website, because the configuration profiles aren't encrypted.

Here's how to set up a VPN by installing a configuration profile you've received in an e-mail message or downloaded from a website:

1. Open the configuration profile:
   - If you've received the configuration profile in an e-mail message, as shown here, tap the configuration profile's button. Your iPad then displays the Install Profile screen, as shown in Figure 5-11.

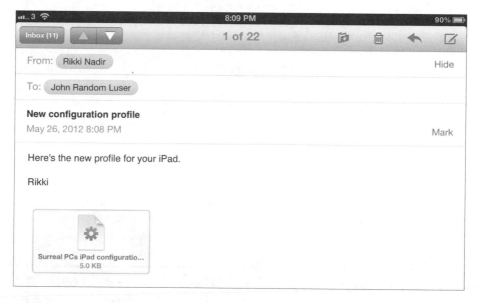

   - If the configuration profile is posted on a web page, open that page in Safari, and then tap the profile's download link. Your iPad then displays the Install Profile screen.

2. Look at the information on the Install Profile screen to make sure you want to install the profile. To see more information about the profile, tap the More Details button, which displays the profile's information screen (shown in Figure 5-12). Tap the Install Profile button in the upper-left corner to go back to the Install Profile screen.

3. Check the profile's status: Unsigned, Not Verified, or Verified. See the nearby sidebar "Understand the Unsigned, Not Verified, and Verified Terms on the Install Profile Screen" for an explanation of these terms and advice on how you should treat the profiles they mark.

4. Tap the Install button on the Install Profile screen to start installing the profile. You'll need to provide your username (see Figure 5-13) and means of authentication, such as your password and shared secret, to set up the VPN.

**FIGURE 5-11**   On the Install Profile screen, tap the Install button to start installing the configuration profile.

DOUBLE GEEKERY

## Understand the Unsigned, Not Verified, and Verified Terms on the Install Profile Screen

The readout to the left of the Install button on the Install Profile screen shows the profile's status:

- **Unsigned**   Whoever created the profile didn't apply a digital signature to the profile to protect it against changes.
- **Not Verified**   The creator did apply a digital signature to the profile, but your iPad can't confirm the digital signature is authentic.
- **Verified**   The iPad has confirmed the digital signature applied to the profile is authentic.

In an ideal world, you'd install only profiles that were verified as coming from whom they claim. But many companies and organizations still use unsigned profiles, so you have a fair chance of running into them. If in doubt, check with an administrator that the profile is safe to install.

**FIGURE 5-12**    The profile's information screen shows you the details of what the profile contains—in this case, the signing certificate and the VPN payload.

**FIGURE 5-13**    Your iPad walks you through the process of setting up the VPN. You enter your username on the Enter Username screen, and then provide your means of authentication—for example, a password and a shared secret.

5. When the Profile Installed screen appears, tap the Done button. Your iPad takes you back to where you started the installation—either the e-mail message containing the configuration profile or the web page from which you downloaded the profile.

You can now start using the VPN. Skip ahead to the section "Connect to a VPN," later in this chapter.

## Set Up a VPN Manually

If your administrator has supplied you with a list of configuration details for the VPN rather than with a configuration profile, you'll need to set it up the hard way. Because you have to type in all the details on your iPad, this is somewhat laborious, but you need to do it only once for any connection. Follow these steps:

1. Press the Home button to reach the Home screen.
2. Tap the Settings icon to display the Settings screen.
3. Tap the General button to display the General screen.
4. Tap the Network button to display the Network screen (shown here).

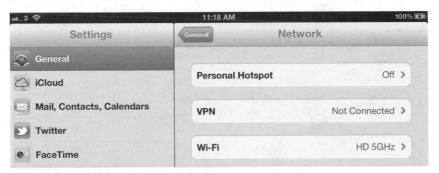

5. Tap the VPN button to display the VPN screen (shown here).

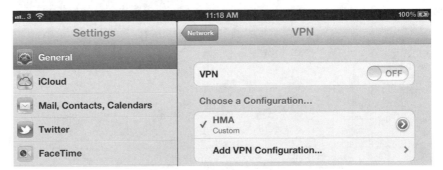

6. Tap the Add VPN Configuration button to display the Add Configuration dialog box, shown in Figure 5-14.

**FIGURE 5-14**   On the Add Configuration screen, enter the information for the connection.

7. Near the top of the screen, click the button for the security type the VPN uses: L2TP, PPTP, or IPSec. The iPad displays a list of the information required for the connection.

8. Type in the details for the VPN configuration on the screen:
   - **Description**   This is the name under which the VPN appears in the list of VPNs. Choose a descriptive name that suits you.
   - **Server**   Type the computer name (for example, vpnserver.surrealmacs.com) or IP address (for example, 216.248.2.88) of the VPN server.
   - **Account**   Type your login name for the VPN connection. Depending on your company's network, this may be the same as your regular login name, but in most cases it's different for security reasons.
   - **Password**   If the administrator has given you a password rather than a certificate (discussed next), you can enter it here and have your iPad provide it for you each time you connect. For greater security, you can leave the password area blank and enter the password manually each time you connect. This prevents anyone else from connecting using your iPad, but it's laborious, especially if your password uses letters, numbers, and symbols (as a strong password should).
   - **RSA SecurID**   (PPTP and L2TP only) If the administrator provided you with an RSA SecurID token, move this switch to On to use it. The iPad then hides the Password field, because you don't need to use a password when you use the token.

- **Use Certificate**   (IPSec only) If the administrator provided you with a configuration profile that installed a certificate for authenticating you on the connection, move this switch to On. To save you from temptation, the switch is available only when a certificate is installed.
- **Secret**   (L2TP only) Type the preshared key, also called the *shared secret*, for the VPN. This preshared key is the same for all users of the VPN (unlike your account name and password, which are unique to you).
- **Group Name**   (IPSec only) Type the name of the group to which you belong for the VPN.
- **Send All Traffic**   (L2TP only) Leave this switch set to On (the default position) unless the administrator has told you to turn it off. When Send All Traffic is on, all your Internet connections go to the VPN server; when it is off, Internet connections to parts of the Internet other than the VPN go directly to those destinations.
- **Encryption Level**   (PPTP only) Leave this set to Auto to have the iPad try 128-bit encryption (the strongest) first, then weaker 40-bit encryption, and then None. Choose Maximum if you know you must use 128-bit encryption only. Choose None only in desperate circumstances—no sane administrator will recommend it.

9. When you've finished entering the information, tap the Save button to save the connection. The VPN connection then appears on the VPN screen.

You're now ready to connect to the VPN, as described in the next section.

## Connect to a VPN

After you've installed or created your VPN connection, you can connect to it quickly and easily. Follow these steps:

1. Press the Home button to reach the Home screen.
2. Tap the Settings icon to display the Settings screen.
3. Start the VPN connection in one of these ways:
   - **If you have only one VPN connection**   On the Settings screen (shown here), move the VPN switch to the On position.

- **If you have two or more VPN connections**   Tap the VPN button to display the VPN screen. In the Choose A Configuration list (shown here), make sure the correct VPN is selected; if not, tap the one you want, putting a check mark next to it. Then move the VPN switch to the On position.

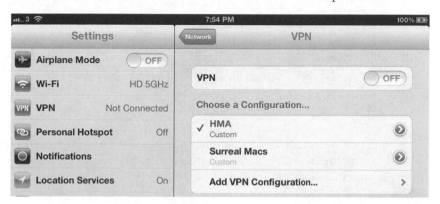

If the administrator set you up to authenticate yourself with a password, and you chose not to store the password in the VPN connection, you'll be prompted for your password. Enter it, and the iPad establishes the connection. The Status readout on the VPN screen shows the connection is active, as shown here, and the VPN indicator also appears in the status bar as a reminder you're using the VPN.

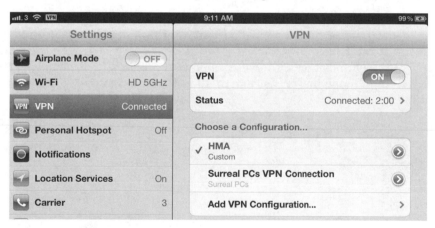

You can tap the Status readout to see the details of the connection, including your iPad's IP address, as shown next.

Once you've established the connection, you'll be able to work on the VPN. What exactly you'll be able to do depends on the permissions the administrator has granted you, but you'll typically be able to access your e-mail and shared information resources.

## Disconnect from a VPN

When you've finished using the VPN, close any files that you have been using, and then disconnect like this:

1. Press the Home button to reach the Home screen.
2. Tap the Settings icon to display the Settings screen.
3. If you have a single VPN set up, move the VPN switch on the Settings screen to the Off position. Otherwise, tap the VPN button to display the VPN screen, and then move the VPN switch on the VPN screen to the Off position.

# 6 Jailbreaking and Advanced Geekery

So far in this book, we've kept your iPad within the ecosystem that Apple has created for iOS devices—the iPad itself, the iPhone, and the iPod touch.

This ecosystem is what's known as a "walled garden"—an area that's tightly protected to help you have a safe computing experience in mostly pleasant surroundings. For example, in its normal state, iOS allows you to install only apps from the App Store, which are all approved by Apple. This helps you avoid installing apps that contain malware or that try to ship your credit card details to people who will use them vigorously until you get your bank to issue a cease-and-desist order.

To get outside this walled garden, you need to "jailbreak" your iPad.

We'll start this chapter by backing up your iPad's contents so that you can restore them if anything goes wrong during the jailbreak or other moves. Then we'll perform the jailbreak so that we can start performing advanced moves with your iPad.

Once your iPad is jailbroken, you'll learn how to find and install unapproved apps and back them up so that you can reinstall them later as needed. You'll connect to your iPad via SSH from your computer, explore your iPad's two partitions, and learn how to manage your files directly on the iPad. You'll also apply themes to make your iPad look different, make Wi-Fi–only apps run over 3G connections when necessary, and play console and arcade games under emulation on your iPad. You'll even get to control your iPad using your computer.

At the very end of the chapter, we'll put your iPad back in its Apple jail—but only if you want.

Let's get started.

## Project 38: Back Up Your iPad's Contents and Settings

Before you jailbreak your iPad (as described in the next project), back it up to make sure that your precious data and settings are safe. If necessary, you will then be able to restore your data and settings when needed.

To back up your iPad, follow these steps:

1. Connect your iPad to your computer via the USB cable.
2. If iTunes doesn't automatically display the iPad's control screens, click the iPad's entry in the Devices category in the Source list to display them.
3. If the Summary screen isn't displayed, click the Summary tab to display it.
4. In the Backup box, make sure the Back Up To This Computer option button is selected rather than the Back Up To iCloud option button.

DOUBLE GEEKERY

# Understand What an iPad Backup Contains

Before you use iTunes' feature for backing up your iPad, it's vital you understand what the backup includes and what it doesn't. Otherwise, if you need to restore your iPad from backup, you may not be able to restore all the files you need.

Your iPad can contain a huge amount of files—a 64GB iPad has around 57GB of space available to you—but most of the files will normally be either on your computer or in iCloud as well. For example, if you sync your music, video files, TV shows, and so on with your iPad, your computer still has these files—so your iPad backup doesn't need to include them.

So when you back up your iPad, iTunes syncs your calendars, contacts, notes, text messages, and settings, but not the media files or your iPad's firmware.

This means that if you create files in third-party apps on your iPad, you must copy them to your computer or to online storage to keep them safe, because backing up your iPad doesn't keep copies of them. If you have to erase your iPad's contents and settings and then restore the iPad from backup, these files won't be included.

5. If you want to encrypt the backup, follow these substeps:
   a. Select the Encrypt Local Backup check box. iTunes displays the Set Password dialog box. The next illustration shows the Mac version of the Set Password dialog box.

 If you plan to jailbreak your iPad, don't encrypt the backup, because you'll most likely need to remove the encryption in order to perform the jailbreak.

   b. Type a password in the Password box and the Verify Password box.
   c. On the Mac, select the Remember This Password In My Keychain check box if you want OS X to store your password in the Keychain, so that it can enter the password automatically for you.
   d. Click the Set Password button. iTunes starts backing up the iPad.
6. If you didn't start the backup from the Set Password dialog box, start it by right-clicking (or CTRL-clicking on the Mac) your iPad's entry in the Devices category in the Source list, and then clicking the Back Up item on the context menu.

# Project 39: Jailbreak Your iPad on Windows

After backing up your iPad as described in the previous project, you're ready to jailbreak it. Jailbreaking your iPad lets it get out of the walled garden that Apple has penned it in and enables you to install third-party apps and customizations that haven't passed Apple's stringent approvals process.

At this writing, there are several tools you can use to jailbreak your iPad. Some tools, and some versions of tools, work only with particular models of iPad, so make sure you choose a tool and version that will work with the iPad model you have. The best jailbreaking tool at the moment for the iPad is Absinthe, which I'll show you how to use in this project.

 The Redmond Pie website (www.redmondpie.com) is a good place to find out about jailbreaking tools and techniques. You can also find plenty of other sites by searching using terms such as **jailbreak iPad 3** or **jailbreak new iPad**.

To jailbreak your iPad using Absinthe on Windows, follow these steps:

1.  Locate and download the appropriate version of Absinthe. For example, go to a site such as Redmond Pie (www.redmondpie.com) and search for Absinthe.

 When downloading Absinthe, make sure you click the Download link for Absinthe rather than any button temptingly marked Download. Such buttons may be for other software that you likely don't want.

2.  Unzip the Absinthe Zip file. For example, in Windows Explorer, use the Extract All Files command.

 **DOUBLE GEEKERY**

## Understand Tethered Jailbreaks and Untethered Jailbreaks

Depending on your iPad model and the version of iOS it's running, you may be able to choose between a tethered jailbreak and an untethered jailbreak:

*   **Tethered jailbreak**   You must connect the iPad to your computer and use the jailbreaking application each time you want to restart the iPad in jailbroken mode. We'll perform a tethered jailbreak in the next project.
*   **Untethered jailbreak**   After you've jailbroken the iPad, you can restart it without connecting it to your computer. We'll perform an untethered jailbreak in this project.

As you can see, an untethered jailbreak is far preferable—so you'll probably want one if it's available for your iPad and version of iOS. But for some iPad models, versions of iOS, and computer operating systems, you may find that only tethered jailbreaks are available.

3. Double-click the Absinthe application file to open it. At this point, Windows normally displays the Open File – Security Warning dialog box, shown here, because the file doesn't have a valid digital signature. This is normal for unofficial software such as this.

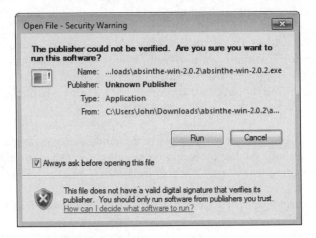

4. Click the Run button. You'll see a Command Prompt window as Absinthe extracts the files it needs. The Command Prompt window then closes, and you'll see a new Absinthe folder in the folder from which you ran the application file.
5. Double-click the new Absinthe folder to open it.
6. If there's a readme.txt file, double-click to open it in Notepad or your default text editor so that you can read the latest information.
7. Double-click the Absinthe application file in the new Absinthe folder to run Absinthe. When you do this, Windows normally displays a User Account Control dialog box, as shown here, asking if you want to allow this program from an unknown publisher to make changes to your computer.

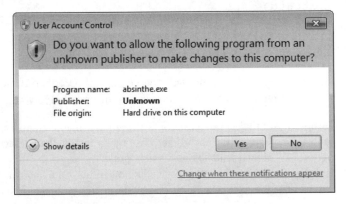

8. Click the Yes button. Next, you'll see the first Absinthe screen, which prompts you to plug in your iDevice.
9. Connect your iPad to your PC. When Absinthe detects your iPad, it makes the Jailbreak button available, as shown next.

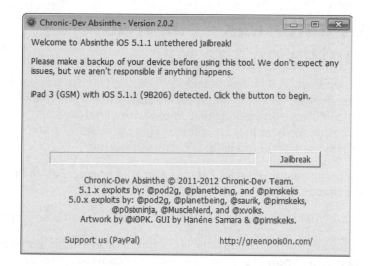

 If Absinthe displays an Error dialog box warning that your iPad has a backup password set, you must use iTunes to remove the backup password before you can proceed. In iTunes, click the iPad's entry in the Devices category in the Source list, click the Summary tab, and then clear the Encrypt Local Backup check box. Type your password in the Enter Password dialog box and click the OK button. iTunes then creates an unencrypted backup of your iPad.

10. Click the Jailbreak button to start the jailbreaking process. Absinthe shows a progress bar as it works (see the next illustration), and you'll see your iPad's screen indicating what's happening—for example, you'll see the Restore In Progress message.

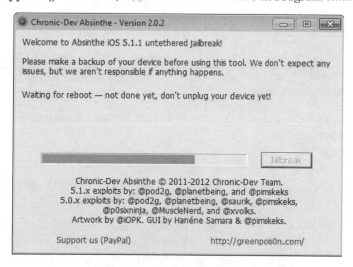

11. When the Absinthe screen shows the message "Done, enjoy!", click the Close button (the × button) to close Absinthe.

Your iPad is now jailbroken, and you can use Cydia as explained in Project 41.

# Project 40: Jailbreak Your iPad Using Absinthe on the Mac

After backing up your iPad as described in Project 38, you can use your Mac to jailbreak it. Jailbreaking lets your iPad escape Apple's walled garden and allows you to install third-party apps and customizations that Apple hasn't approved.

At this writing, the best tool for jailbreaking your iPad on a Mac is Absinthe, which lets you perform an untethered jailbreak.

 Before performing a jailbreak, back up your iPad as described in Project 38, earlier in this chapter.

To jailbreak your iPad using Absinthe and a Mac, follow these steps:

1. Locate and download the appropriate version of Absinthe. For example, go to a site such as Redmond Pie (www.redmondpie.com) and search for Absinthe.

 When downloading Absinthe, make sure you click the Download link for Absinthe rather than any button temptingly marked Download. Such buttons may be for other software that you likely don't want.

2. If OS X doesn't automatically mount the Absinthe disk image and open a Finder window displaying its contents, mount the disk image yourself. For example, click the Downloads icon on the Dock, and then click the Absinthe disk image on the Downloads stack. OS X displays a Finder window showing the contents of the disk image.
3. If there's a readme.txt file, double-click to open it in TextEdit or your default text editor so that you can read the latest information.
4. Double-click the Absinthe application to launch Absinthe.

 If you plan to run Absinthe frequently, drag the Absinthe icon to your Applications folder. If you plan to run it only once or twice, it's easier to run it from your Downloads folder.

5. If OS X double-checks that you want to run Absinthe, as shown here, click the Open button.

6. Absinthe displays its first screen, which prompts you to plug in your iDevice.

7. Connect your iPad to your Mac. When Absinthe detects your iPad, it makes the Jailbreak button available, as shown here.

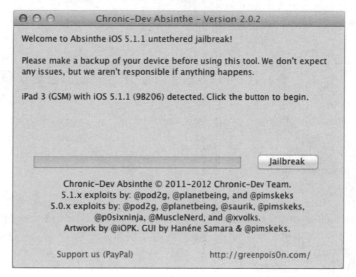

 If Absinthe displays an Error dialog box warning that your iPad has a backup password set, you must use iTunes to remove the backup password before you can proceed. In iTunes, click the iPad's entry in the Devices category in the Source list, click the Summary tab, and then clear the Encrypt Local Backup check box. Type your password in the Enter Password dialog box and click the OK button. iTunes then creates an unencrypted backup of your iPad.

8. Click the Jailbreak button to start the jailbreaking process. Absinthe shows a progress bar as it works (see the next illustration), and you'll see your iPad's screen indicating what's happening: a restore operation, a reboot, and so on.

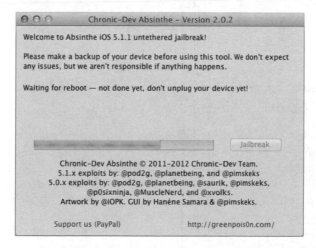

9. When the Absinthe screen shows the message "Done, enjoy!", CTRL-click or right-click the Absinthe icon on the Dock, and then click Quit to quit Absinthe.

Your iPad is now jailbroken, and you can use Cydia as explained in Project 41.

# Project 41: Find and Install Unapproved Apps

As you know, the official source for apps for your iPad is Apple's App Store, which you can access either using iTunes on your computer or using the App Store app on your iPad. The App Store has more than a half-million apps available at this writing, with more being added each day—so there's a wide variety you can choose from.

These are all apps that Apple has approved as being suitable for the iOS devices—the iPad, the iPhone, and the iPod touch.

To gain approval, an app not only must be programmed following Apple's guidelines but must also not violate any of its rules about content. For example, an app containing hardcore adult content won't get approved even if its coding is immaculate. Nor will an app that uses the underlying parts of iOS in ways that Apple doesn't permit, no matter how ingenious or useful the app is.

Because of this approval process, some developers choose not to submit their apps to the App Store. Instead, they make them available through other sources.

At this writing, Cydia is the main tool for installing unapproved apps on iOS devices. After you install it on a jailbroken iPad, Cydia gives you access to a wide range of repositories for iOS software. This software includes both free apps and paid apps that you buy through the Cydia Store.

 This project assumes you've jailbroken your iPad and installed Cydia as described in the previous two projects. If not, go back and do so. If you used a tethered jailbreak rather than an untethered jailbreak, use the jailbreaking software to boot into the jailbroken state.

 DOUBLE GEEKERY

## Understand Why Cydia Needs to "Prepare" the File System

Your iPad obviously has a fully functional file system—if it didn't, it wouldn't be running. So you may well wonder why Cydia needs to "prepare" the file system.

What's happening here is that Cydia is moving apps and various other files from the OS partition to the Media partition and replacing them with symbolic links so that they'll continue to work. By moving the apps, Cydia frees up space on the OS partition, which enables you to put other apps on it.

We'll get into the details of the file system in Project 44.

## Open Cydia

To open Cydia, tap the Cydia icon on one of your Home screens, just like any other app, as shown here.

The first time you run Cydia, you'll see the Preparing Filesystem message for a few minutes while Cydia gets itself into shape. When Cydia finishes preparing the file system, it automatically quits.

Tap the Cydia icon to restart the app. Cydia displays the Who Are You? screen (shown in Figure 6-1), which lets you choose your type of Cydia usage:

- **User**   Tap this button to make apps, tweaks, and themes available. This is usually the best choice to start with.
- **Hacker**   Tap this button to make apps, tweaks, themes, and command-line tools available.
- **Developer**   Tap this button to make all the Cydia apps and utilities available.

After tapping the appropriate button, tap the Done button. You'll then see the Cydia app's interface, which consists of six screens, among which you switch by tapping the tabs at the bottom of the screen. Figure 6-2 shows the Cydia screen, which you'll see at first.

## Find Apps in Cydia

You can find apps in Cydia by using the Cydia screen, the Sections screen, the Changes screen, and the Search screen, which you access by tapping the tabs at the bottom of the screen.

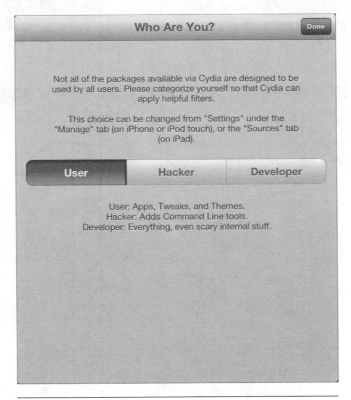

**FIGURE 6-1** On the Who Are You? screen, tap the User button, the Hacker button, or the Developer button, as appropriate, and then tap the Done button.

- **Cydia** From this screen, you can quickly access the Featured list, the Themes list, and the Cydia Store. You can also see the User Guides list, the Extensions Useful On iPad list, and the Products Designed For iPad list.
- **Sections** Tap this tab to display a screen containing a list of different categories (sections) of apps and utilities, as shown in the upper part of Figure 6-3. Tap a category to display its contents, as shown in the lower part of Figure 6-3.

 In the Cydia listings, item names that appear in black are free. Item names that appear in blue are pay software. For pay software, you can pay using either Amazon Payments or PayPal.

- **Changes** Tap this tab to display the Changes screen (shown in the upper part of Figure 6-4), which provides a list of the latest software.
- **Installed** Tap this tab to display the apps and packages you've installed using Cydia. From here, you can remove an app.

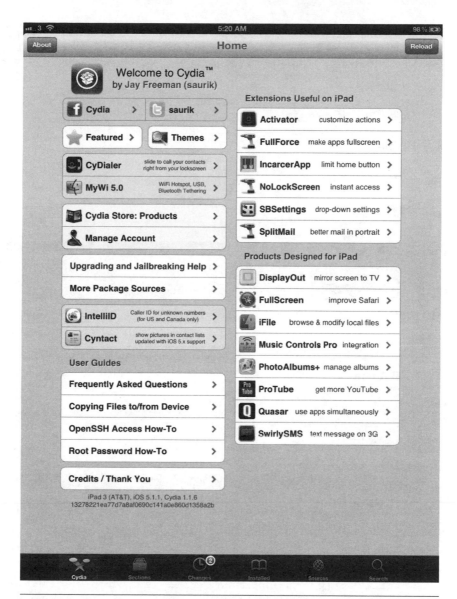

**FIGURE 6-2**   Cydia's interface consists of six main screens. You switch among the screens by tapping the tab buttons at the bottom of the screen.

- **Sources**   Tap this tab to display a list of the sources of the apps you've installed using Cydia.
- **Search**   Tap this tab to display the Search screen (shown in the lower part of Figure 6-4). You can then type a search term to find matches.

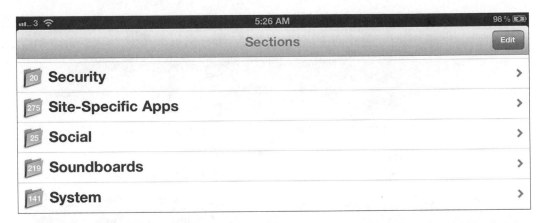

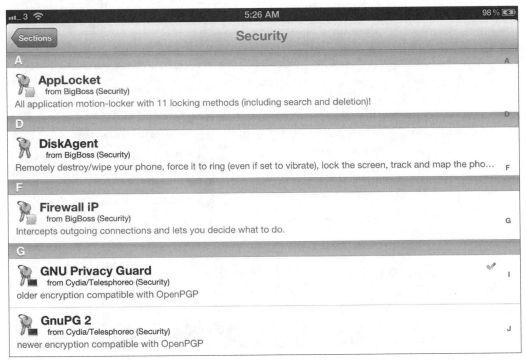

**FIGURE 6-3**   Use the Sections screen (above) to browse the available software by categories. Tap a category to display its contents (below).

## Install an App with Cydia

When you've found an app that interests you, tap its button to display the Details screen (shown in Figure 6-5). You can then tap the Install button to install the app if it's free or the Purchase button to buy the app if it's not free.

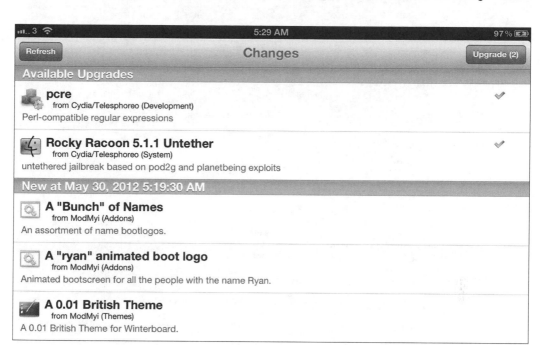

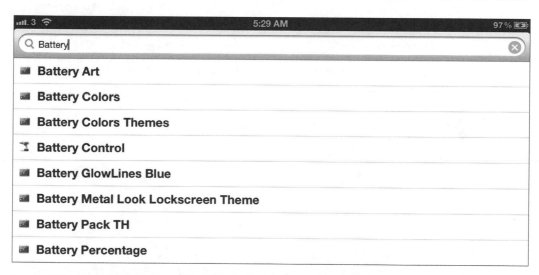

**FIGURE 6-4**   The Changes screen (above) lists the latest software. The Search screen (below) lets you search by keyword.

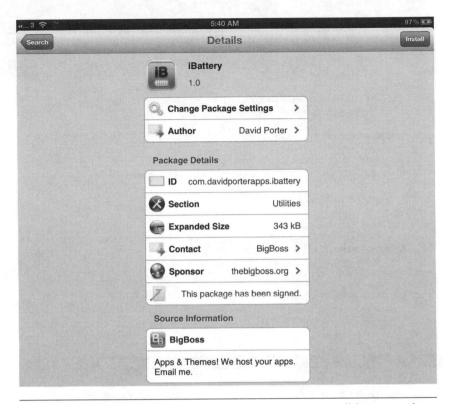

**FIGURE 6-5** On the Details screen for an app, tap the Install button or the Purchase button.

In the Confirm dialog box that appears (shown here), tap the Confirm button to go ahead with the installation.

You'll then see the installer run. When the installer displays the Complete screen, as shown in Figure 6-6, tap the Return To Cydia button to close the installer and return to Cydia.

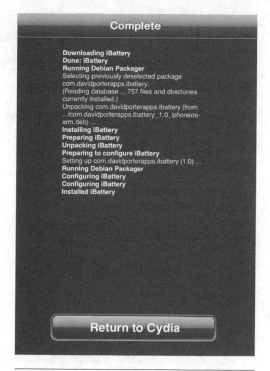

**FIGURE 6-6**   The installer downloads the app's file and then installs it. When the installation process finishes, tap the Return To Cydia button.

 After installing some apps, you may need to restart Springboard, the iOS feature that runs the Home screen. If so, the installer displays a Restart Springboard button in place of the Return To Cydia button.

## Run an App You've Installed with Cydia

After installing an app with Cydia, the app appears on one of your iPad's Home screens, just like when you install an app from the App Store.

Tap the app's icon to open the app. Figure 6-7 shows BatteryInfoLite, an app installed using Cydia.

 One difference between installing an app from the App Store and an app from Cydia is that you may need to restart your iPad to get a freshly installed Cydia app to work. If you used a tethered jailbreak, you'll need to connect your iPad to your computer and use the jailbreaking tool to perform the restart.

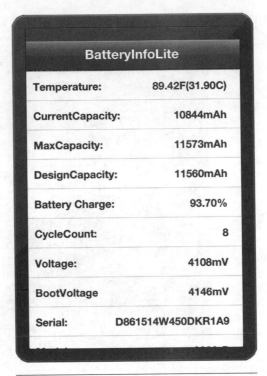

| BatteryInfoLite | |
|---|---|
| Temperature: | 89.42F(31.90C) |
| CurrentCapacity: | 10844mAh |
| MaxCapacity: | 11573mAh |
| DesignCapacity: | 11560mAh |
| Battery Charge: | 93.70% |
| CycleCount: | 8 |
| Voltage: | 4108mV |
| BootVoltage | 4146mV |
| Serial: | D861514W450DKR1A9 |

**FIGURE 6-7**    After you install an app
using Cydia, tap its icon on the Home screen
to launch the app.

## Uninstall an App You've Installed with Cydia

To uninstall an app you've installed with Cydia, follow these steps:

1. From the Home screen, tap the Cydia icon to launch Cydia.
2. Tap the Installed tab to display the Installed screen (see Figure 6-8).
3. Tap the button for the app you want to remove. Cydia displays the Details screen for the app (see Figure 6-9).
4. Tap the Remove button. Cydia displays the Confirm dialog box.
5. Tap the Confirm button. Cydia runs the installer, which uninstalls the app.
6. Tap the Return To Cydia button to return to Cydia.

# Project 42: Back Up Your Jailbroken iPad

If you've followed through the previous two projects, you've now jailbroken your iPad, installed some unapproved apps on it, and are enjoying using them.

Now for the bad news: If you update your iPad's firmware to a new version, you may well lose the jailbroken apps. This is because iTunes doesn't include the folders

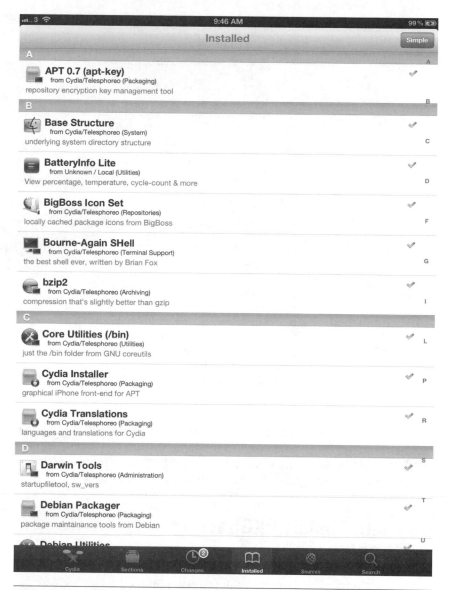

**FIGURE 6-8**   On the Installed screen, tap the button for the app you want to remove.

that contain the jailbroken apps in the backup—so when it restores your iPad after the firmware upgrade, those apps won't be there.

This doesn't mean you can't update your iPad—it just means that you need to back up your jailbroken apps so that you can restore them after a firmware upgrade.

In this project, we'll use PKGBackup to back up your iPad's jailbroken apps and to restore them. PKGBackup is a paid app that costs $7.99 at this writing.

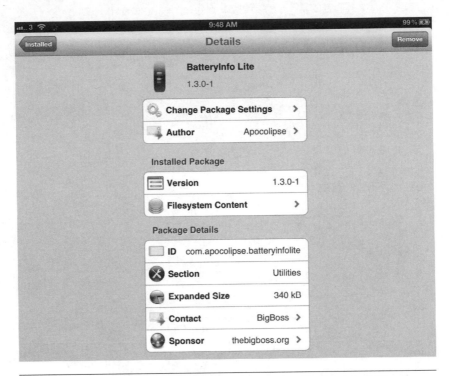

**FIGURE 6-9** On the Details screen for the app, tap the Remove button for the app you want to remove.

 Instead of using PKGBackup or a similar app, you can back up your jailbroken files manually if you prefer. See Project 43 for instructions on connecting to your iPad via Secure Shell from your computer and Project 44 for instructions on exploring your iPad's file system to find the files you need to back up.

## Buy and Install PKGBackup

To get PKGBackup, follow these general steps:

1. Run Cydia as explained in the previous project.
2. Tap the Cydia Store button to display the Cydia Store screen.
3. Locate PKGBackup, and then tap its button to display the Details screen.
4. Tap the Purchase button, and follow through the payment process. After your payment goes through, the Install button takes the place of the Purchase button.
5. Tap the Install button to install PKGBackup.
6. In the Confirm dialog box, tap the Confirm button.
7. When the Complete screen appears, tap the Return To Cydia button.
8. Press the Home button to return to the Home screen.

# Run PKGBackup and Back Up Your Jailbroken Apps

After you install PKGBackup, run PKGBackup, choose settings, and back up your jailbroken apps. Follow these steps:

1. Tap the PKGBackup icon on the Home screen to launch the app.

 If your iPad displays the "PKGBackup" Would Like To Use Your Current Location dialog box, tap the Don't Allow button.

2. If PKGBackup displays the Apps & Packages Scans Disabled dialog box (shown here), follow these steps to configure PKGBackup:

   a. Tap the Settings button in the Apps & Package Scans Disabled dialog box to display the PKGBackup screen in the Settings app. Figure 6-10 shows the PKGBackup screen in Settings.

 If tapping the Settings button in the Apps & Package Scans Disabled dialog box doesn't display the Settings app, go to the Settings app manually. Press the Home button to display the Home screen, tap the Settings icon to open the Settings app, and then tap the PKGBackup button in the Extensions section, which you'll find just above the Apps list.

   b. In the At Startup box, set the Scan Applications switch, the Scan Packages switch, and the Automatic Backup switch to the On position.
   c. If you want to choose other settings, choose them. For example, in the Dialogs box, you can choose whether to confirm backups, whether to confirm restores, and whether to enter a backup memo (a note about what a particular backup contains).
   d. When you finish choosing settings, press the Home button twice to display the app-switching bar, and tap PKGBackup to display the app again.
3. At this point, you should be seeing the PKGBackup screen (shown on the left in Figure 6-11). Tap the Settings button (the cog wheel icon) in the upper-left corner to display the Settings screen (shown on the right in Figure 6-11).
4. In the Select Where To Store Your Data box, tap the Connect To Dropbox button. PKGBackup displays the Link Account screen (shown on the left in Figure 6-12), which you use to link your Dropbox account so that PKGBackup can store data in it.

 If you don't have a Dropbox account yet, tap the Create An Account link at the bottom of the Link Account screen to start one.

5. Tap the Email box and type the e-mail address you use for your Dropbox account.
6. Tap the Password box and type the password for your Dropbox account.

**FIGURE 6-10**    On the PKGBackup screen in the Settings app, set the Scan Applications switch, the Scan Packages switch, and the Automatic Backup switch to the On position. You can also choose which alerts and which dialog boxes to use.

7.  Tap the Link button. PKGBackup establishes the link, and then displays the Settings screen again.

8.  In the # Of Backups To Keep box, either enter a specific number of backups (for example, 5) or leave the default setting, 0, which allows an unlimited number of backups.

**FIGURE 6-11**   On the main PKGBackup screen (left), tap the Settings button (the cog wheel) to display the Settings screen (right).

 You may need to limit the number of backups to prevent PKGBackup loading your Dropbox account chock-full. But at first you may prefer to leave the 0 setting (for unlimited backups) until you see how much space each backup takes in Dropbox. You can then decide how many backups to keep, and enter that number in the # Of Backups To Keep box.

9. If you want to create a scheduled backup, use the controls in the Repeat Schedule section of the Settings screen to specify the details—for example, Daily at 03:00 or Weekly at 22:00 every Sunday.
10. Tap the Accept Changes button to save the changes you've made. PKGBackup returns you from the Settings screen to the main screen.
11. Tap the Do Backup button in the lower-right corner of the screen to run a backup now. You'll see a progress indicator as PKGBackup backs up your data. When PKGBackup displays the Backup Done dialog box, as shown on the right in Figure 6-12, tap the OK button.

## Restore Your Jailbroken Apps with PKGBackup

When you need to restore your jailbroken apps, follow these steps:

1. Tap the PKGBackup icon on the Home screen to launch PKGBackup.

 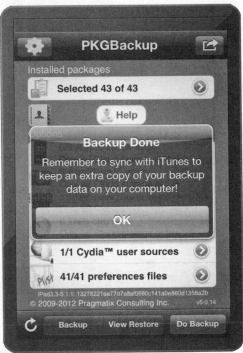

**FIGURE 6-12** On the Link Account screen (left), enter the details of your Dropbox account or start creating a new account to link to PKGBackup. On the main PKGBackup screen, you can then tap the Do Backup button in the lower-right corner. When the Backup Done dialog box (right) appears, tap the OK button.

 If the reason you need to restore your jailbroken apps is that an iPad firmware update has removed them, you will need to get PKGBackup up and running first. This means jailbreaking the iPad, installing Cydia, using Cydia to install PKGBackup, and then connecting PKGBackup to your Dropbox account so that it can access your backups.

2. Tap the View Restore button at the bottom of the screen to display the Restore screen (shown on the left in Figure 6-13).
3. Tap the Select Backup button to display the list of available backups (shown on the right in Figure 6-13).
4. Tap the backup you want to use.
5. Tap the Select button. PKGBackup displays its main screen with the backup's details.
6. Tap the Do Restore button. PKGBackup restores the apps and then displays the Restore Done dialog box (shown here).
7. Tap the Reboot button if you're ready to restart your iPad to make the changes take effect.

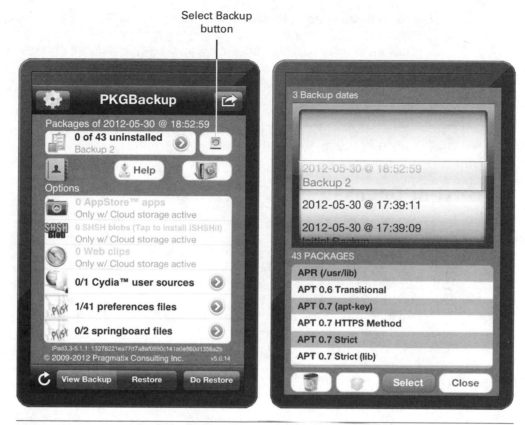

**FIGURE 6-13**   On the Restore screen (left), tap the Select Backup button to display the Device Backups screen (right). Tap the backup you want to use, and then tap the Select button.

# Project 43: Connect to Your iPad via SSH from Your Computer

In this project, we'll look at how to connect to your jailbroken iPad using Secure Shell (SSH). Connecting via SSH enables you to access your iPad's file system and transfer files back and forth.

 SSH is a networking protocol that you use to establish a secure connection between two computers. One computer is an SSH server, set up to accept connections from SSH clients. In this project, your iPad is the SSH server and your computer is the SSH client.

Here's what we'll do in this project:

- Install the free SSH app called OpenSSH on your iPad. This is the app that runs the SSH server on your iPad.

- Install the free utility app called SBSettings on your iPad. This app enables you to control Springboard settings and turn system services on and off. You need SBSettings to turn OpenSSH on and off, because OpenSSH doesn't have a user interface.
- Install the free SSH-capable application called FileZilla on your PC or Mac.
- Connect to your iPad.

After you've established the connection, as discussed in this project, you can explore your iPad's system partition and media partition (as discussed in Project 44).

## Install OpenSSH and SBSettings on Your iPad

To install OpenSSH and SBSettings on your iPad, follow these steps:

1. Tap the Cydia icon on the Home screen to launch Cydia.
2. Tap the Search button at the bottom of the screen to display the Search screen.
3. Search for **openssh**, and then tap its button to display the Details screen.
4. Tap the Install button. Your iPad displays the Confirm dialog box.
5. Tap the Confirm button to confirm the installation. Cydia then downloads OpenSSH and runs the installer.
6. When the installer displays the Complete screen, tap the Return To Cydia button to return to Cydia.
7. Tap the Cydia button at the bottom of the screen to display the Cydia Home screen.

 If the SBSettings button doesn't appear in the Extensions Useful On iPad list on the Cydia Home screen, tap the Search button at the bottom of the screen, and then search for **sbsettings.**

8. In the Extensions Useful On iPad list, tap to the SBSettings button to display the Details screen.
9. Tap the Install button to display the Confirm dialog box.
10. Tap the Confirm button to start the installation.
11. When the Complete screen appears, tap the Restart Springboard button to restart Springboard.

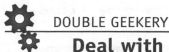

DOUBLE GEEKERY

## Deal with the "Cannot Locate Package" Message

If Cydia displays the "Note: Cannot Locate Package" message when you try to locate an app or utility, you may need to refresh your Cydia package catalog or add more package sources.

Start by refreshing your Cydia package catalog, because this will usually clear up the problem. Follow these steps:

1. Tap the Changes button at the bottom of the screen to display the Changes screen.
2. Tap the Refresh button in the upper-left corner. Cydia displays the Updating Databases message as it gets the latest package catalog information. You'll then see a Reloading Data message in the middle of the screen while Cydia loads the new information.

After Cydia loads the new information, try accessing the app or utility again. You should be able to find it this time—but if not, you'll need to add more package sources.

To add a package source, follow these steps:

1. In your web browser, search for the package source. This depends on the app or utility you're trying to install, so use that item's name in your search. At this writing, major package sources include the following three—but note that Cydia may already have some of these sources added already:

   - **BigBoss**  http://apt.thebigboss.org/repofiles/cydia/
   - **Cydia/Telesphoreo**  http://apt.saurik.com
   - **iJailbreak**  www.ijailbreak.com/repository/

2. In Cydia, tap the Sources button at the bottom of the screen to display the Sources screen (shown here).

*(continued)*

3. Tap the Edit button in the upper-right corner to turn on Edit mode. The Done button replaces the Edit button, as shown here.

4. Tap the Add button to display the Enter Cydia/APT URL dialog box (shown here).

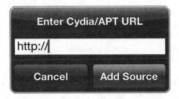

5. Type in the address for the package source you want to add.
6. Tap the Add Source button. You'll see the Updating Sources screen as Cydia updates its list of sources.
7. When the Complete screen appears, tap the Return To Cydia button to return to Cydia. You can now access packages from the package source you added.

# Install FileZilla on Your Computer

Next, download FileZilla and install it on your PC or Mac. Follow these steps:

1. Open your web browser and go to the FileZilla website, http://filezilla-project.org.
2. Download and install the latest version of the FileZilla Client for Windows or for Mac, as appropriate.
   - **Windows**   Run the file you download, and then follow through the setup routine. If you are an Administrator for your PC, you can choose whether to install FileZilla for all users or only for you. And on the Choose Components screen (shown next), choose which of the optional items to install. The Shell Extension component lets you drag files between Internet Explorer and FileZilla and is usually helpful; whether to install the Icon Sets, Language Files, and Desktop Icon components is up to you.

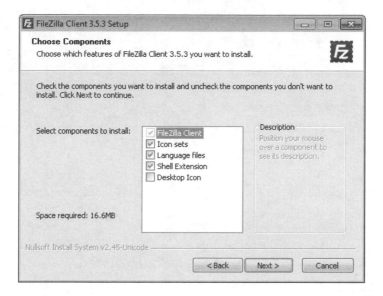

- **OS X**  Open the compressed file if Safari doesn't open it for you, and then drag the FileZilla application to the Applications folder. Leave the Applications folder open for now so that you can open FileZilla in the next step.
3. Open FileZilla:
   - **Windows**  On the Completing The FileZilla Client Setup screen of the installer, select the Start FileZilla Now check box, and then click the Finish button. In the future, choose Start | All Programs | FileZilla FTP Client | FileZilla.
   - **OS X**  In the Finder window showing the Applications folder, hold down OPTION and double-click the FileZilla icon. (Holding down OPTION as you double-click the icon makes the Finder window close as the application opens.)
4. If FileZilla displays the Welcome To FileZilla dialog box, click the OK button to close it. You'll then see the main FileZilla window. Figure 6-14 shows the Mac version.

## Use SBSettings to Find Your iPad's IP Address and Turn On SSH

Now run SBSettings and use it to find your iPad's IP address and to turn on SSH. Follow these steps:

1. From the Home screen, tap the SBSettings icon to launch SBSettings.
2. Press the Home button to display the Home screen again.

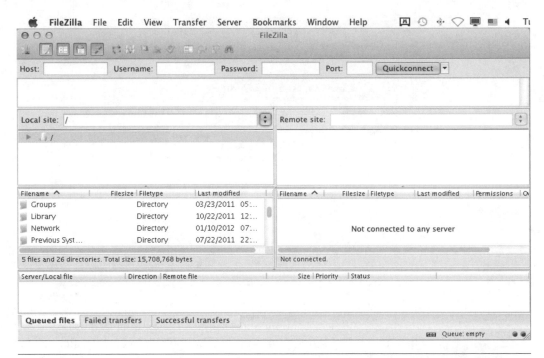

**FIGURE 6-14** From the main FileZilla window, you can quickly connect to your iPad via SSH.

3. Swipe your finger from left to right across the status bar at the top of the Home screen to display the SBSettings panel (shown here).

4. Note the IP address shown in the Wi-Fi IP Address readout near the bottom—for example, 10.0.0.43 or 192.168.1.153.

5. If the SSH icon on the right side of the second line is red (indicating that SSH is off), tap the icon. When the icon turns green, SSH is on.

6. Tap the Close button (the × button) at the upper-left corner to close the SBSettings panel.

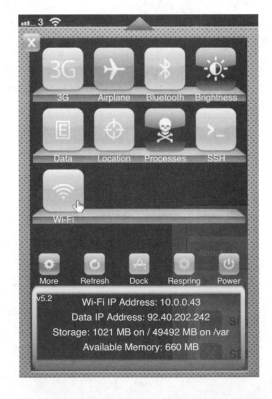

# Create the Connection in FileZilla

Now create the connection to your iPad in FileZilla. Follow these steps:

1. Click the Site Manager button at the left end of the toolbar, or choose File | Site Manager, to display the Site Manager dialog box (shown in Figure 6-15 with a site for the iPad being created).
2. Click the New Site button. FileZilla creates a new entry in the My Sites list in the Select Entry pane and names it New Site.
3. Type the name for the site—for example, **My iPad**—over the default name and press ENTER (on Windows) or RETURN (on the Mac) to apply the new name.
4. Click in the Host box and type the IP address you learned in the previous section.
5. Leave the Port box blank.
6. Open the Protocol drop-down list and choose SFTP – SSH File Transfer Protocol.
7. Open the Logon Type drop-down list and choose Normal.
8. Click in the User box and type **root**.

 The root user is the super-administrator on Unix-based systems.

9. Click in the Password box and type the standard password, **alpine**.

Leave the Site Manager open so that you're ready to connect as described in the next section.

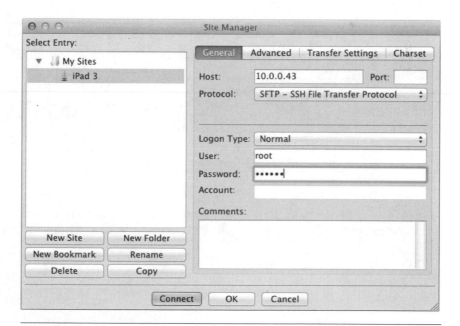

**FIGURE 6-15**   From FileZilla's Site Manager dialog box, you can create FTP sites, manage them, and connect to them.

## Connect to Your iPad

Now that you've created a site for your iPad in FileZilla, you can connect to it quickly. Follow these steps:

1. Make sure that your PC or Mac is connected to the same network as the iPad.

 Your PC or Mac doesn't necessarily have to be connected to the same *wireless* network as the iPad. If you have a network that combines wired and wireless portions, your computer can be connected to the wired portion and the iPad can be connected to the wireless portion.

2. In the Site Manager window in FileZilla, click your iPad's site, and then click the Connect button.

 If the password **alpine** doesn't work for connecting to your iPad, and you haven't set a different password by using a jailbroken utility, search online for other standard passwords to try. Use search terms such as **connect ipad ssh password**.

3. If you see the Unknown Host Key dialog box (shown here), which warns you that your computer doesn't know the SSH server's host key and so can't confirm its identify, verify the IP address on the Host line, and then click the OK button. If you're feeling trusting, you can select the Always Trust This Host, Add This Key To The Cache check box before clicking the OK button.

FileZilla then displays your iPad's file system in the right pane, as shown in Figure 6-16. The left pane shows the current folder on your PC or Mac.

You're now ready to explore your iPad's partitions. See the next project for details.

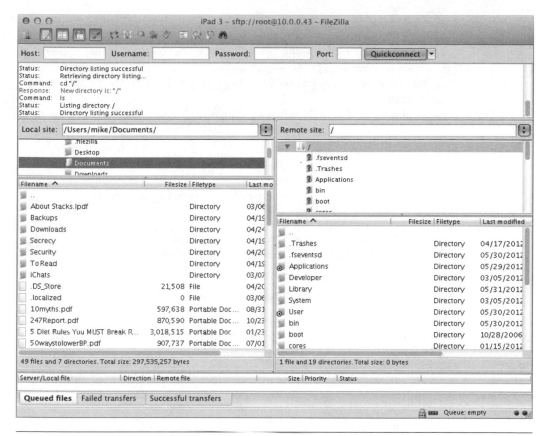

**FIGURE 6-16**   FileZilla displays your iPad's file system in the right pane.

DOUBLE GEEKERY

# Change Your iPad's Root Password

When you read in the main text that most iPads use the same root password, "alpine," did you think "Uh-oh..."?

As I'm sure you're all too well aware, a password known is a password blown. So if you want to be able to connect safely to your iPad via SSH, you need to change your iPad's root password.

Apple doesn't give you a way to do this, so you need to turn to jailbroken software. What you need is a terminal app called MobileTerminal—the iOS equivalent of Command Prompt (in Windows) or the Terminal utility (on the Mac), which you use to give the commands for changing the password.

Open Cydia, tap the Search tab at the bottom, and then search for **mobileterminal**. Tap the search result and read the description.

If the description says MobileTerminal is compatible with the version of iOS you're using (iOS 5 at this writing), tap the Install button to download and install it.

*(continued)*

If the description says MobileTerminal isn't compatible with that version of iOS, you'll need to use the external repository at iJailbreak.com. Add this repository as a package source by following the instructions in the sidebar titled "Deal with the 'Cannot Locate Package' Message," earlier in this project. Then search for **mobileterminal** again, and you'll be able to find and install the version from iJailbreak.com.

You can now use MobileTerminal to change your password. Follow these steps:

1. On the Home screen, tap the Terminal icon to launch MobileTerminal.
2. Type the following command:

    ```
    su root
    ```

3. Tap the Return button. MobileTerminal prompts you for the password.
4. Type the default password:

    ```
    alpine
    ```

5. Tap the Return button. You'll see another prompt, like this:

    ```
    iPad:/variable/mobile root#
    ```

6. Type the command for changing the password:

    ```
    passwd
    ```

7. Tap the Return button. MobileTerminal prompts you to enter the new password.
8. Type the new password you want to use.
9. Tap the Return button. MobileTerminal prompts you to retype the new password.
10. Type the new password again, and tap the Return button again. You'll then see the prompt again:

    ```
    iPad:/variable/mobile root#
    ```

11. Type the exit command:

    ```
    exit
    ```

12. Tap the Return button.
13. Press the Home button to return to the Home screen.

Your iPad is now using the new root password you set. From now on, you will need to use this password to connect via SSH.

# Project 44: Explore Your iPad's OS Partition and Media Partition

Once you've connected to your iPad via SSH, as described in the previous project, you're ready to explore its partitions. In this section, you learn about the two partitions, how to explore them, how to copy files to or from your iPad, and how to disconnect from the iPad when you finish.

 To follow this project, you must already have connected to your iPad via SSH, as described in Project 43.

# Understand the Two Partitions

Your iPad uses two partitions, the OS partition and the Media partition.

## OS Partition

The OS partition contains the files for iOS and other essential files.

This partition is relatively small—the size varies depending on the version of iOS, but for iOS 5 it is typically between 1GB and 2GB.

The OS partition is normally set to be read-only, and iOS is designed not to write to it. Under normal use, the only times the OS partition is written to is when you install firmware updates and when you restore the iPad.

Cydia makes the OS partition readable so that it can make changes to it. Cydia makes space for itself, plus extra space for apps that need to be on the OS partition, by moving the Applications folder (which contains the built-in apps) and various other folders from the OS partition to the Media partition. Cydia creates a symbolic link to the Applications folder and the other folders so that the apps still run as usual and iOS works normally.

 A *symbolic link* or *symlink* is a file that refers to another file or folder, much like a shortcut in Windows or an alias on the Mac.

## Media Partition

The Media partition contains your media files—songs, videos, podcasts, and so on. This partition takes up all the space left on your iPad after the chunk taken by the OS partition.

For example, say you have a 64GB iPad. Those 64 gigabytes are "marketing gigabytes" of a billion bytes each rather than true gigabytes of 1,073,741,824 bytes ($1024 \times 1024 \times 1024$ bytes), so the actual capacity is 59.6 true gigabytes. The OS partition takes up between 1GB and 2GB, leaving you with 57–58GB free on the Media partition.

To create space on the OS partition for itself and for any apps that can run only from the OS partition, Cydia moves various folders from the OS partition to the Media partition.

 DOUBLE GEEKERY

## Understand Why Some Apps Must Run from the OS Partition

Most apps that are written using normal coding practices can run either from the OS partition (as Apple intends) or from the Media partition using symbolic links. After you jailbreak your iPad and install Cydia on it, Cydia puts such apps on the Media partition, leaving space on the OS partition.

But some apps are *hard-coded*—they have the paths to the files they require written into the code, rather than using variables that point to where the files actually are. Hard-coded apps have to go on the OS partition, because they won't run correctly from the Media partition.

# Meet the Partitions and Folders in Your iPad's File System

After connecting to your iPad's file system with FileZilla, you'll see the folders it contains. In this section, we'll take a quick tour through the key folders. This example uses Windows screens, but the moves are the same on the Mac.

To take the tour, follow these steps:

1. Set up the FileZilla window along the lines of Figure 6-17 so that you have a good view of the Remote Site pane:
   - Choose View | Message Log, removing the check mark from the menu item, to hide the message log. This is the pane that shows the commands—for example, Status: Directory Listing Successful.
   - Choose View | Transfer Queue, removing the check mark from the menu item, to hide the transfer queue. This is the pane at the bottom of the FileZilla window that shows the progress of file transfers.
   - If the Remote Directory Tree pane isn't displayed, choose View | Remote Directory Tree (placing a check mark next to the command) to display it.
   - Drag the vertical bar between the Local Directory Tree pane and the Local Site pane (on the left) and the Remote Directory Tree pane and Remote Site pane so that the Remote Site pane is wide enough to show all its files. You may need to adjust the width of this pane while you're browsing. You may also need to change the width of the columns in the Remote Site pane by dragging the divisions between the column headings to the left or right. Alternatively, double-click the bar at the right side of a column heading to size the column automatically to fit its contents.

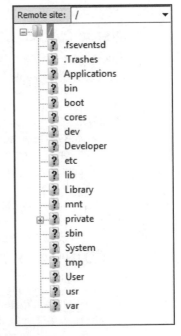

2. At the top of the Remote Directory Tree pane, you'll see the root directory, represented by a forward slash (/) as is the custom on Unix-based file systems. Click the root directory to display a list of its contents in the Remote Site pane, as shown in Figure 6-17.

3. If the root directory is collapsed, click the + sign or disclosure triangle to its left to expand it. You can also simply double-click the item. This illustration shows the list of folders you'll see.

 As in Windows Explorer, a + sign in a box to the left of a folder in FileZilla indicates that you can expand it, and a – sign indicates that you can collapse it. Similarly, on the Mac, a gray downward-pointing disclosure triangle indicates that you can expand it, and a gray right-pointing disclosure triangle indicates that you can collapse it.

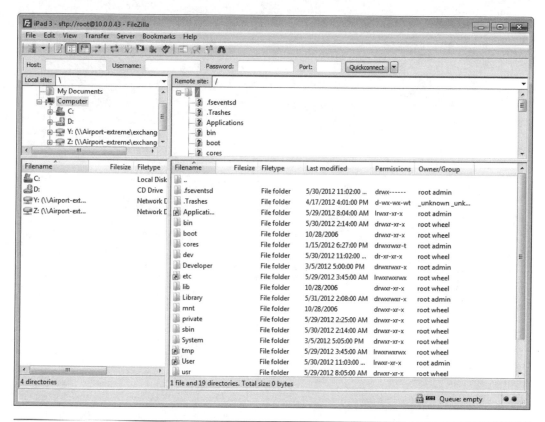

**FIGURE 6-17**  In the FileZilla window, hide the message log and the transfer queue, and then drag the main vertical divider bar to the left to give more space for the Remote Directory Tree pane (upper right) and the Remote Site pane (lower right).

4.  The OS partition is mounted at the root, so the contents of the OS partition appear directly inside the root folder—the Applications folder, the bin folder, the boot folder, and so on. The Media partition is mounted in the private folder, which we'll visit in a minute.

5.  In the iPad's normal, non-jailbroken state, the Applications folder contains the apps—Safari, Mail, Phone, and all the others. But as you read earlier, Cydia moves the contents of the Applications folder to give itself space on the OS partition. Try double-clicking the Applications folder. Instead of displaying the folder's contents, FileZilla follows the symlink and displays the contents of the /private/variable/ stash/Applications folder (see Figure 6-18), which is where Cydia has moved the Applications folder. This folder's name ends with a unique string of text—for example, Applications.PStTBz.

6.  With the Applications folder selected in the Remote Directory Tree pane, look at the Remote Site pane. Here, you can see the list of apps in the folder, including AppStore.app, Camera.app, and Cydia.app.

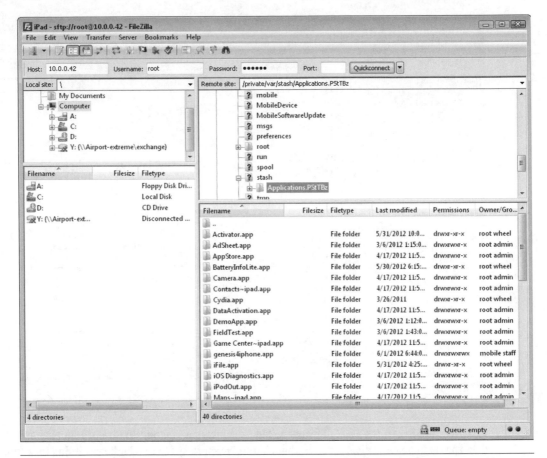

**FIGURE 6-18**   Double-clicking the Applications folder in a jailbroken iPad takes you to the /private/var/stash/Applications folder, where Cydia has stored the apps.

7. Scroll up the Remote Directory Tree pane until you can see the mobile folder (still under /private/var/), and then double-click it to expand it.
8. Now, let's find your songs. First, expand the Media folder under the mobile folder.
9. Next, expand the iTunes_Control folder under the Media folder.
10. Then expand the Music folder under the iTunes_Control folder.
11. Last, click one of the folders whose names begin with F—for example, the F00 folder. The list of song files it contains appears in the Remote Site pane (see Figure 6-19).

 Looking at the songs listed in the Remote Site pane, you'll notice that they have cryptic, four-character names—for example, BWYH.m4a or ZFID.mp3. iTunes and your iPad's Music app use these filenames, instead of the songs' titles (or mutations of them), to identify songs on the iPad uniquely.

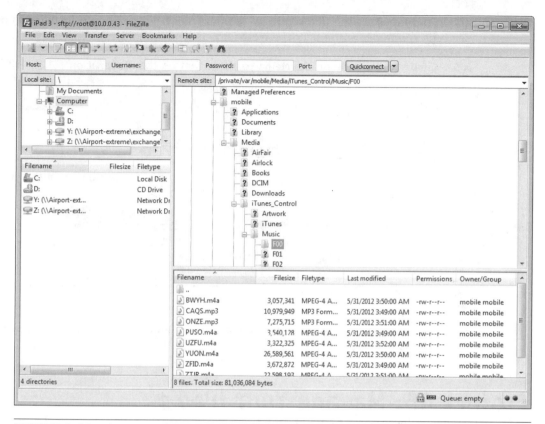

**FIGURE 6-19**   Open a subfolder of the /private/var/mobile/Media/iTunes_Control/Music/ folder to see the songs you've loaded on your iPad.

As you can see, your iPad has many other folders, but we'll stop the tour there for now. Leave the FileZilla window open if you want to copy or move files to or from your iPad, as described next.

# Copy Files to and from Your iPad

After connecting to your iPad with FileZilla, you can easily copy files to it or from it by dragging them between the Local Site pane and the Remote Site pane.

For storing your files on your iPad, you'll probably want to create one or more of your own folders rather than using the iPad's existing folders. To create a folder, follow these steps:

1. In the Remote Site pane, right-click (or CTRL-click on the Mac) the folder in which you want to create the new folder, and then click Create Directory on the context menu. FileZilla displays the Create Directory dialog box (shown here).

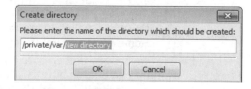

2. In the Please Enter The Name Of The Directory Which Should Be Created box, type the folder name over the New Directory placeholder.

 Create folders only on the Media partition, not on the OS partition.

3. Click the OK button.

## Disconnect FileZilla from Your iPad

When you finish FTP-ing to your iPad, click the Disconnect button (the button with the red ×) on the toolbar to disconnect from your iPad.

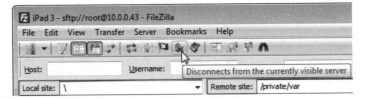

 You can also disconnect by choosing Server | Disconnect or by pressing CTRL-D (on Windows) or ⌘-D (on the Mac).

# Project 45: Manage Your iPad's Files—on Your iPad Itself

If you use your iPad as your main computer, you'll probably want to be able to manage the iPad's file system directly rather than having to work through FTP from your computer. You can manage the file system by using an app such as iFile. This app is shareware, so you can try it and see how you like it before paying.

 iFile and similar file-management apps are especially useful when you're running out of space on your iPad and you need to remove some files quickly to make room for others.

## Install iFile on Your iPad

To install iFile on your iPad, follow these steps:

1. Tap the Cydia icon on the Home screen to launch Cydia.

 Before searching for iFile, look at the Products Designed For iPad list on the Cydia Home screen. If you find an iFile button, tap it to display the Details screen.

2. Tap the Search button at the bottom of the screen to display the Search screen.
3. Search for **ifile**, and then tap its button to display the Details screen.

4. Tap the Install button. Your iPad displays the Confirm dialog box.
5. Tap the Confirm button to confirm the installation. Cydia then downloads iFile and runs the installer.
6. When the installer displays the Complete screen, tap the Return To Cydia button to return to Cydia.

## Manage Your iPad's Files with iFile

Now press the Home button to display the Home screen, and then tap the iFile icon to launch iFile.

You can use iFile in either landscape orientation or portrait orientation. Usually, landscape orientation is easier, because there's space on the left to display the sidebar, the main navigational tool (see Figure 6-20). In portrait orientation, the sidebar doesn't appear until you tap the Sidebar button at the upper-left corner of the screen, making the sidebar appear as a pop-up panel.

iFile is pretty straightforward to use. Following are the five operations you're likely to need the most.

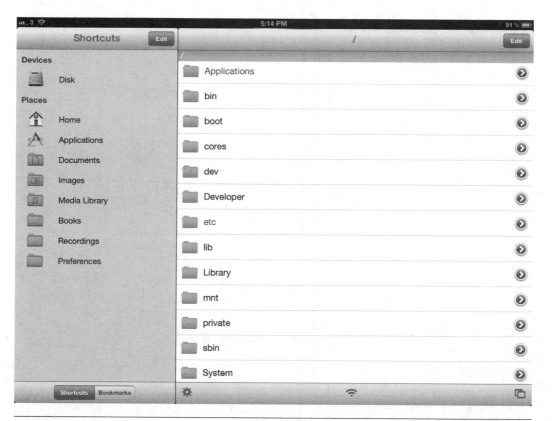

**FIGURE 6-20**  In landscape orientation, the sidebar appears on the left, and you can navigate quickly among the devices in the Devices list and the places in the Places list.

- **Navigate to a folder**  In the Shortcuts list, tap the Disk icon in the Devices category if you want to display the root folder. Otherwise, tap one of the places in the Places list to display that place. For example, tap the Home icon in the Places list to display the contents of the /var/mobile/ folder, which acts as your home folder on the iPad.
- **Navigate to a file**  Tap the folder that contains the file to display the folder's contents.
- **Open a file**  Tap the file to display a pop-up panel containing a list of the apps that can open the file, and then tap the app you want to use.
- **Manipulate one or more files**  Navigate to the folder that contains the files, and then tap the Edit button in the upper-right corner of the screen to turn on Edit mode. A selection button appears to the left of each file, and a bar of action icons appears at the bottom of the screen (see Figure 6-21). Tap the selection button for each file you want to affect, and then tap the appropriate action icon. For example, tap the Trash icon to delete the files. Tap the Done button when you finish using Edit mode.

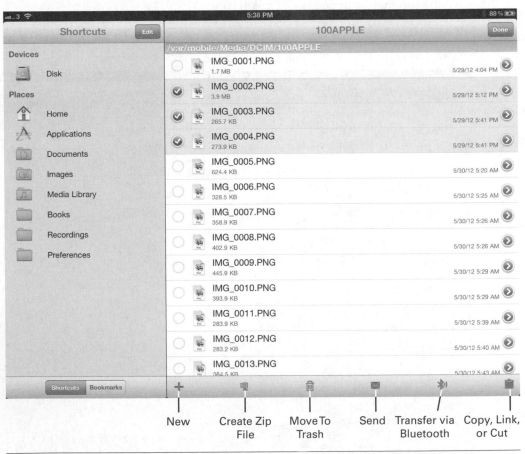

**FIGURE 6-21**  In Edit mode, use the selection buttons to the left of the filenames to select the files you want to manipulate, and then tap the appropriate action icon on the bar at the bottom of the screen.

**FIGURE 6-22** Select the Directory item on the Type button in the Attributes list in the New dialog box to create a new folder. You can also create a new file or a new symbolic link by tapping the Type button and then using the Type dialog box to choose the item.

- **Create a new folder** Tap the Edit button to turn on Edit mode, and then tap the New button to display the New dialog box (see Figure 6-22). Type the name in the Name box, make sure Directory is selected on the Type button in the Attributes list, and then tap the Create button.

# Project 46: Control Your iPad from Your Mac or PC

Controlling your PC or Mac from your iPad is great—but there may be times when you want to turn the tables and control your iPad from your PC or Mac. This project shows you how to do so by installing a VNC server on your iPad and connecting to it using a VNC client on your computer.

This project is mostly fun, but it can be handy when you use your iPad as your main computer and you need to be able to work quickly on it using another computer.

 Your iPad must be jailbroken for you to control it remotely as described here.

To control your iPad from your computer, you need to take the following steps:

- Install the Veency app on your iPad.
- Configure Veency to accept incoming connections.
- Install a VNC client on your computer.
- Connect your computer's VNC client to your iPad.

Let's take it from the top.

## Install the Veency App on Your iPad

First, install the Veency app on your iPad. Follow these steps:

1. Run Cydia by tapping the Cydia icon on the Home screen.
2. Tap the Search button to display the Search screen.
3. Start typing **Veency** until you get a narrow enough list of matches.
4. Tap the Veency button to display the Details screen for Veency.
5. Tap the Install button. Cydia displays the Confirm dialog box.
6. Tap the Confirm button to set the installation running.
7. When the Complete screen appears, tap the Restart Springboard button to restart Springboard.

## Configure Veency to Accept Incoming Connections

After Springboard restarts, drag the slider to unlock your iPad, and type your passcode if you're using one. When your iPad displays the Home screen again, follow these steps to configure Veency to accept incoming connections:

1. Tap the Settings icon to display the Settings screen.
2. Scroll down to the Extensions section, and then tap the Veency button to display the Veency screen (shown here).

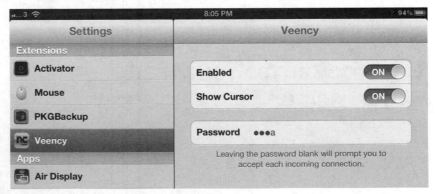

3. Set the Enabled switch to the On position.
4. Set the Show Cursor switch to the On position.
5. Tap the Password field and type the password you will use.
6. Press the Home button to display the Home screen again.

# Install a VNC Client

Next, you need to install a VNC client on your PC or Mac. This section recommends two VNC client programs for the PC and two VNC client applications for the Mac.

## Install and Run RealVNC on Windows

Many different VNC clients are available for Windows, but a good one to start with is RealVNC. This program comes in several different editions, of which two are good for our purposes here:

- **RealVNC Free Edition**  This version is free and works well, but it cannot adapt the screen resolution.

 If you have the New iPad, you'll do better with a VNC client program that can display an adapted screen resolution—otherwise, the iPad's resolution is likely to be too high to fit on your computer's display all at once. RealVNC Personal Edition can reduce the screen resolution, while RealVNC Free Edition cannot.

- **RealVNC Personal Edition**  This version costs $30. It has many more features than the Free Edition, but the crucial feature is Desktop Scaling—the ability to display the VNC server's desktop at a different size than it actually is. You can try the Personal Edition for free before paying for it.

You can download either edition from http://realvnc.com/products/download .html. Choose the Executable file rather than the Zip Archive file.

After downloading the file, double-click it to run the VNC Setup Wizard. Setup is straightforward, with just a couple of decisions to make:

- **Select Components**  On the Select Components screen (shown here), you can choose whether to install the VNC Server, the VNC Viewer, or both. Normally, you'll want to install only the VNC Viewer, so clear the VNC Server check box.

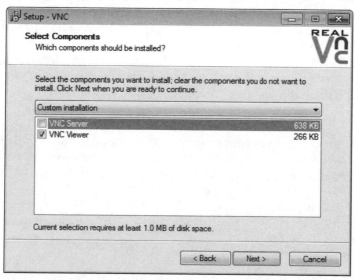

- **Select Additional Tasks**   On the Select Additional Tasks screen, clear the Create A VNC Viewer Desktop Icon check box unless you want an icon for VNC Viewer on your Desktop. Similarly, clear the Create A VNC Viewer Quick Launch Icon check box unless you want an icon on your Quick Launch toolbar.

When the Completing The VNC Setup Wizard screen appears, click the Finish button. You can then launch VNC from the Start menu—choose Start | All Programs | RealVNC | VNC Viewer—or from the Desktop icon or Quick Launch toolbar icon if you allowed the Wizard to create either.

## Install and Run a VNC Client Application on the Mac

You can get various different VNC clients for the Mac, but at this writing these two are your best bets:

- **Chicken of the VNC**   This app is free, and you can download it from SourceForge .net (http://sourceforge.net/projects/cotvnc/files/latest/download). Chicken of the VNC is a capable VNC client, but it can't adapt the screen resolution.

If you have the New iPad, you'll do better with a VNC client program that can display an adapted screen resolution to make the iPad's high-resolution screen fit on your computer's screen. JollysFastVNC can reduce the screen resolution, but Chicken of the VNC cannot.

- **JollysFastVNC**   This app is a full-featured VNC client whose features include adapting the screen resolution. JollysFastVNC costs $19.99. The easiest place to get it is the Mac App Store—but if you do so, you must pay immediately. If you want to try JollysFastVNC without paying until you know whether it suits you, go to the developer's website, www.jinx.de.

After downloading Chicken of the VNC or the trial version of JollysFastVNC, open the disk image file if OS X doesn't open it automatically for you. For example, click the Downloads icon on the Dock to display the Downloads stack, and then click the disk image file you downloaded.

In the Finder window showing the contents of the disk image, click the Chicken of the VNC icon or the JollysFastVNC icon and drag it to your Applications folder. You can then click the app's icon in the Applications folder to launch the application, or launch it using Launchpad if you find that more convenient.

You can also run Chicken of the VNC or JollysFastVNC directly from the disk image if you want: Simply double-click the application's icon. But if you plan to use the application regularly, add it to your Applications folder.

When you buy JollysFastVNC from the Mac App Store, your Mac automatically installs it. You can then launch JollysFastVNC by clicking its icon on the Launchpad screen.

# Connect to Your iPad via VNC

With your VNC client installed, you can connect to your iPad via VNC.

 To get a VNC connection working, you may need to connect your computer to the same wireless network as your iPad. If your computer is on a wired part of the same network, the VNC connection may not work.

## Connect to Your iPad via VNC with RealVNC on Windows

To connect to your iPad using RealVNC, follow these steps:

1. Choose Start | All Programs | RealVNC | VNC Viewer to launch VNC Viewer. You'll see the VNC Viewer window, shown here with settings chosen.
2. Type your iPad's IP address in the VNC Server box.
3. In the Encryption drop-down list, select the Let VNC Server Choose item.

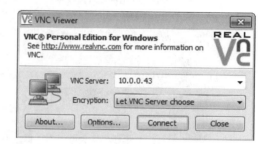

4. If you're using RealVNC Personal Edition rather than RealVNC Free Edition, click the Options button to display the Options dialog box (shown here). In the Display area, select the Scale To Window Size check box. Then click the OK button.

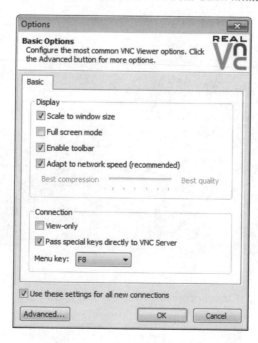

5. Click the Connect button. RealVNC then displays the Authentication Credentials dialog box (shown here).

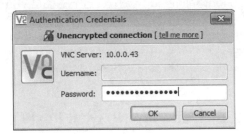

6. Type your VNC password in the Password text box.
7. Click the OK button. RealVNC establishes the connection and displays your iPad's screen in a window (see Figure 6-23).

**FIGURE 6-23** When RealVNC displays your iPad's screen, you can get to work. Move the mouse pointer to the top of the window when you need to display the toolbar.

When you're ready to end your VNC session, either simply click the Close button (the × button at the right end of the window's title bar) or move the mouse pointer to the top of the screen and click the Close Connection button on the toolbar that appears.

## Connect to Your iPad with Chicken of the VNC on the Mac

To connect to your iPad with Chicken of the VNC, follow these steps:

1. Launch Chicken of the VNC. For example, click the Launchpad icon on the Dock, and then click the Chicken of the VNC icon on the Launchpad screen. Chicken of the VNC displays the VNC Login dialog box (shown here).

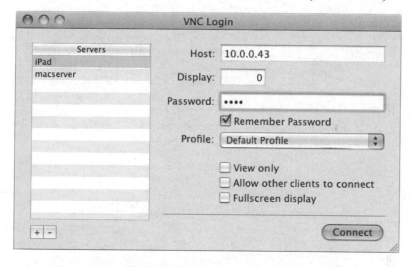

2. Click the + button in the lower-left corner to add a new entry to the Servers list.
3. Type the name for the connection—for example, **iPad**.
4. Type the iPad's IP address in the Host box.
5. Type the password in the Password box.
6. Select the Remember Password check box if you want to store the password.
7. Click the Connect button. Chicken of the VNC connects to your iPad, and your iPad's screen appears in the VNC window. You can start using your iPad from your Mac.

When you're ready to end your VNC session, choose Chicken of the VNC | Quit Chicken of the VNC.

## Connect to Your iPad with JollysFastVNC on the Mac

To connect to your iPad with JollysFastVNC, follow these steps:

1. Launch JollysFastVNC. For example, click the Launchpad icon on the Dock, and then click the JollysFastVNC icon on the Launchpad screen. The Server List window appears.

2. Click the + button in the lower-left corner to add a new entry to the list. The Server List window displays the details pane on the right (see Figure 6-24).
3. Type the name for the connection—for example, **My iPad**—in the Name box.
4. Type the IP address in the Network Address box.
5. Leave the other settings to their defaults.
6. Click the Connect button. JollysFastVNC displays the Authenticate dialog box (shown here).

7. Type the password in the Password box.
8. Select the Remember This Password In My Keychain check box if you want OS X to store the password for future use.

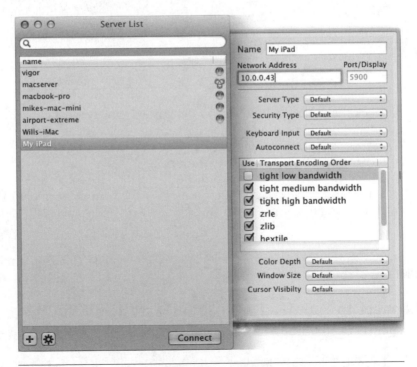

**FIGURE 6-24**   Enter the iPad's details in the Server List window, and then click the Connect button.

**FIGURE 6-25**   Your iPad's screen appears in the JollysFastVNC window. The colors here are a little off, but performance is good.

9. Click the OK button. JollysFastVNC displays your iPad's screen in a window (see Figure 6-25), and you can start using your iPad.

 To resize the iPad's screen, choose View | Half Size or press ⌘-0 (zero). You can also choose View | Actual Size (⌘-1) or View | Double Size (⌘-2) if you want things larger.

When you're ready to end your VNC session, choose JollysFastVNC | Quit JollysFastVNC.

# Project 47: Apply a Theme to Your iPad

If you want to make your iPad's user interface look different, you can apply a theme to it. A *theme* is a different look—wallpaper, icons, and so on.

You can either download a theme using Cydia or find themes on the Web and then apply them yourself.

## Install a Theme Using Cydia

To install a theme using Cydia, follow these steps:

1. If Cydia isn't running, tap the Cydia button on the Home screen to launch it.
2. Tap the Sections button to display the Sections screen.

 You can also search for themes. For example, tap the Search button, and then type **theme** on the Search screen—or, if you're looking for a theme whose name you know, type a distinctive word in the name.

3. Scroll down to the Themes part of the list. You'll find a large number of different items here—Themes, Themes (Carrier), Themes (Complete), Themes (System), and so on.
4. Tap the category of themes you want to browse.
5. Tap the theme you want to view. The Details screen appears.
6. If you want to install the theme, tap the Install button. The Confirm dialog box appears.
7. Tap the Confirm button. Cydia launches the installer, which downloads the theme and installs it.
8. Tap the Return To Cydia button to return to Cydia or the Reboot Device button if the theme requires a reboot.

 Most themes you install by using Cydia include the WinterBoard app for choosing the theme. If the app you choose doesn't include WinterBoard, or if you download a theme and install it manually, search for **winterboard** in Cydia and install it yourself.

## Install a Theme Manually

Installing a theme using Cydia is handy, but you'll find other themes on the Web that aren't available in Cydia packages. You need to install such themes manually. Follow these steps:

1. Download the theme to your computer.
2. Unzip the Zip file that contains the theme. You'll get a folder containing the files for the theme.
3. Connect to your iPad using FileZilla, as explained in Project 43.
4. Copy the folder containing the theme's files to the /var/stash/Themes/ folder.

You can now apply the theme using WinterBoard, as described in the next section.

## Apply a Theme Using WinterBoard

After installing a theme using Cydia (or installing it manually), use WinterBoard to apply the theme. Follow these steps:

1. Press the Home button to display the Home screen.

2. Tap the WinterBoard button to launch the WinterBoard app (shown here).

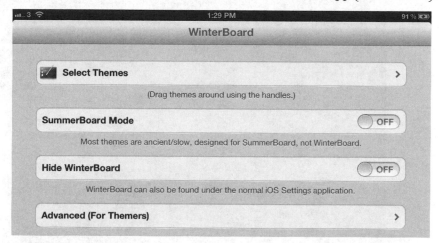

3. Tap the Select Themes button to display the theme screen (see Figure 6-26).

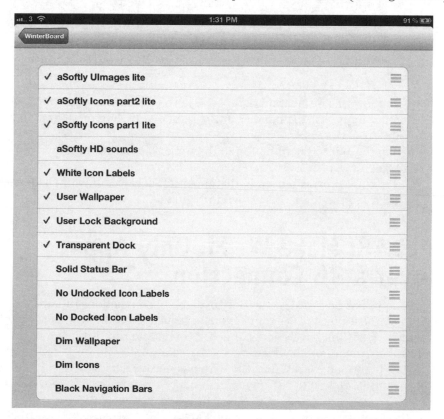

**FIGURE 6-26**   Place a check mark on each theme item you want to use. You can also drag items up or down the theme by grabbing the handles at the right end of each button.

**FIGURE 6-27**    Your chosen theme appears after you relaunch Springboard.

4. Tap to place a check mark on each item you want to use.
5. Optionally, use the handles at the right end to drag the theme items into a different order.
6. Tap the WinterBoard button in the upper-left corner to return to the WinterBoard screen.
7. Tap the Respring button in the upper-left corner to relaunch Springboard. You'll then see the theme, as shown in Figure 6-27.

# Project 48: Make Wi-Fi–Only Apps Run over a 3G Connection

Some apps are designed to run only over Wi-Fi connections rather than over both Wi-Fi connections and 3G connections. The usual reason for this is that the app typically transfers large enough amounts of data to run through a normal data allowance uncomfortably fast.

But if you have a cellular iPad with a generous data plan, or if the app is so vital that you're prepared to pay any extra costs you run up, you may want to run an app over 3G.

To do this, you need an app called My3G. My3G costs $3.99 from the Cydia Store, but there's a three-day free trial you can test first to see if the app suits you.

## Get and Install My3G

Run Cydia, tap the Search tab to display the Search screen, and then search for **my3g**. Tap the search result to display the Details screen, tap the Install button, and then tap the Confirm button. When the Complete screen appears, tap the Restart Springboard button to restart Springboard.

Tap the My3G icon on the Home screen to launch My3G. If you're using the trial version, tap the Start Trial button on the Welcome To My3G screen. My3G then downloads a trial license, after which you have to restart Springboard.

The easiest way to restart Springboard is to display SBSettings by dragging your finger across the status bar on the Home screen, and then tap the Respring button.

Now tap the My3G icon on the Home screen to launch My3G again, and you'll be in business.

## Specify Which Apps to Run over 3G

What you need to do now is specify which apps you want to run over 3G. Normally, you'll pick only certain apps rather than letting the whole herd of apps run hog-wild through your data allowance.

On the My3G screen (shown on the left in Figure 6-28), tap the button for each app you want to use, putting a check mark next to it.

## Run Your Apps over 3G

You can now run those apps you chose over the 3G network instead of a wireless network. If you try to run an app, and it gives a message saying it requires Wi-Fi, turn on the direct flag for it like this:

1. Go back to the My3G app. For example, press the Home button twice in quick succession, then tap the My3G icon on the app-switching bar.
2. Tap the > button on the app's button to display the Settings screen (shown on the right in Figure 6-28).
3. Tap the Use Direct Flag switch and move it to the On position.

Now try the app again, and it should work over 3G.

# Project 49: Play Games Under Emulation

You can find a vast number of games at the App Store—but there are many older games that people want to play: Sega Genesis, Nintendo and Super Nintendo, Game Boy Advance, PlayStation ... and even old arcade games.

To play games that aren't designed to run on the iPad, you need to install and use an emulator.

This project shows you how to get an emulator up and running, how to install games on the emulator, and how to run the games.

**FIGURE 6-28**    On the My3G screen (left), tap to place a check mark on each app you want to use over 3G. If you find an app displays messages warning that it requires Wi-Fi, tap the > button on the app's button on the My3G screen to display the Settings screen (right), and then move the Use Direct Flag switch to the On position.

## Install Your Emulator and Get It Running

Your first step is to get a suitable emulator and get it running. Here's the list of the emulators you'll need:

| Game Console | Emulator | Cost |
|---|---|---|
| Sega Genesis | genesis4iphone | Free |
| Game Boy Advance | gpSPhone | $4.99 |
| Arcade games | mame4iphone | Free |
| Nintendo | NES | $5.99 |
| Super Nintendo | snes4iphone | Free |
| PlayStation | psx4iphone | $2.99 |

To get one of these emulators, follow these general steps:

1. Open Cydia by tapping its icon on the Home screen.
2. Tap the Search tab to display the Search screen.
3. Search for the emulator by name.
4. Tap the search result to display the Details screen.
5. Tap the Install button. Cydia displays the Confirm dialog box.
6. Tap the Confirm button. Cydia launches the installer, which downloads and installs the app.
7. Tap the Return To Cydia button or the Relaunch Springboard button.

## Install Games on the Emulator

To install a game, connect to your iPad using FileZilla, as described in Project 43, earlier in this chapter. Then use FileZilla to copy the game's ROM to the appropriate folder on your iPad:

- **Sega Genesis**   /var/mobile/Media/ROMs/GENESIS/

A ROM is a read-only memory file containing the game. If you don't have the ROMs for the game consoles you want to install, you can almost certainly find them on the Internet. It's a good idea to check that whoever is distributing them is doing so legally.

- **Game Boy Advance**   /var/mobile/Media/ROMs/GBA/

For Game Boy Advance, you must also install a file named gba_bios.bin in the /var/mobile/Media/ROMs/GBA/ folder. You can find this file by searching online.

- **Multiple Arcade Machine Emulator**   /var/mobile/Media/ROMs/MAME/ roms/
- **Nintendo**   /var/mobile/Media/ROMs/NES/
- **Super Nintendo**   /var/mobile/Media/ROMs/SNES/
- **Sony PlayStation**   /var/mobile/Media/ROMs/PSX/

For PlayStation, you must also install a file named scph1001.bin in the /var/mobile/Media/ROMs/PSX/ folder. You can find this file by searching online. If you can't find the file by searching with Google, try Yahoo!.

## Run the Games on the Emulator

After installing the games, you're ready to run them. Launch the emulator from the Home screen, pick the game from the list of those you've installed, and then start

**FIGURE 6-29**   Choose the game in the emulator (left) and then start playing (right).

playing. The left screen in Figure 6-29 shows the list of games in the genesis4iphone emulator. The right screen in Figure 6-29 shows Sonic the Hedgehog launching into action.

# Project 50: Restore Your iPad to Its Jail

After jailbreaking your iPad as described at the beginning of this chapter, you may find you need to undo the jailbreak. This project shows you how to do so.

 When you restore your iPad to its jail, you get rid of Cydia and all the jailbroken apps you've installed.

To restore your iPad to its jail, follow these steps:

1. Connect your iPad to your computer, and wait for it to appear in the Source list in iTunes.
2. Click your iPad's entry in the Devices category in the Source list to display the iPad screens.

3. Click the Summary tab if it's not already displayed.
4. Click the Restore button. iTunes displays a confirmation dialog box, as shown here, to make sure you know that you're about to erase all the data from the device.

> **Are you sure you want to restore the iPad "iPad3" to its factory settings? All of your media and other data will be erased.**
>
> iTunes will verify the restore with Apple. After this process is complete, you will have the option to restore your contacts, calendars, text messages and other settings.
>
> Cancel      Restore

If a new version of the iPad software is available, iTunes prompts you to restore and update the iPad instead of merely restoring it. Click the Restore And Update button if you want to proceed; otherwise, click the Cancel button.

5. Click the Restore button to close the dialog box. iTunes wipes the device's contents, and then restores the software, showing you its progress while it works.
6. At the end of the restore process, iTunes restarts your iPad. iTunes displays an information message box for ten seconds while it does so. Either click the OK button or allow the countdown timer to close the message box automatically.
7. After your iPad restarts, it appears in the Source list in iTunes. Instead of the iPad's regular tabbed screens, the Set Up Your iPad screen appears.
8. To restore your data, make sure the Restore From The Backup Of option button is selected, and verify that the correct iPad appears in the drop-down list.
9. Click the Continue button. iTunes restores your data and then restarts the iPad, displaying another countdown message box while it does so. Either click the OK button or allow the countdown timer to close the message box automatically.
10. After your iPad appears in the Source list in iTunes following the restart, you can use it as normal.

# Index